Autobiography of a Princess

A JOAN KAHN BOOK

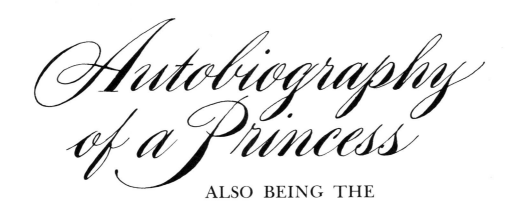

Autobiography of a Princess

ALSO BEING THE

ADVENTURES OF AN AMERICAN FILM DIRECTOR

IN THE LAND OF THE MAHARAJAS

Compiled by

JAMES IVORY

Photographs by

JOHN SWOPE

and others

Screenplay by

RUTH PRAWER JHABVALA

HARPER & ROW, PUBLISHERS

New York, Evanston, San Francisco, London

AUTOBIOGRAPHY OF A PRINCESS.

Printed in the United States of America.

For information address Harper & Row, Publishers, Inc.,
10 East 53rd Street, New York, N.Y. 10022.
Published simultaneously in Canada
by Fitzhenry & Whiteside Limited, Toronto.

FIRST EDITION

Designed by Dorothy Schmiderer

Calligraphy by Robert Paul Blessin

ISBN 0-06-012149-1 (Cloth)
ISBN 0-06-012151-3 (paper)

Library of Congress Catalog Card Number: 75-6341

75 76 77 78 79 10 9 8 7 6 5 4 3 2 1

Contents

Acknowledgments   vii

Foreword   ix

I   FROM WARRIOR TO SYBARITE:
A Portrait Gallery, 1870–1900   1

II   DAZZLING RULERS AND THEIR DAZZLED GUESTS:
The 1920's and 1930's   33

III   DEPOSED AND DISPOSSESSED   55

IV   THE LAND OF DEATH   79

V   PALACES AS SETS: *Alwar and Bikaner*   105

VI   *Autobiography of a Princess*   131

VII   SETS FOR A FILM TO COME   163

Glossary   173

Photo Credits   176

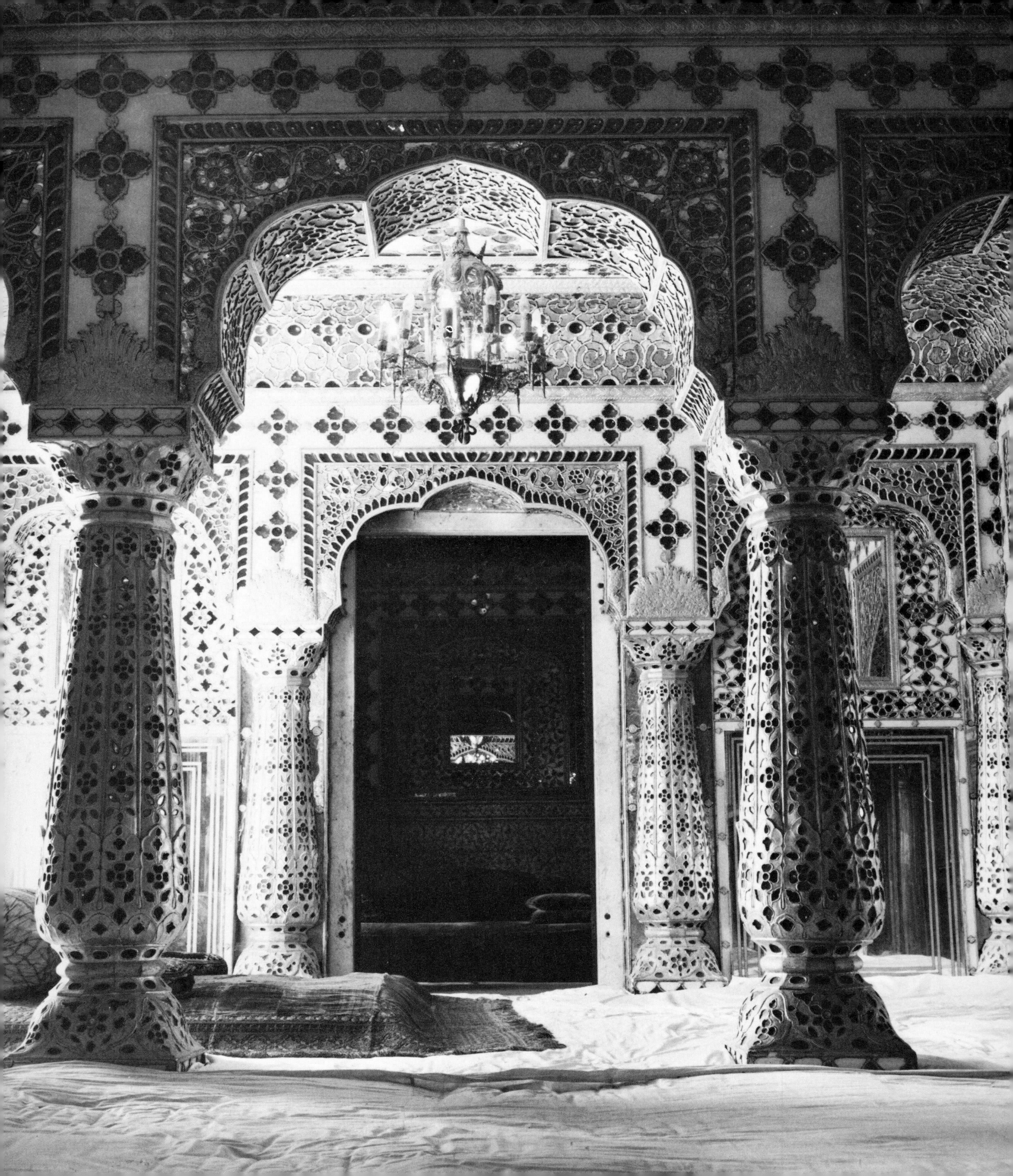

Acknowledgments

I would like to express my appreciation for all the help given to me by my various collaborators in the preparation of this book. John Swope, who took most of the photographs, is the first of these. I think it was a difficult assignment sometimes, with me in New York issuing instructions by letters, most of which arrived too late. But that doesn't seem to have mattered; he brought back exactly what I wanted. He must be the only photographer to have gone around the princely states systematically recording the later Maharajas' passion for building palaces. I doubt that anybody will bother to do it again. In the future, people who want to know about these palaces—Indianized versions of English country houses and French châteaux—as well as how their owners lived in them in the days of their splendor can find out from John Swope's photographs, just as they can find out how the Maharajas themselves looked from the photographs Bourne and Shepherd took of them in the last century.

The Bourne and Shepherd portraits that I have used in this book have been lent by Sven Gahlin and Kasmin, who are lucky to possess some wonderful albums of Indian photographs, and I'm deeply grateful to them, as well as to the India Office Library for giving me permission to publish some of theirs.

I am also grateful to Methuen, publishers of Yvonne Fitzroy's *Courts and Camps in India*, for their generous permission to quote at such length, and to Hodder and Stoughton Ltd. for material from Iris Butler's excellent book, *The Viceroy's Wife*.

To the royal families of the former princely states of Hyderabad, Jaipur, Jodhpur, and Bikaner: my special gratitude.

I want to thank Richard Macrory and Nick Young, who helped me research my book, and also worked very hard on the film, doing

Jaipur. The City Palace

all the dirty work like loading trucks and that kind of thing. I'd especially like to thank Antony Korner, Renana Jhabvala, Lloyd and Susanne Rudolph, Lee Thaw, Mary Ellen Mark, and the staff of the Photography Collection in the Humanities Research Center at the University of Texas, for their valuable assistance. Finally, I want to thank Ismail Merchant and Ruth Jhabvala, my companions in Royal India. There would have been no book without them and, of course, no film.

—JAMES IVORY

Alwar. A locked door in the Old Palace.

Foreword

This book is a film maker's response in print and not on celluloid to what is called Royal India—land of Maharajas. It contains the overflow from my films in which Royal India appears: *Shakespeare Wallah*, *The Guru*, and *Autobiography of a Princess*, of which the screenplay is included here. It is a collection of photographs, anecdotes, and odds and ends which I think are worth saving— a kind of journal after the fact of the travels I went on and the work I did from 1959 to 1973 involving what the British used to call the "native princes." It is neither a history of India's princely states nor a guide to what to see there. Also—because, as many film directors do, I've developed into some sort of connoisseur of rooms —this is a book of rooms. Were there ever any like those of the Maharajas? All that heavy furniture, all those yards and yards of brocade, those chandeliers, the carpets and dinner services and bathtubs carved like sarcophagi—all dragged out to the deserts and into the jungles, where they lie now, closed up and forgotten, like the contents of some huge tomb: the tomb of decades of rich men's taste, from 1870 to 1940.

When India became independent in 1947, the princes were guaranteed their titles, properties, and certain privileges. But more and more their special status came to be seen as an anachronism, and it has now been legally abolished. For the princes, it was like the French Revolution, except that none of them went to the guillotine; they merely became private citizens. Many of these former rulers are still doing very well. Some have large investments in industry and, like defunct noblemen elsewhere, are turning their palaces into hotels and their collections into trusts. Some are members of Parliament, even cabinet ministers. Some have become ambassadors, others have opened boutiques. In a generation, the peculiar mentality of the Indian ruler will have disappeared, as no more young men are brought up to perform as Maharajas. The popular attitude toward them is also changing. When an ex-Maharaja stands for Parliament, he can no longer expect his former subjects automatically to vote for him but has to woo them as hard as any common candidate—and even then may lose.

There has also been a transfer of transcendental powers. The Maharaja had always been credited with superhuman attributes which he was called upon to exercise for the good of his people. In 1970 a problem arose in Surendranagar, a city in Gujerat, about propitiating the angry Bhogavo River. Traditionally, during times of flood the ruler would toss a coconut and sprinkle a few drops of blood from his finger into the river. The Bhogavo was in high spate following the incessant rains in Surendranagar on Monday, September 7—the day on which the order on the de-recognition of the princes was tabled in the Indian Parliament. Since the ruler of Surendranagar had officially ceased to be its ruler, losing all his princely privileges, he could no longer exercise the right to propitiate the river. But the people believed that the flood havoc befalling them was the result of the order dispossessing their former prince. Something had to be done fast, and a local official of the revenue department took over. He cut his finger and offered a few drops of plebeian blood and the coconut to the angry river. The waters started receding in a few hours—proving before the eyes of all that the bureaucrat had the sanction of the highest Authority to replace the prince.

Lake Pichola, Udaipur, in the 1870s. The peculiarly shaped boat was used for the Maharana of Mewar's nocturnal outings. In eighteenth century miniature paintings of such events the decks are always crowded with beautiful girls singing and tossing flower petals at the Rana, who reclines on fat cushions with his favorite. The dark skies are split by lightning or illuminated by gilt swirls of fireworks. Later on, these boats were strung with electric lights. On the water, as seen in old film footage of princely revels in the 1930s, it appears as if the Fun House at an amusement park has broken loose and floated out to sea.

I

Warrior to Sybarite

A Portrait Gallery, 1870~1900

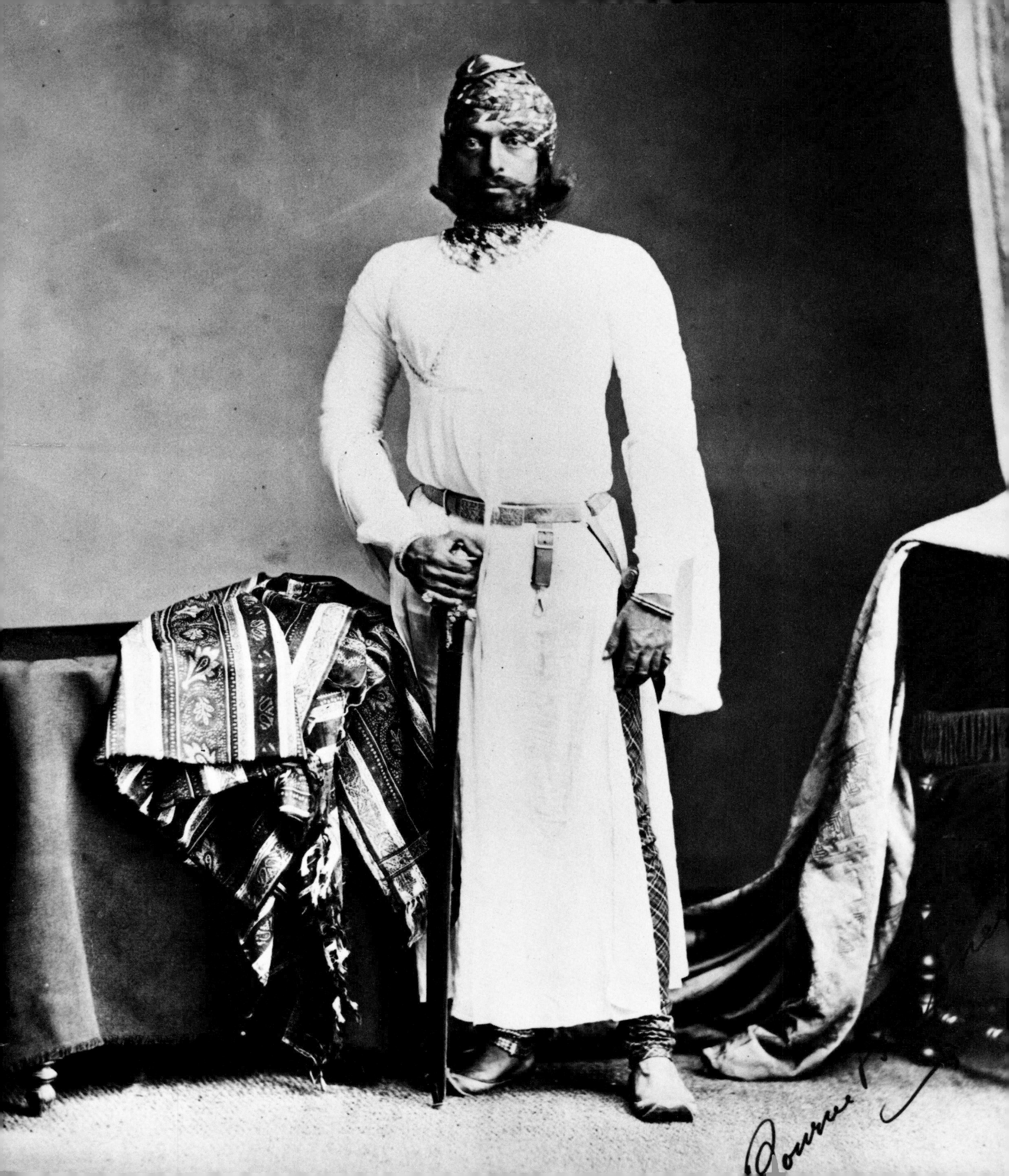

IN THEIR composition, the last miniatures painted of the Maharajas in the nineteenth century resemble the formal photographs of the era. The princes sit in Victorian armchairs beside Victorian fringed tables—facing us, which is a big change from the Indian tradition of profile portraits. A curtain is draped behind them, pulled back to let us see some bit of landscape no more real than a photographer's backdrop. These pictures are like icons; we don't get much idea of the sitter's personality unless, as sometimes happened, the painting is a copy of a photograph. When the first itinerant photographers—men like Bourne and Shepherd—began to travel around the native states in the 1860s they found the rulers more than ready to have their pictures taken. They posed them like eminent Victorians, in plush chairs or standing next to what look like prop thrones. But the faces of these men aren't those of Victorians—at least not eminent ones. If as a class they resemble any other group, it is the desperadoes of the American frontier, who too were a law unto themselves in a wild, desert land.

There are no photographs of women here—another waste of the purdah system. One would do almost anything to have pictures of the Ranis and Begums of a century ago, but of course no camera was ever taken into the *zenana* (in the same way that not a single artist during the centuries that miniatures were being painted seems to have had access for the purpose of portrait making. The history of Indian photography, like the history of Indian art, is devoid of any record of those strong female personalities whose lives are otherwise very well documented by court historians and by the British, who learned to respect—and sometimes to fear—the powerful purdah ladies). The only Indian women the Victorians were permitted to photograph were songstresses and nautch girls or poor women glimpsed in the bazaar. One or two enlightened Parsis from Bombay sat for their potraits, but that is all.

(*page 1*) **Identified Simply as "Pertab Singh" in the Sven Gahlin Album, No State Given. c. 1870.**

◄**A Proud Oriental King: Maharaja Jaswant Singh of Jodhpur (reigned 1873–1895).**

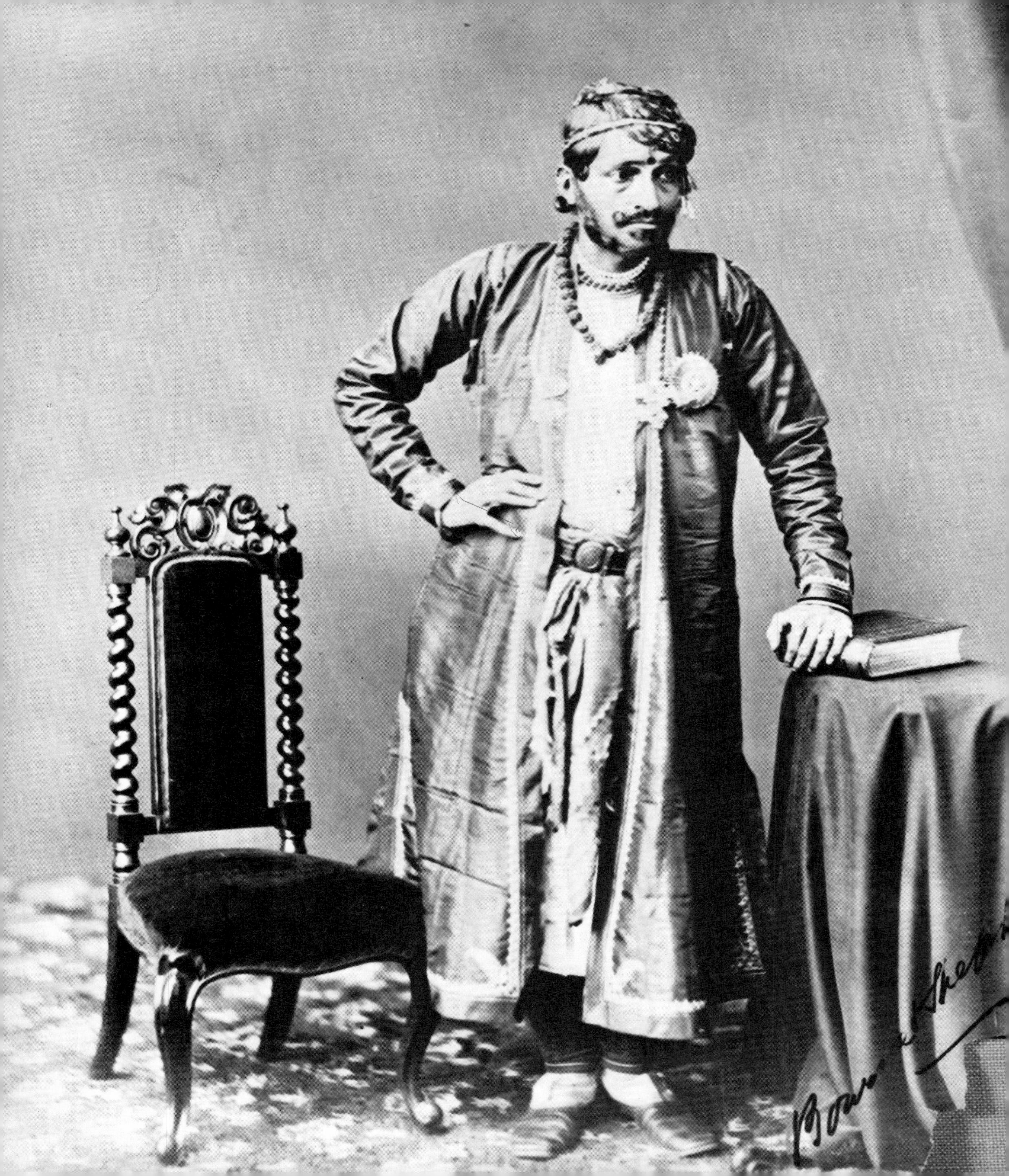

Maharaja Ram Singh of Jaipur (1835–1880). His Highness appears, from the evidence of this photograph, to have been quite a tough character; nevertheless, he was taking dancing lessons and learning to master the steps of the quadrille. The photograph hardly squares with the description of him as "sickly-looking" in the following *Times of India* account of a grand ball in Simla (August 6, 1869). The Maharaja's dancing partner, the Countess of Mayo, was the wife of the Viceroy, Lord Mayo: ". . . The Ball opened with quadrilles. In the leading double quadrille, the Maharaja had the honour of having the Countess of Mayo for partner; in fact it had been arranged that His Highness should open the Ball with her Ladyship, and for fully a week previously he had been under Terpsichorean instruction. Contrary to the expectations of nearly all present, His Highness acquitted himself remarkably well—with great composure and with such tolerable knowledge of the figures, that the very worst that could be said of his performance would be that it was stiff. His Highness, however, took a long time to put on his white kids, a feat which he executed without the slightest hurry, though, at the moment the observed of all observers, for the other "sets" had involuntarily broken up, and, with the whole company, ladies and all, had grouped themselves round the leading set, to see how His Highness would get through his first quadrille. At first there was a slight inclination to titter, but it soon passed away, for there was really nothing to laugh at, and when the quadrille had concluded, the universal verdict was 'that Jeypore had done remarkably well!' The bearing of the Countess of Mayo was very kind and encouraging, and such as to make the native Prince feel that the great honour vouchsafed him was not grudgingly accorded. Her Ladyship once or twice, with a good humoured smile, prevented the Maharaja from making a dancing blunder, and the whole five figures of the quadrille (a simple one) were got through without a single mistake. His Highness 'walked' through the figures somewhat slowly, but with the most profound attention to the novel and arduous task he had to get through. He is about thirty-four years of age, low-statured, and sickly-looking. He speaks English, but after the manner of one who has tried to acquire it in adult years, and not been very successful. His first quadrille is, however, a matter of great prospective social importance as regards the native population. The *tout ensemble* of the scene was pronounced to be as imposing as anything of the kind Simla had previously seen . . ."

Maharaja Mahendra Singh of Patiala in the 1870s with the Viceroy, Lord Northbrook.
Patiala was a vastly rich Sikh state in the Punjab whose rulers were much admired by the British for their manliness, straight dealing, and loyalty to the Crown.

Maharaja Raghuraj Singh of ▶ Rewah. His dates are 1834–1880. Whether this means he reigned for forty-six years—a very long time for a nineteenth century Rajput ruler—or whether he lived, however furiously, only to be that age, is unclear. But the uncertainty raises a question: Assuming the latter was the case, could even the most stupendous dissipation, combined with the nearly absolute powers of life and death over his subjects that a Maharaja in those days possessed, produce a face like this one in just four decades? The answer would probably have to be Yes.

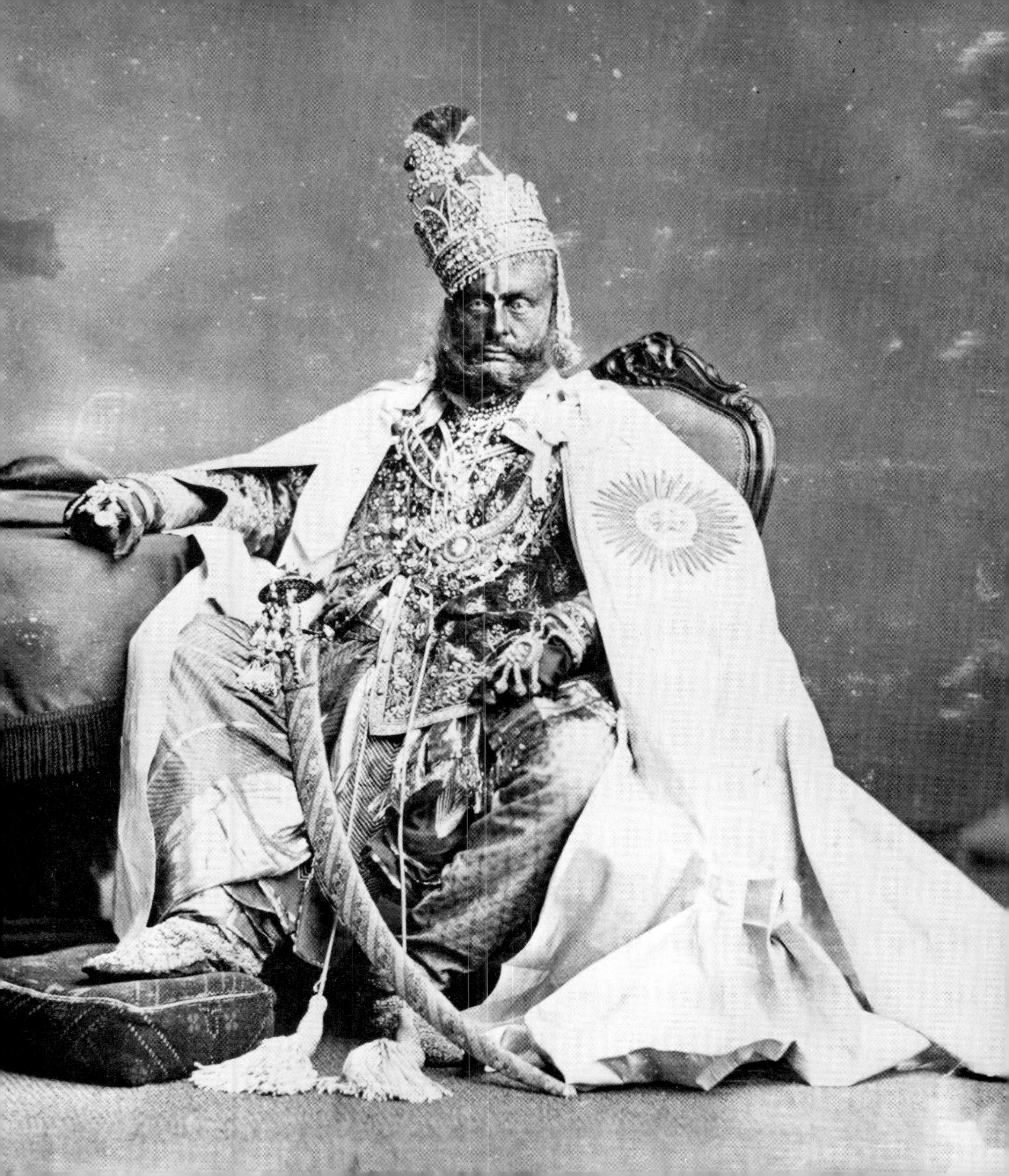

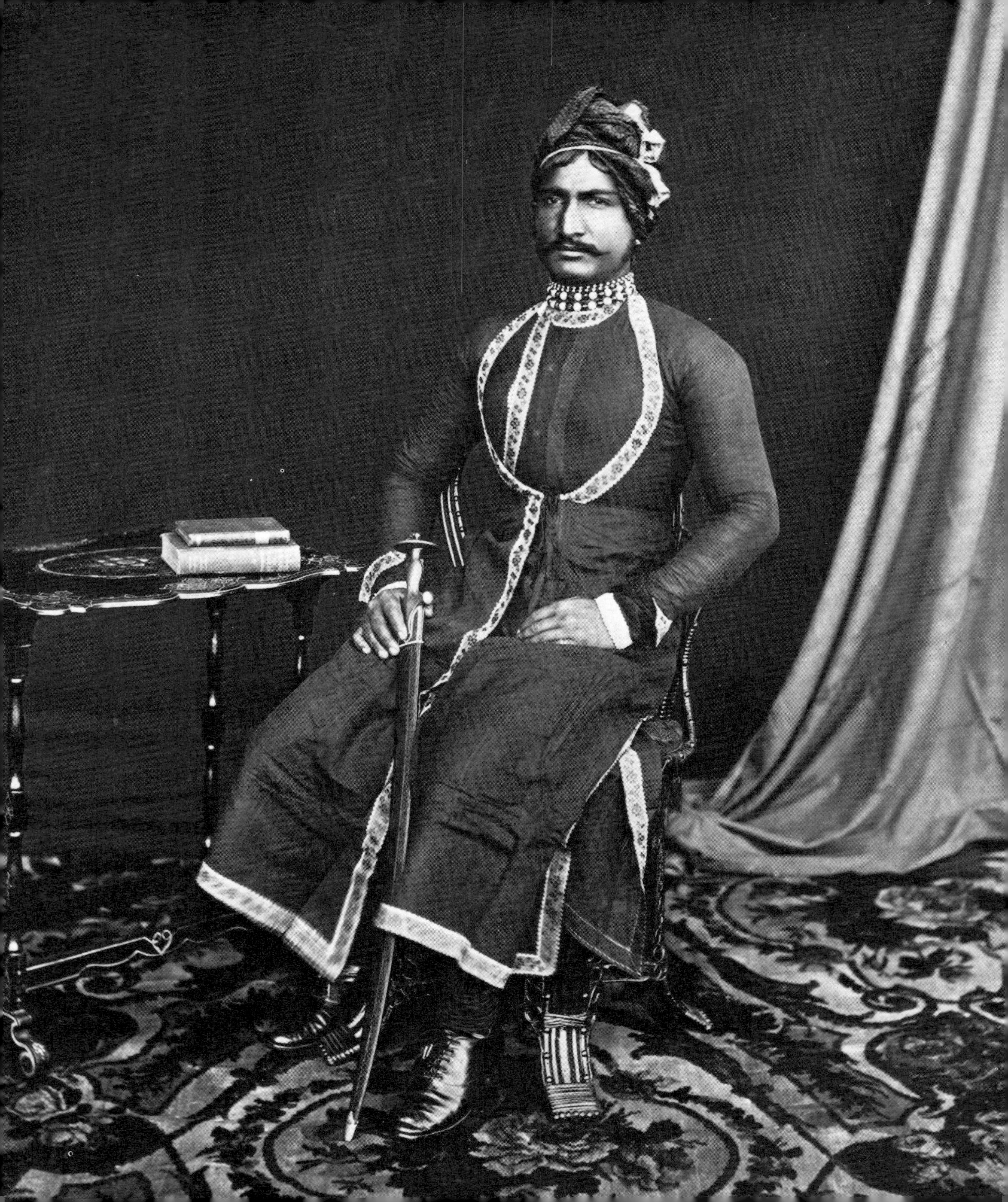

**Anand Rao, the Raja of Dhar,►
Sometime in the 1870s.** Though
a dwarf, Anand Rao was
intelligent and well educated;
in 1877 the British conferred the
title of Maharaja on him as a
personal distinction. Along
with the yards of pearls that
festooned him here, he is
wearing an order bestowed by
Queen Victoria.

◄**Mangal Singh of Thana,
Maharaja of Alwar (reigned
1874–1892).**

Gorgeous Fashion Shows:

◄ **Maharaja Ranjit Singh of Rutlam (reigned 1864–1892).**

**The Nawab of Bahawalpur, ►
Sadiq Muhhamad Khan (reigned 1866–1889).** A Muslim prince from a state now incorporated into Pakistan. Looking at his dress—the long coat, the loose pajamas, the amazing turban— specialists in traditional Indian costume could place him quite exactly even if there were no identification on the photograph.

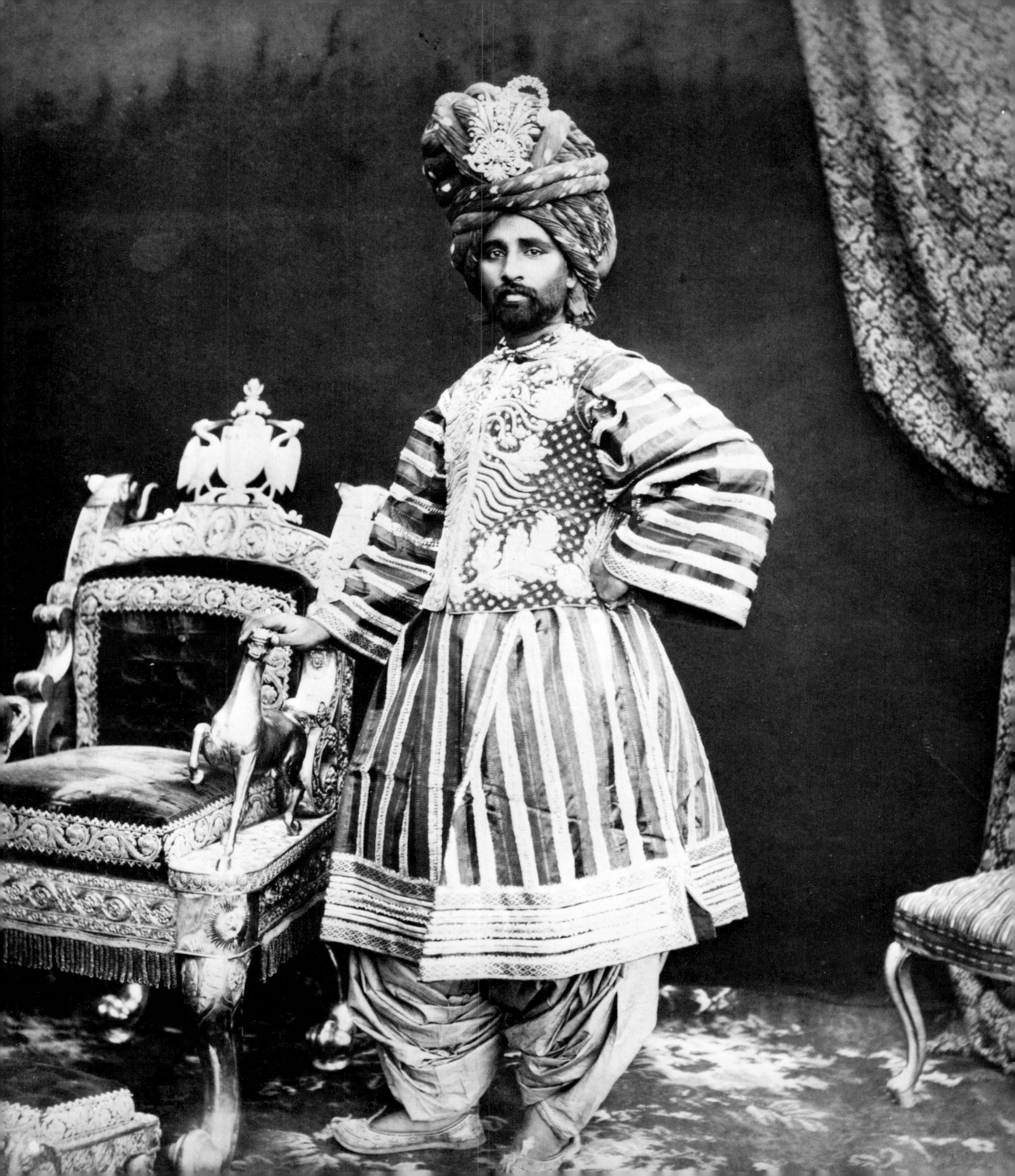

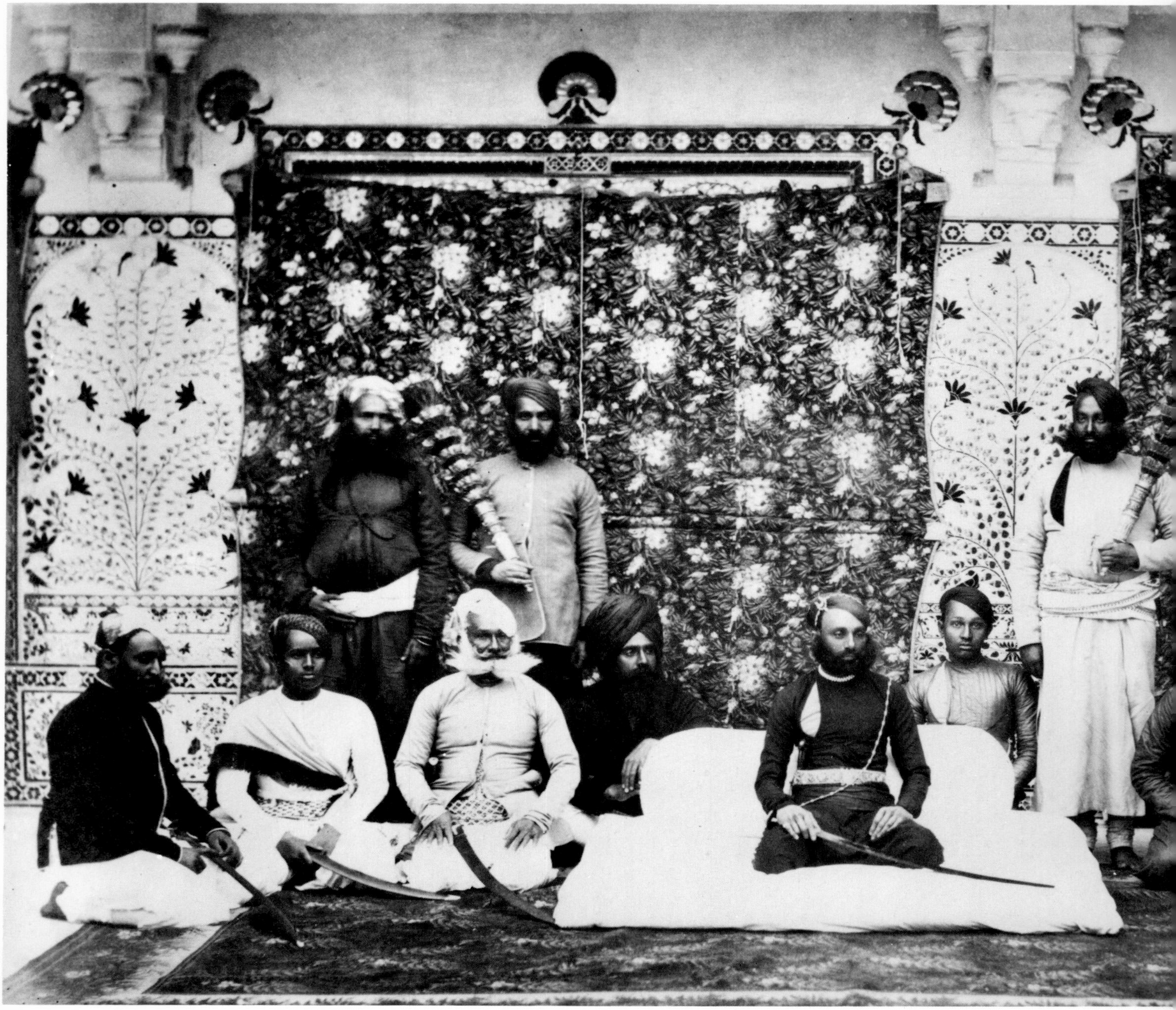

The Maharana of Mewar, Fatah Singh, in Council, c. 1880. Louis Rousselet, a French traveler in India in the early 1870s, describes a banquet the previous Maharana gave in his palace in Udaipur for his foreign guests: ". . . The royal banquets are always given in the Khoosh Mahal, i.e. 'Palace of Pleasure,' a most graceful edifice crowning the hill. The tables are spread in an immense saloon, richly but simply decorated, the vaulted roof of which rests upon indented arches, supported by columns of white marble, and which is brilliantly illuminated by crystal chandeliers whose lights are reflected by a thousand mirrors. . . . The dinner itself, which comes from the kitchens of the Residency, naturally is quite in the European style; and the wine, which comes from the royal cellars, is first rate.

"The Rana receives his guests, but only waits till they are seated at the table, when he retires; considering that, his religion forbidding him to take part in our repast, his presence as a spectator would be a restraint upon his guests. He returns with the principal Raos when the dessert is served, and graciously accepts the silver cup of champagne, which the Resident offers him. Numerous toasts soon remove all constraint, and Rajpoots and Europeans vie with each other in doing honour to the wines of the West and to the Manilla and Havannah cigars.

"The inevitable Nautch girls soon make their appearance, as no entertainment here can be given without them. Taking advantage of the conviviality of their superiors, they boldly take part in the conversation, and intersperse their dances with pleasantry, which is much relished by the courtiers. Towards midnight the Rana rises and dismisses his guests, after throwing garlands of flowers round their necks . . ." [From *India and Its Native Princes* (London: Chapman & Hall, 1876)]

A Nautch Girl and Her Musicians. *Tabla* on the left, *sarangi* on the right. The word *nautch* means "dance" in many Indian languages, so "nautch girl" simply means a dancing girl. Traditionally, a nautch girl danced before princes and noblemen (and quite a few Englishmen), sometimes solo, sometimes in groups. Often, she was a prostitute who danced to allure; on a higher scale, she might be a star dancer or a courtesan who was expert in giving lessons in refined manners to the sons of princes, somewhat like a Japanese geisha. The presence of the nautch girls made up, in some degree, for the absence of the ladies shut away in their *zenana*.

The English viewpoint on nautches changed the longer they stayed in India; a 1903 description is less sympathetic than Rousselet's. This was written for Lord Curzon's Coronation Durbar Album: ". . . During the Durbar wealthy natives kept high holiday, and nautch dancers were in great requisition, this form of entertainment being to them irresistible, though quite monotonous to Europeans, who must not look for a dance in the ordinary acceptation of the word, for posturing and attitudes, with a continual shuffling of the feet and occasional whirling, seem the whole of the nautch girl's idea of dancing. They are loaded with gaudy silks and jewels, quite enough to hamper any other movement of the limbs. The music is supplied by cymbals, tom-toms, and peculiar stringed instruments, which create a tumultuous discord . . ."

And another English viewpoint: ". . . the songs the girls sang weren't as gay as they were supposed to be. I always found them rather sad. And the girls too, in their tawdry dresses. Some of them were no longer in their first youth. What happens to the singing and dancing girls when they get old? When I asked His Highness, he said, 'They die of pox in the bazaar.' He laughed when he said it, so I suppose he was joking . . ." [Cyril Sahib, in *Autobiography of a Princess*]

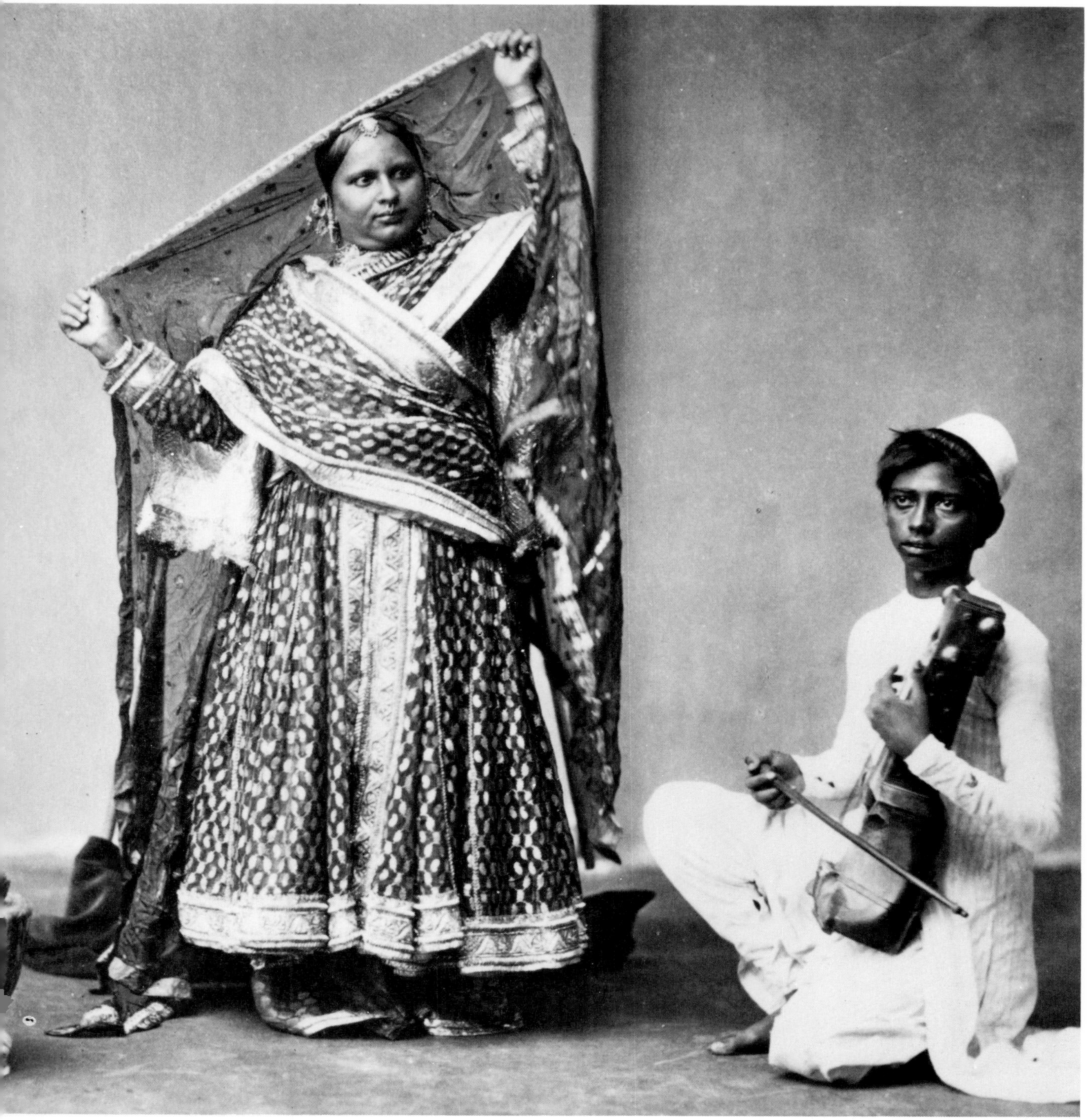

Maharana Fatah Singh After a Hunt, c. 1880. When Rousselet visited Udaipur, the previous Maharana, Sambhu Singh, was eighteen or nineteen years old. He describes him as follows: ". . . The expression of his countenance was pleasing and agreeable, and did not wear that look of cunning which, in general, characterizes his race; his manner was affable, engaging, and full of dignity. . . . He listened with attention to what I said as to the object of my journey, questioning me minutely about France . . ."

The Maharana, like most of his fellow princes right down to the present, was a passionate hunter. Rousselet writes that he had carefully studied the habits of the animals with which his forests abounded and appeared to possess great knowledge of them. When Rousselet expressed his surprise at the absence of tigers in a recent hunt, the Maharana told him that wild boars, collecting in great numbers, had succeeded in expelling them whenever they trespassed on their domain, or even killing them. When the Frenchman finally left Udaipur, there was this exchange between the two: ". . . The chamberlains ushered us into the throneroom, arrival. 'But, sahib,' said he, 'you have been here but two days!' 'Two months, Maharaja!' I replied—'two years of pleasure.' This thoroughly Oriental answer elicted the 'Wah! wah!' of the courtiers, who sang my praise in chorus. . . ."

(*overleaf, left*)
The Maharaja of Jodhpur, Sardar Singh, in 1896. A golden age is dawning. His Highness, aged seventeen, is not wearing his forefathers' famous diamond eyebrows, which hooked over the ears like a pair of glasses. Perhaps they were reserved for more important occasions than that of dressing up for this rather Cecil Beaton–like photograph.

(*overleaf, right*)
Maharaja Ganga Singh of Bikaner in 1896. Like the portrait of the Maharaja of Jodhpur, this is a souvenir portrait made on the occasion of a viceregal tour. His Excellency, Lord Elgin, wrote in his photo album of Ganga Singh, "A pleasant and interesting young chief of 16." Here is a description of him in his maturity: ". . . Sir Ganga Singh . . . occupied a great position in Indian politics and social life. A man of striking personal beauty, charm and great ambition, he played a principal part in the founding of the Chamber of Princes and became its first Chancellor. During World War I he was much in London and France, his state having made great contributions to the war effort. He also took part in the peace negotiations at Versailles. A very cosmopolitan, a very sophisticated man, but one who never forgot his Rajput past. He was a wonderful host and did not ignore old friends even if they were quite unimportant people. Neither did he ever fail to keep contact with friends old and new who *were* very important people. . . ."
[Iris Butler, *A Viceroy's Wife* (1969)]

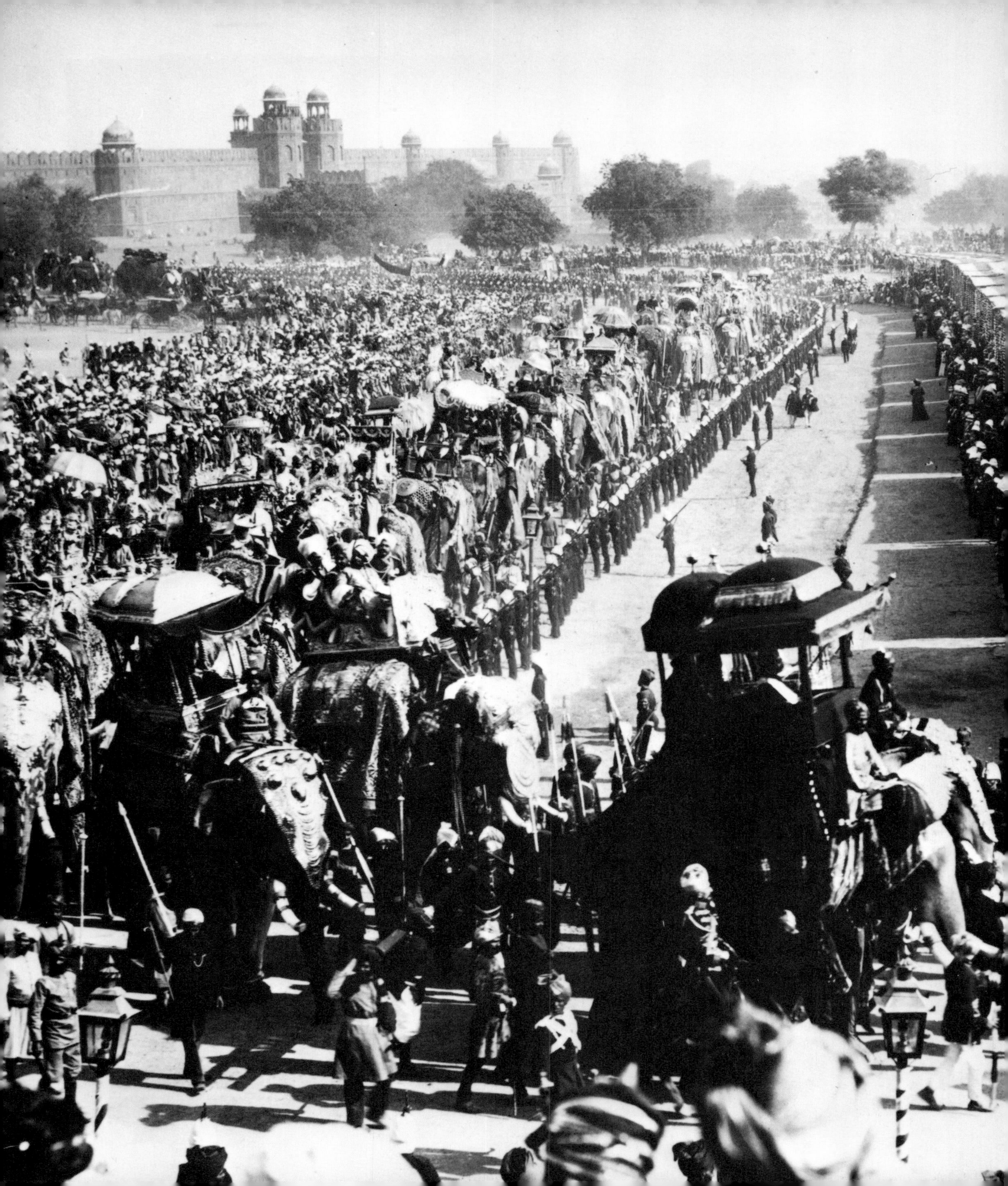

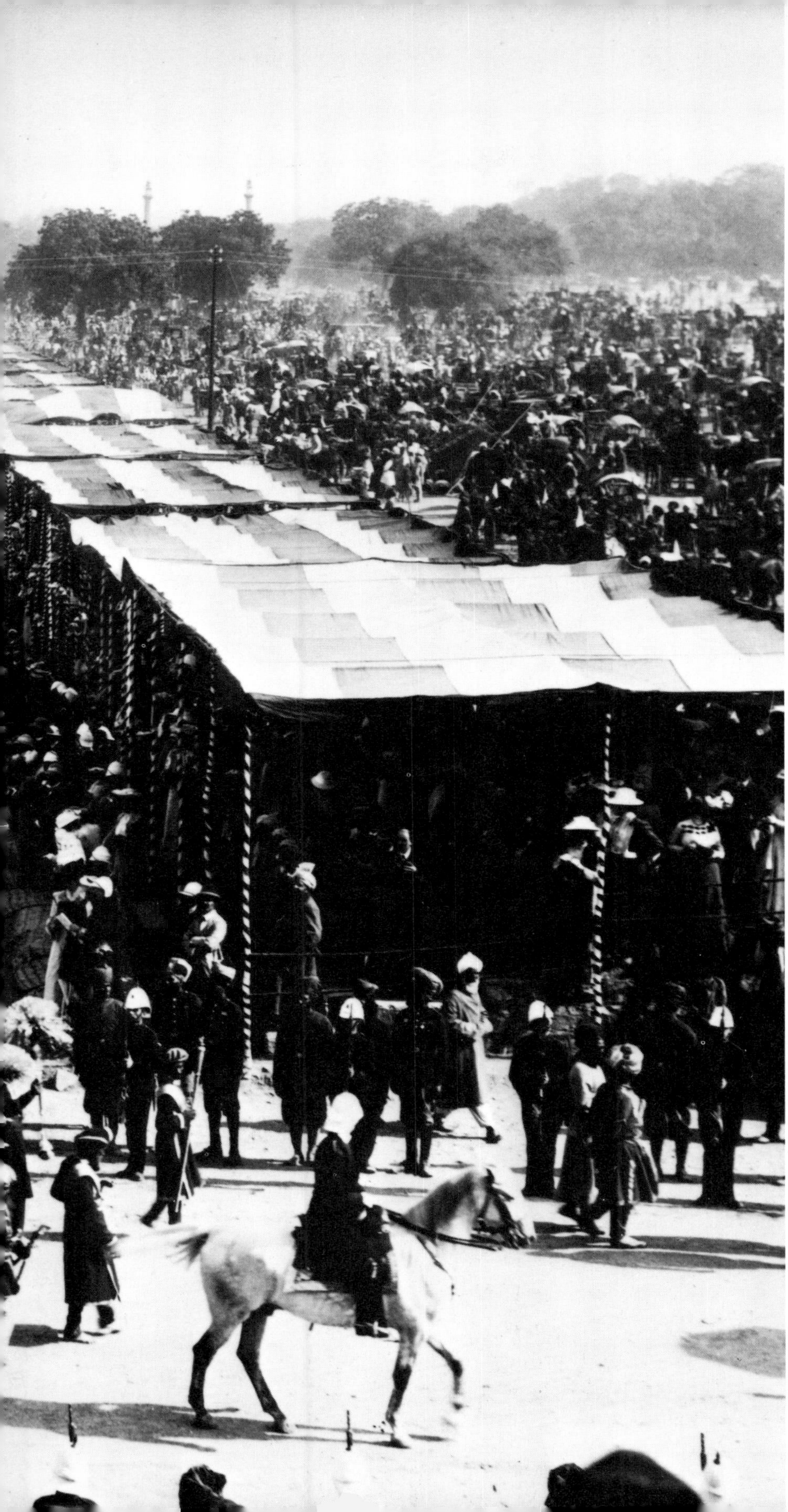

The Parade of the Century. The Princes' State Entry into Delhi at the 1903 Coronation Durbar. The triumphal procession of the vassal lords of the East during the Roman Empire could not have appeared more splendid. Yet, in spite of the sumptuous details, there is always, for a European, an air of shabby theatricality, a kind of circus atmosphere, about these grand Indian events. The phalanxes of spear bearers, the solid-silver howdahs, the cloth of gold, and ropes of pearls: it is all seen through clouds of Indian dust. At the upper left is the Red Fort, seat of the Moghul Emperors from Shah Jehan onwards.

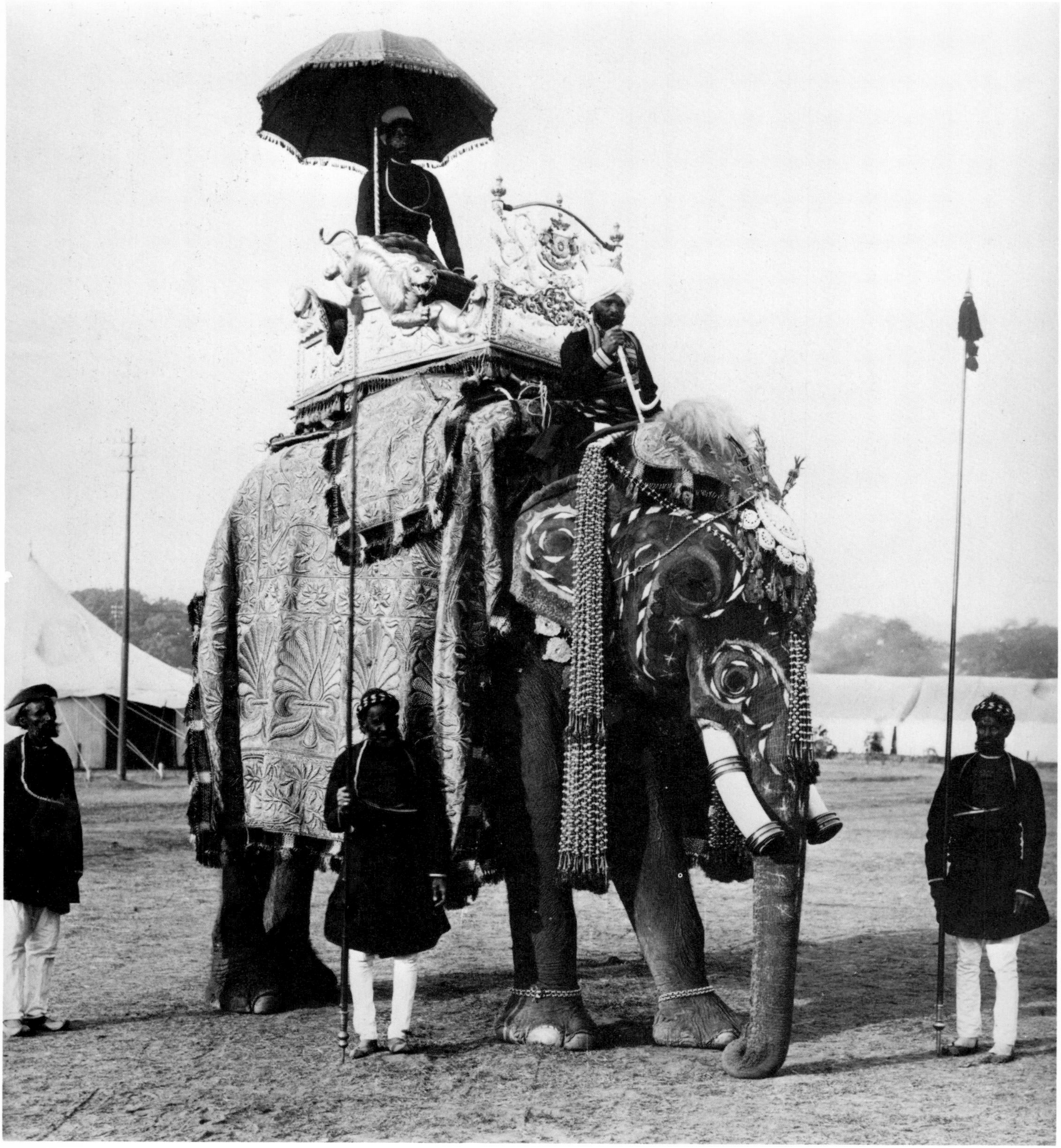

◄ **The Elephant That Carried King Edward VII's Representatives, the Duke and Duchess of Connaught, in State into Delhi, December 29, 1902.** Except for the slightly frontal angle and the absence of a fat Raja on top, this is exactly what we see in miniatures showing caparisoned elephants. The tradition of minutely depicting feudal customs, which was such a marked feature of feudal Indian art, was carried over intact into the days of photography: surely a unique transition.

The Maharaja of Rewah's State Elephant Car at the Coronation Durbar.

**Interior of a Shamiana, or
Tent, Put Up for the Maharaja
of Durbanga at the Time of the
Coronation Durbar.** In these
grand tents the assembled
princes entertained each other
and their English friends, made
courtesy calls, did business, and
brought in the nautch girls to
perform at their all-night
drinking parties.

**A Giant of Kashmir: A Servant
Employed by the Maharaja of
Kashmir, Photographed during
the Coronation Durbar.**

26

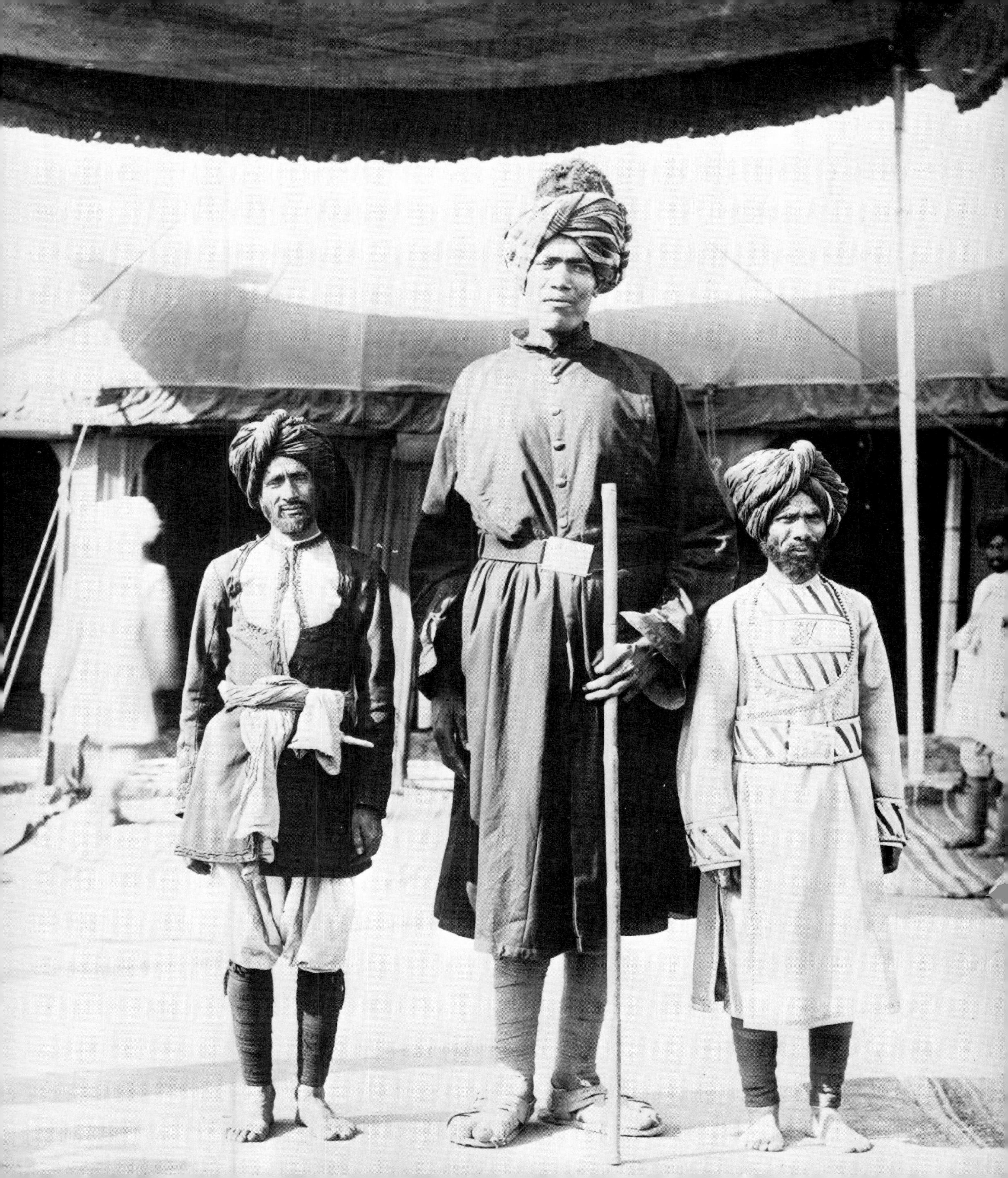

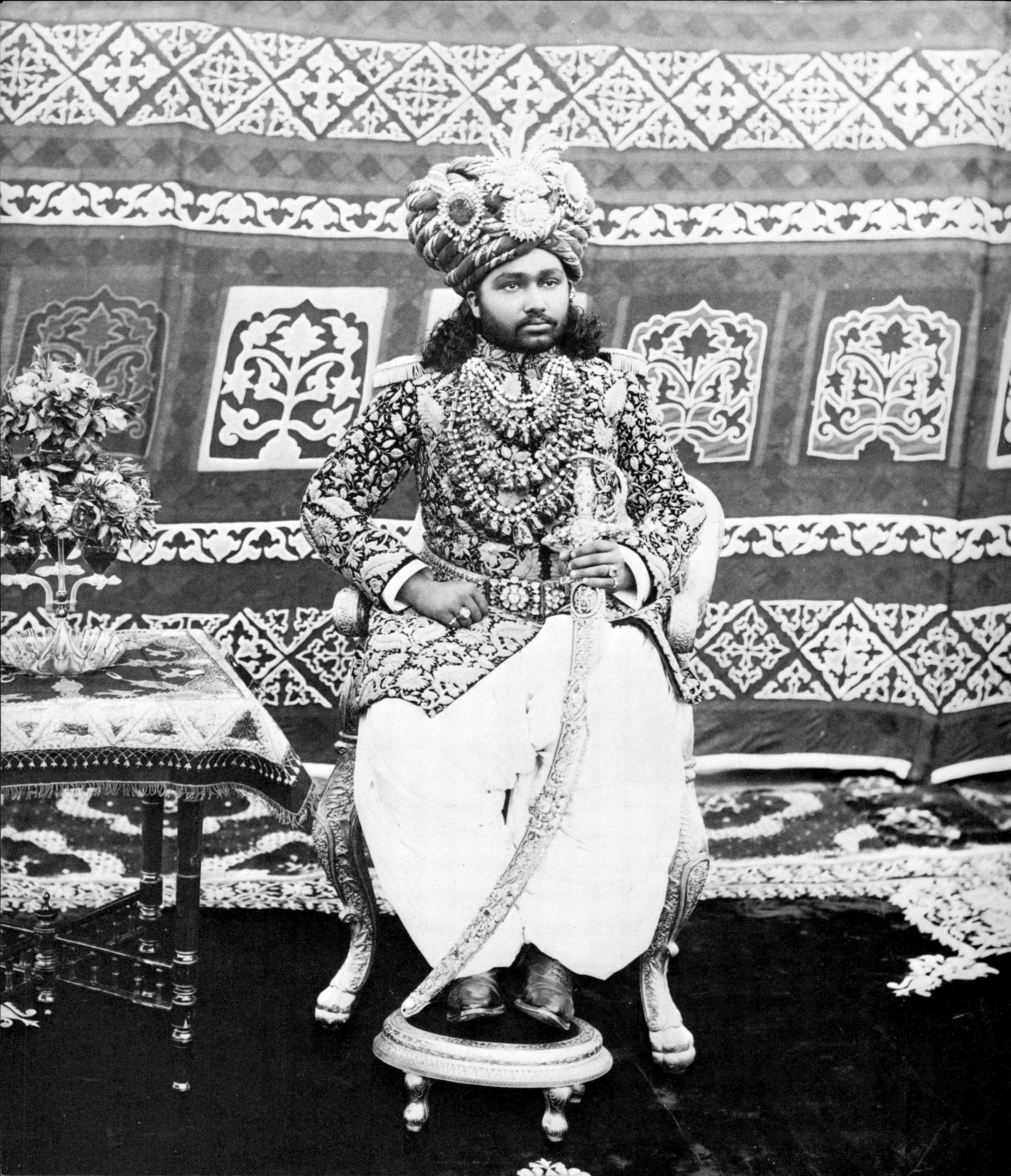

◄ **The Nawab of Bahawalpur, Mohomed Bahawal Khan, in 1903 at Age Nineteen.** The reader may ask: Why all these teen-age Maharajas? The answer frequently is that their fathers' livers gave out very early.

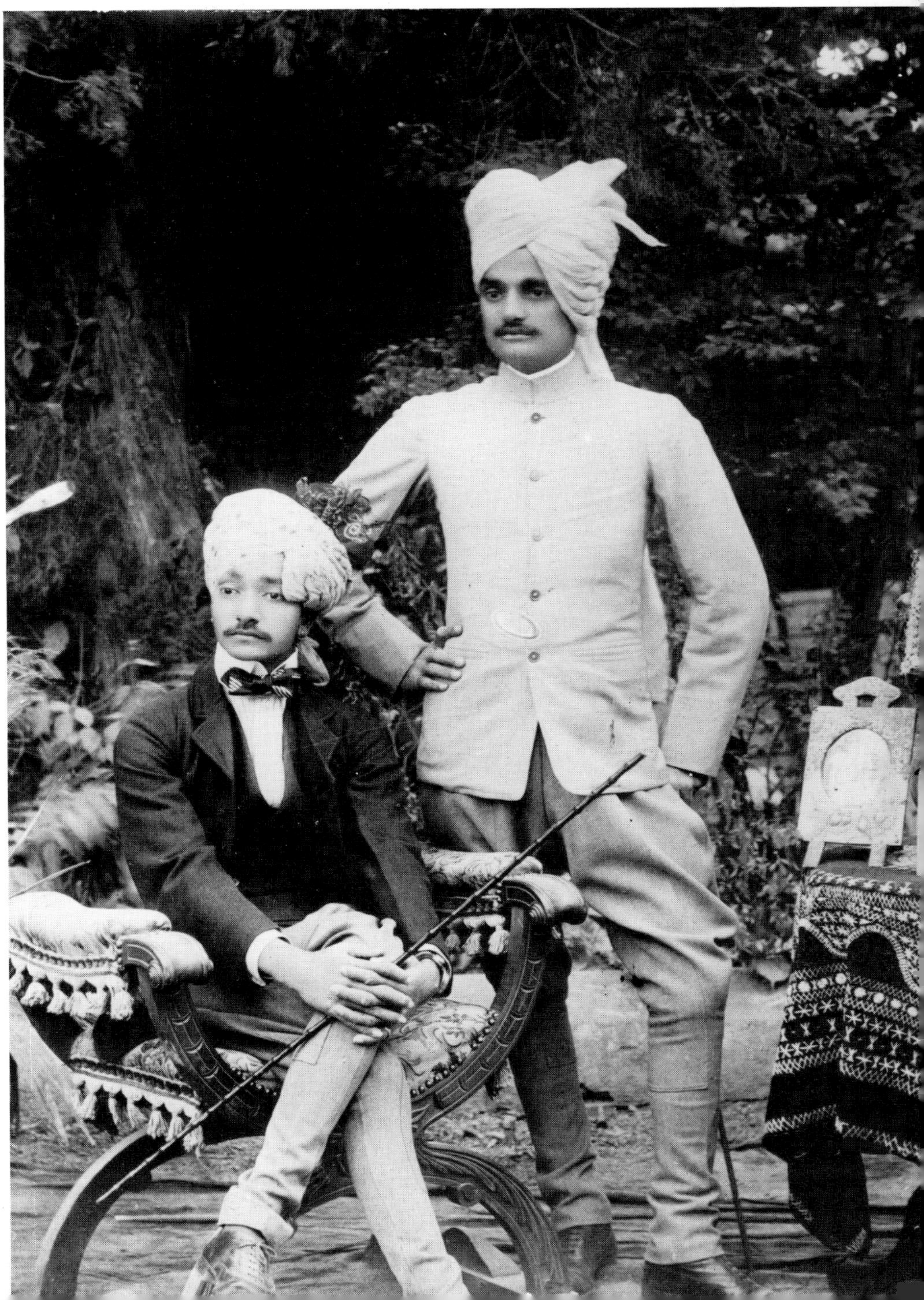

Madan Singh, Maharaja of Kishengarh (seated), with the Diarist, Amar Singh, c. 1903. ► Amar Singh, a young nobleman who later became commanding general of the Jaipur State Forces, left an 87-volume diary spanning four decades of life in Rajasthan. At an Indian court, however, a young man's private diary could sooner or later be expected to fall into the wrong hands. When he wrote, apropos of Maharaja Sardar Singh of Jodhpur (page 20) ". . . As I have now made up my mind to depict if possible the features and manners of any man I come across who interests me, I think I can do no better than first to begin with His Highness himself . . ." what must have been a compromising description of a troublesome young ruler breaks off in mid-passage and two pages are excised. At one point, Amar Singh showed his diary to his tutor, Bharat Ram Nathjee, who scolded him as follows: ". . . Sorry to say that though this diary has been written at its end during the months of the greatest famine of the century [1899], yet nothing has been written about it or the suffering humanity. Very sorry to say that you have left to the world only a record of so many animals killed in such and such a manner . . ."

Maharaja Jai Singh of Alwar in 1903 at Age Twenty-One. The process is complete: English knight and gentleman, Honorary Colonel in the British Army, *and* Maharaja. The princes were now ready to take their place on a new and very brightly lit stage—that of international society. Alwar's full title was His Highness Raj Rajeshwar Shri Sawai Maharaj Lt. Colonel Sir Jai Singhji Veerendra Shiromani Dev Deo, G.C.S.I., G.C.I.E.

Alwar was a small, come-lately state adjoining Jaipur. But Maharaja Jai Singh made up for his state's lack of size and ancient pedigree by eccentricity, social smartness, prowess as a hunter, and a reputation for bizarre vice said to rival the Marquis de Sade's. However, his reputedly sinister character did not hinder his social success among the British, who seem to have found him, at least for a while, quite fascinating. The Marchioness of Reading, wife of the Viceroy, was his frequent hostess in New Delhi and Simla; she liked him very much and thought he was altogether the cleverest of the princes. She describes him in a letter (1922): ". . . His Highness of Alwar, young, cultured (as to education), voluble, not difficult to entertain, which is my first thought as they always sit on my right at lunch and dinner. He is gorgeous to look at, came down to dinner in a brocade coat stiff with embroideries of pink roses. An old rose velvet cap (not turban) with magnificent ruby ornament. He varied it last night by wearing a striped velvet coat and the most magnificent necklace of emeralds . . ."

Lady Reading tells her correspondent, in another letter, how he was ". . . in mourning for his 'Grand-ma,' all in black with his moustache gone and head shaved, but on his last night he relented as to the black and appeared gorgeous in dark blue and gold with a diamond necklace, ear-rings and bracelet. . . ."

But not all her descriptions dealt wth his brocade coats and jewelry. Though she found him a supremely interesting person, with all his talk of the transmigration of souls and suchlike subjects, there was also "something intensely weird about him": ". . . Alwar nearly always wears gloves for fear he should touch anything made of cowskin (the gloves are of chamois or silk), he holds the cow so sacred, but goes nearly mad when he sees a dog and writes beforehand when paying a visit asking all dogs to be removed. Report says he kills them when he sees them. . . ."

To Yvonne Fitzroy, Lady Reading's secretary, he remained a puzzle, a mystery. Against her own experience of him as a thoughtful and considerate host, she had to balance all those stories she heard about him, no doubt mostly apocryphal but nevertheless "significant": ". . . Stories indeed of amazing feats of courage but more often of hideous cruelty and, sometimes, darker inferences that remind one of tales of black magic and evil possession. You may think of him as Poet and Hero until—you catch the gleam of that wild animal smile or hear the goat wail once too often!"

He was ultimately deposed by the British for (what else?) cruelty to animals; he had set a polo pony on fire for its unsatisfactory performance. He went to live in Paris, where he died in 1937. His body was brought back to Alwar, propped up in his gold-plated Lancaster automobile, and driven in state through the streets of his capital. For this last journey he was as exquisitely dressed as ever, wearing gloves and dark glasses.

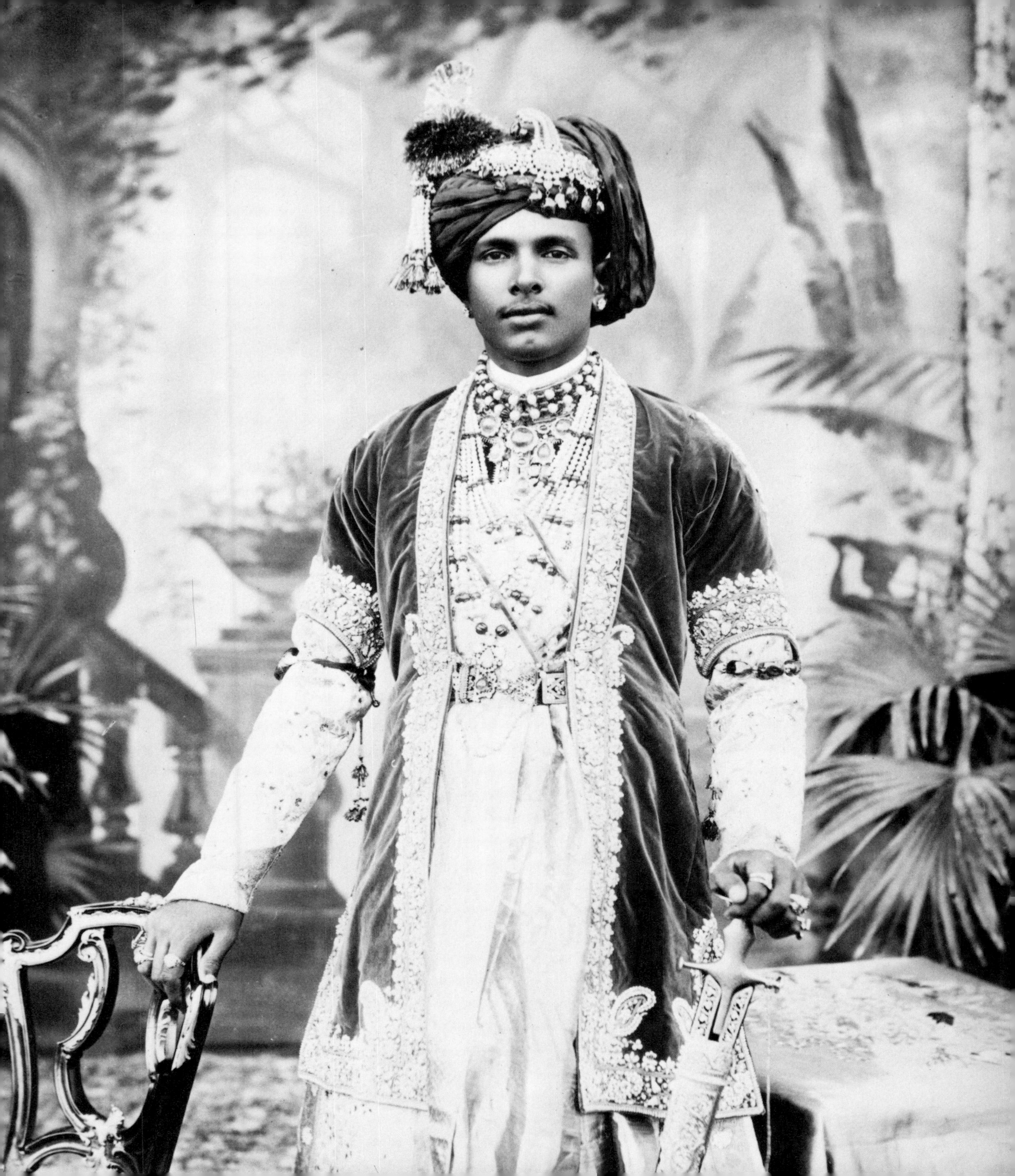

II

Dazzling Rulers
and Their Dazzled Guests

The 1920's and 1930's

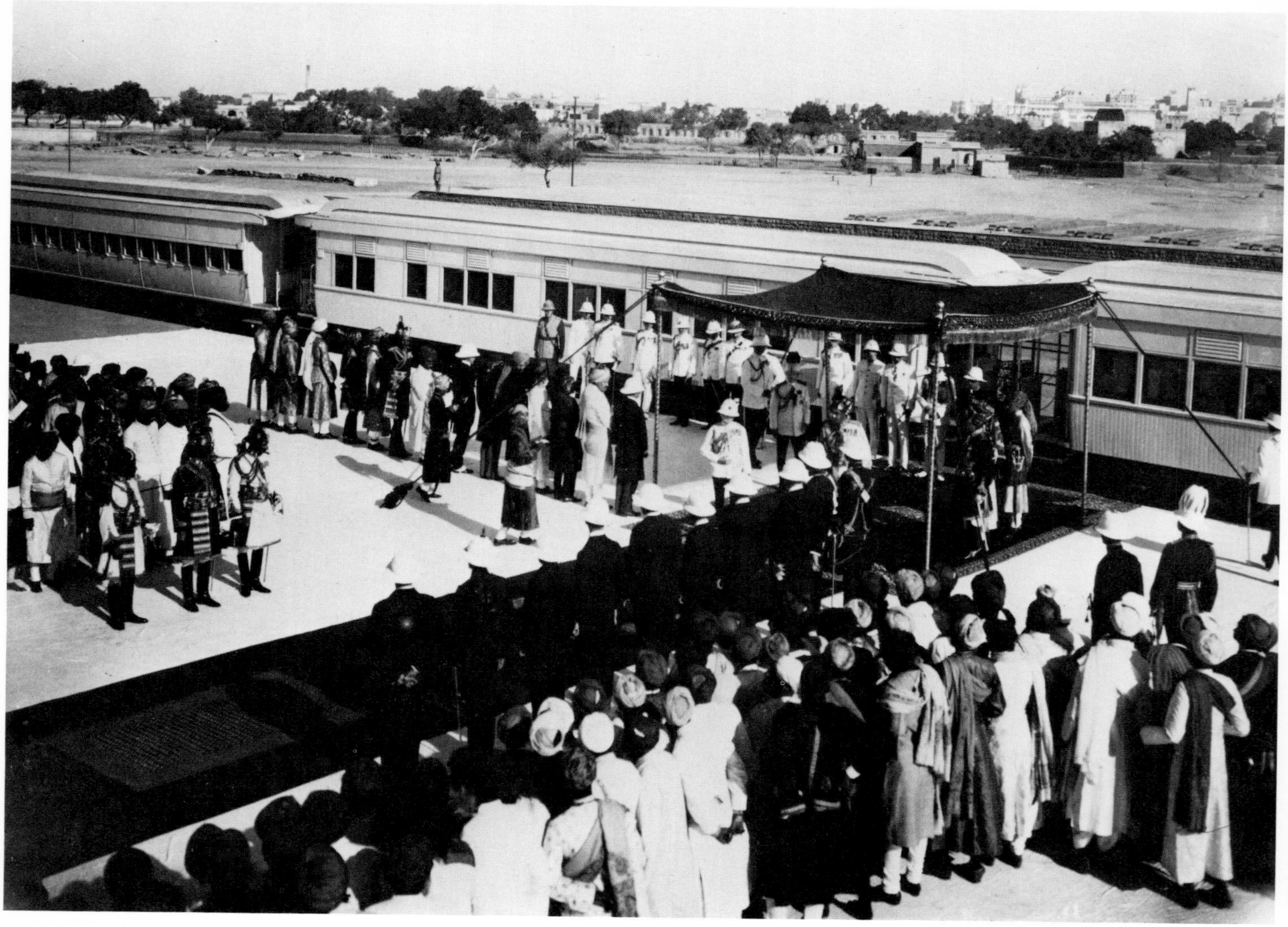

A Ceremonial Line-up at the Railway Station on the Arrival of the Prince of Wales at Bikaner in 1921. The arrivals and departures of the Viceroy, and even of lesser British officials, were also conducted in style. The ladies in the party found early-morning arrivals after nights spent on trains particularly trying. Perhaps that is why we don't see them here: they are still trying to pull themselves together on the train. But once they do, they will appear in their white hats and gloves, smiles fixed, ready to meet the local notables and submit to the drill laid down for them. This might be quite exacting. For an idea of how Lady Reading, the Viceroy's wife, must have spent many of her afternoons, see pages 36 and 37.

ow the Maharajas had everything ready—the new palaces built and furnished, fleets of superb automobiles, the private planes and trains full of merrymaking European guests. Since there were no longer any first-class miniature painters left to record this last chapter of Royal India, cameramen were hired instead. These cameramen were usually English, but sometimes they were German or American. And what a lot of footage they used up! A director's dream, the film stock as lavishly supplied as the champagne served at the feasts they had been brought in to photograph.

With a few modern additions, like the opening of an aerodrome or the visit of the Viceroy, the subjects were the same as those the miniature painters had painstakingly recorded: durbars, weddings, religious processions on holy days, cremations, elephant fights, polo matches, and hunts. Always hunts! Especially pig-sticking. The cameraman had to be quick and a good rider in order to follow the hunt right up to the last close-up of the dying pig, stuck through with spears, twitching in the dirt.

Most of the footage is in very bad condition now. Time and a terrible climate have caused it to deteriorate, and a lot of it is on old nitrate stock, which decomposes very quickly. When it can be projected, the viewer gets only a vague sense of what is actually going on. The ceremonials all seem to look the same, with crowds of salaaming minor nobles coming up to some royal personage who seems scarcely to acknowledge their presence. But suddenly a European face, usually on the side somewhere, is glimpsed in the sea of Indian faces. It is as startling a sight as the Englishmen who occasionally appear in the old miniature paintings. One feels intensely curious about these anomalous apparitions, especially if they are feminine and with the bobbed hair and plucked eyebrows of fifty years ago.

These European women stand out, not only because they're Western, but because they seem to be having fun. In posed photographs the same women look bored, but in this old footage they laugh and smile. Their movements are quick and free, and many of them seem unattached. Who brought them here, out to this strange place, and what became of them? We know some were sight-seeing weekend guests, moving on from state to state and party to party, doing the Indian "season" with highly placed friends living in India; others were hunting for husbands among the unmarried Englishmen they met along the way, civil or military; some were stranded adventuresses, who cadged jobs from the Maharajas as companions to the purdah ladies or as ghost-writers of royal memoirs; and some ended up romantically attached to their hosts.

Any European woman who lived with a Maharaja was asking for trouble sooner or later. She got it from his wives and old female relatives, who schemed for her removal. She got it from the official British, who snubbed and despised her, and tended to regard her as an unsettling influence, a threat to stability in the state. And sometimes she got it from her protector, who might turn out to be an opium addict, a drunkard, or a brute. Their stories would make good films, good period pieces. These young women are still around today—no longer following Maharajas, but swamis. Whereas the followers of the Maharajas used to move from palace to palace in private trains with a trunkful of pretty dresses and evening slippers, the swamis' admirers travel from ashram to ashram in third-class cars on the Indian railway with a bedroll and a knapsack containing a cotton sari, an extra T-shirt, and some cheap plastic sandals from the bazaar.

In the early 1920s, one young woman who visited princes in the company of highly placed friends was Yvonne Fitzroy, personal secretary to Lady Reading, wife of the Viceroy. She traveled with the Readings on their official trips to many parts of India, and everywhere, of course, they were lavishly entertained by the rulers who received them. The Viceroy made these visits for a number of reasons. He went to show himself, as the representative of the Crown, to the prince's subjects—to give *darshan*, as it were, in his own right, in the time-honored Indian fashion. He went to talk over the prince's problems, since the Viceroy often had a lot to do with the internal matters of a state, such as succession. Sometimes

WORK CARD

Arrival of Her Excellency the Countess of Reading

His Highness will receive Her Excellency and conduct her to the Shamiana

Royal Salute

Her excellency will take her seat, while the Ceremony of the Consecration of the Flag takes place

After the Puja, Her Excellency will give the signal for raising the flag (by pressing a small knob on the Model, on the table)

Colonel D. B. Girdhar Singh will raise the Flag

Feu-de-Joie

The Bharatpur Anthem will be played by the Herald Trumpeters

His Highness will then present the Model of the Flagstaff to Her Excellency

Her Excellency will then be conducted to her Carrying Chair

Tea and Conjuring

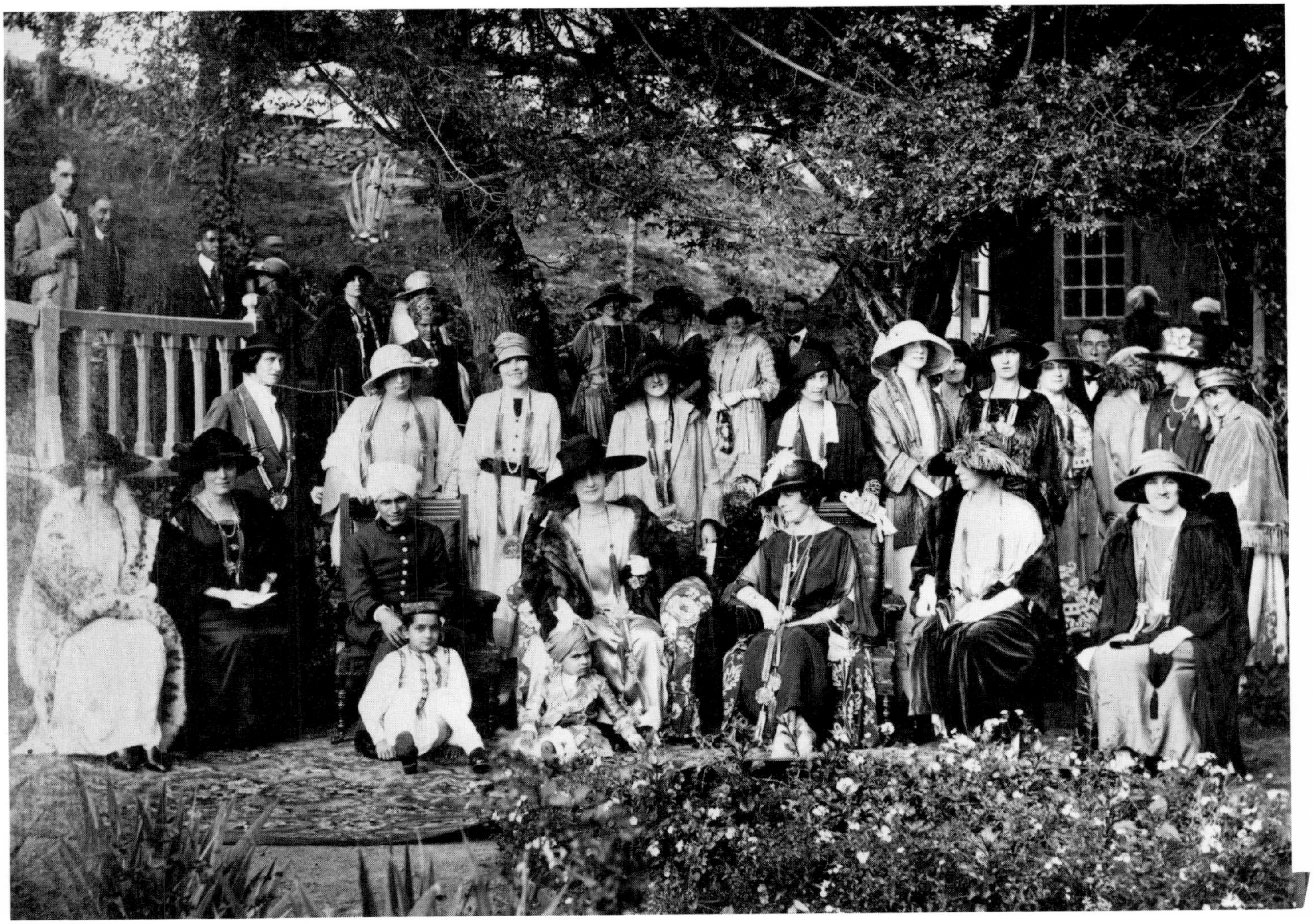

Lady Reading and Her Party with the Maharaja of Bharatpur and His Children. On arrival, Lady Reading (seated in the center in a chintz-covered armchair) would have been presented with what was called a "work card." This is the one she had to follow at Simla, where the Maharaja, like many of the North Indian rulers, had a summer "cottage"—here being opened officially (*see left*).

he went for sport, which meant to hunt. Usually the Viceroy's wife went along on these trips. She was permitted glimpses of Indian life that were denied to her husband; often we are indebted to the wives of British officials for the little we know about what went on—at least on the surface—in the purdah palaces.

Yvonne Fitzroy kept a diary of the trips she made with the Readings and later used portions of it in her book *Courts and Camps in India*, published in 1926. She was a very sympathetic and sensitive observer—sometimes, we feel, almost too sympathetic. She seems to approach her Maharajas with the same uncritical, gushing admiration as her sisters today approach their swamis. But in the pages of her diary she has given a detailed and lively account of princely India as it existed at its height. Here she describes the Viceroy's visit to the Maharaja of Indore; the date is October 21, 1922:

> The station was gay and had all the appearance of several patriotic bazaars rolled into one, and the Maharaja Holkar was there to receive His Excellency. We have arrived on the heels of the Diwali Festival or Festival of Lamps, during which every man worships the implements of his trade. And so in all the villages you see tufts of peacocks' feathers tied to the heads of cows and bullocks, and at Indore one of the former presented a sinister appearance stamped from horns to tail by the hand of her owner dipped in blood-red paint! At night the festival is greeted by illuminations and the houses are all outlined in light.
>
> Their Excellencies processed through the town with the Maharaja and the Agent to the Governor-General in Central India, the rest of us taking a short cut and arriving at the Manikbagh Palace ahead of them. The palace is the Maharaja's country house, and is very comfortable and European. Once installed, there followed, as in all native states, the ceremony of the Mizaj Pursi, when, with due solemnity, His Highness's Staff waits on His Excellency's Staff in order to inquire after the health of the Viceroy. Is he rested after the fatigues of his journey? is he comfortable? and is he ready to receive the formal visit of his host? The reports being satisfactory, the Maharaja arrives, the Viceroy advancing to a fixed spot on the gold carpet to meet him, but not a step beyond! Indeed, the number of paces, and the exact spot on the carpet to which he is to advance, is ordained by strict regulation, and in consideration of the importance of the Prince received, only the most important achieving the carpet's edge. The Viceroy and the Prince then take their seats

The Viceroy Had His Work Cut Out for Him, too. Lord Reading shares the dais at the installation of the new Nawab of Bahawalpur, Sadiq Mohammad Khan.

side by side on two golden chairs. After a few minutes conversation the Maharaja asks the Viceroy's permission to present his Staff, and each member in turn advances, holding a gold *mohur* which His Excellency touches as a token that the tribute is accepted. The presentations over, servants in scarlet and gold enter bearing gold trays, on which repose tall vials of Itr—a very pungent scent—and a neat pile of Pan, covered in gold leaf. Pan is a concoction of betel-nut and spices folded in an aromatic leaf, and though it is dear indeed to the Indian heart, I found it a difficult taste to acquire. The Viceroy himself presents the Itr and Pan to the Maharaja and hangs a gold Har around his neck, whilst lesser dignitaries do as much for the Staff.

An hour later the Viceroy pays a return visit to the Maharaja at his Palace, and his Staff are in their turn freely anointed with Itr—to their intense and lasting dismay! But the ceremony is one of great dignity, and of a grave and ordered courtesy wholly Eastern.

Then they are in Gwalior, visiting Maharaja Scindia. Miss Fitzroy rated him tops:

> One of the greatest and most powerful of the Princes of India, he was utterly unassuming, a tremendous worker, devoted to the interests of his people, an experienced soldier, a generous friend, and a most lovable personality. He had a delightful and prankish sense of humour, and his chuckle as his Staff or his guests fell headlong into the traps laid for them did one good to hear!

Scindia seems to have been one of those perfect Indian hosts (not by any means always a Maharaja) who still today overwhelm their foreign guests not only by their extravagance but also by the refined inventiveness of their hospitality:

> From the farther ramparts I remember watching the moon rise over the new city, and then by its light visiting the twin Sas Bahu (mother-in-law and daughter-in-law) temples, where we ate chocolate

◄ **Gajner, January** 1922. The *Bara Sahibs* and their *Memsahibs* join in at a great hunt arranged by Maharaja Ganga Singh of Bikaner, at which over 4000 birds were shot. Yvonne Fitzroy describes the occasion: "It is an extraordinary sight even when watched, as I watched it, from a respectful distance, and sounds more like a brisk engagement at the front than a morning's pastime. The grouse are kept away from the other tanks in the countryside for some days before the shoot, with the result that they all sweep down on Gajner for the morning drink. Not in hundreds but in thousands, not for half an hour but for three hours on end. From every direction they come, flying at a tremendous rate in perfect military formation—scouts, vanguard, main body, reinforcements, all complete. They make very difficult shooting and in the best butts the business is incessant; the Princes usually use three guns apiece and have two loaders each . . ."

eclairs and drank lemonade with a sublime disregard for appearances. But at Gwalior there was something so akin to the feasts in the enchanter's palace of one's youth in the unexpected way in which refreshment would suddenly appear, however remote your wanderings and just as you were feeling most hot and exhausted. I remember His Excellency [the Viceroy] telling us how at the end of a tiger beat, miles from camp, after hours spent sitting silent in a broiling sun on a hot and naked rock, he was thinking sadly of the long and thirsty journey home when, from nowhere in particular unless it were from heaven, iced tangerines descended like manna on the company!

In great things as well as small I have never met with such perfection or organization, and the greatest of all was perhaps the Durbar. . . . The procedure differed little from the ceremony at Indore but was infinitely more elaborate. To begin with, the Durbar Hall at Gwalior is a very fine Italianate room, and with its orange and yellow hangings, and vast chandeliers, made a wonderful setting for the three hundred odd chiefs and nobles who gathered to be presented to the Viceroy. They were attired in their old state costumes of every shade from purple to rose-pink, each wore the scarlet Mahratta hat, and the Sardars or chief nobles were splendid in golden embroidery and wore long steel cuffs with a deep gold fringe coming right over the hand. They sat on each side of the hall, and on a raised dais at the upper end two chairs of state were placed for the Viceroy and the Maharaja; behind these and round the walls stood the servants in an infinite variety of costume, but the majority wearing long crimson coats bound in emerald green, orange trousers and belts and scarlet hats. The Mahratta hat, which on state occasions is worn by the nobles in place of the pugree or turban, is exceedingly difficult to describe and altogether a most coquettish little affair; but the first time I saw it, worn at a meeting of the Chamber of Princes by the Maharaja Scindia, it reminded me irresistibly of the headdress of a Dresden shepherdess! To which on reflection it does bear some resemblance, being an elaborate confusion of little bows and knots and strings with a tilt to one side and a narrow crown. . . .

Please to imagine the Viceroy and His Highness to have taken their seats, the great hall aglow with colour, the throbbing of the Indian drum, and the nasal, but not unbeautiful, voice of a singing girl alone breaking the stillness. Then at a signal advancing, rank upon rank, an army of perfectly drilled retainers, dressed in dark blue velvet and gold, and bearing golden trays of jewels, of pearls, of diamonds, of emeralds; trays of silks and cloth of gold. At the

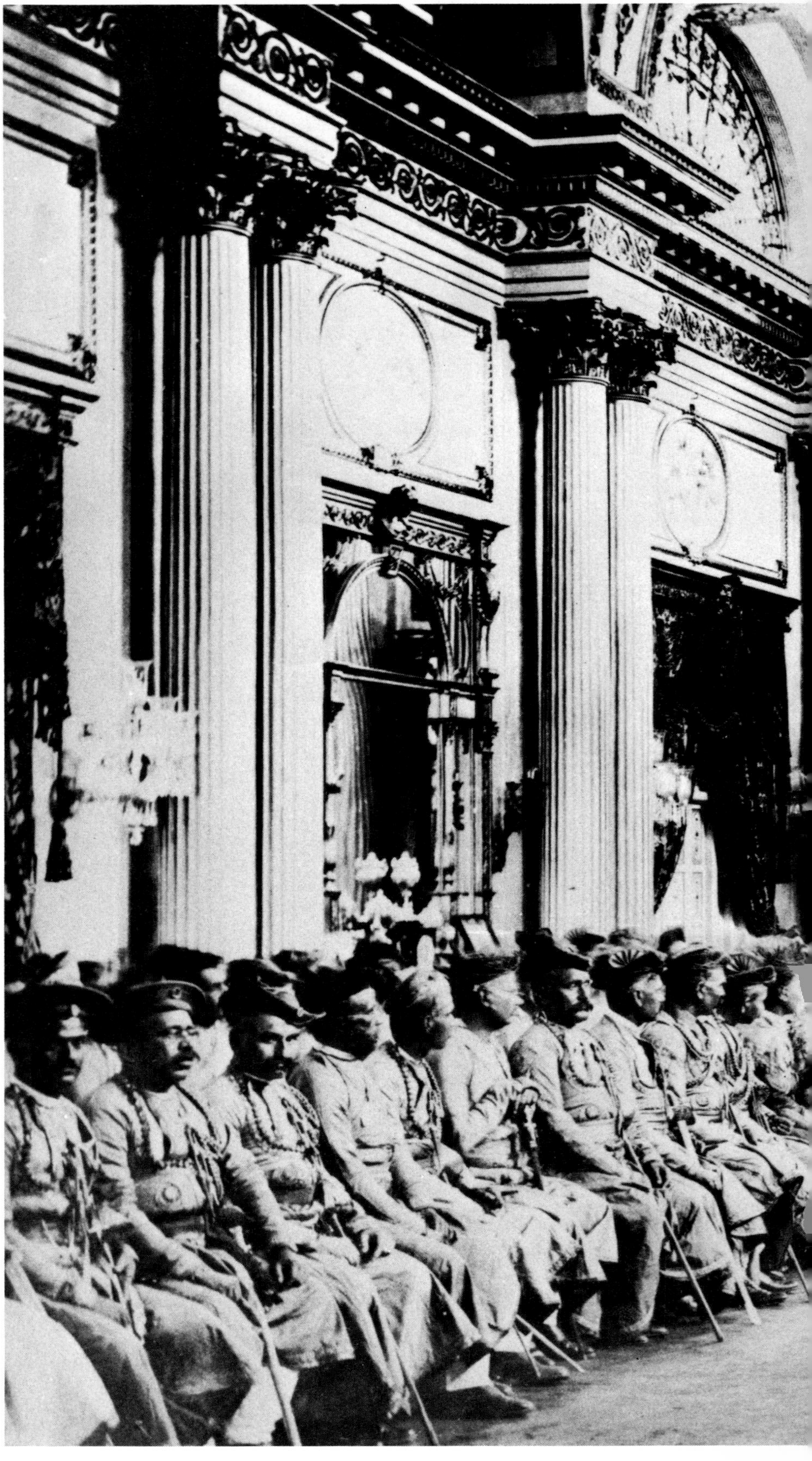

Maharaja Scindia's Durbar. On the left the Mahratta noblemen in the Dresden shepherdess hats described by Yvonne Fitzroy, October 1922.

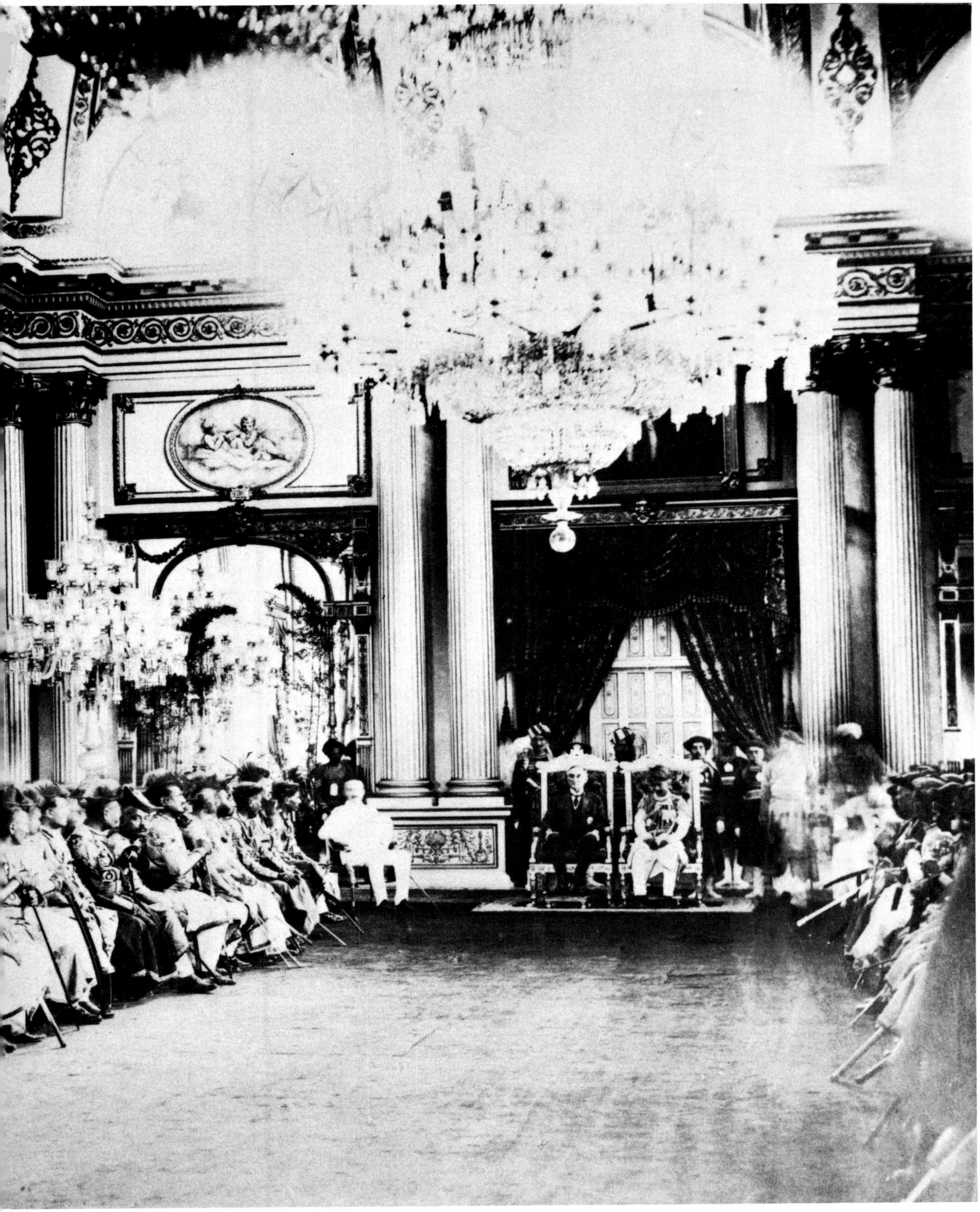

gates of the palace stand six elephants and six horses in all their
state trappings, necklaces of gold mohurs round their necks, anklets
of gold and jewels, and draperies of velvet, silk and gold; these, too,
form part of the Durbar's offerings to the Viceroy. The Trays are
laid at his feet, the servants retire, and with a gesture His Excellency conveys to the assembled company that he gratefully accepts
the spirit of the gift—only! With the same stately ceremonial the
trays are removed, and then the Sardars and Chiefs are in turn
presented; Itr and Pan is brought in, a great golden garland is
hung around the Viceroy's neck by his host, and the Durbar is over.
I have certainly in no other State seen one to equal it.

The programme included visits to the State hospitals and institutions, schools and welfare centres, an inspection of the Maharaja's
jewels and, for Lady Reading, visits to the two Maharanis. The
ladies are, of course, Purdah, but they receive the members of His

The Obligatory Music Party.
The Viceroy sits next to the
Maharaja of Baroda, Sayaji Rao,
who is wearing white spats.
Lady Reading sits between two
royal ladies, who have now
been freed from their purdah
palaces to take part in such
occasions and be photographed.
So we see them at last. Their
heads are modestly covered by
their saris—a nicety of dress
still observed in public by
Indian aristocratic ladies. The
Readings were very receptive
to Indian culture, and here they
are being entertained by a
singer, who sits with her
accompanists on the extreme
left.

Highness's immediate circle, they give parties, play bridge, and moralize on the difficulty of making their lord and master take care of himself, like any emancipated wife! There is a charming club-house for the Purdah ladies of the city, an old pavilion, looking out on one side to a formal garden with tanks and fountains, while, on the other, there are big and shady grounds where they can play badminton and tennis.

There was a review at which George and Mary, the Maharaja's small son and daughter, marched past with their regiment, and the elephants of the elephant battery raised their trunks in grave salute as they passed the base. That evening there were sports and a torch-light tattoo, on another a state banquet, when the pillars of the banqueting hall were wreathed in scarlet and gold, and the walls hung with arms, and silks, and huge silver spears. Opposite each door stood a large white marble bust, the King-Emperor at the one end, the Queen-Empress at the other, buried in flowers and garlanded in gold. The rest of the decorations of the room again savoured engagingly of pantomime, for at the top was an electric rock garden, tiny silver fountains played on the side tables, the centre table was ingeniously lit with revolving coloured balls, and portentous flowers and trees, and down and round it from end to end ran Scindia's famous light railway! A lovely silver train, every detail perfect, run by electricity and dragging seven trucks—brandy, port, cigars, cigarettes, sweets, nuts and chocolates! At dessert the Maharaja presses a button, and the train starts and, if you wish to linger over your choice, you lift out the lining of the truck and the train stops automatically! The most engaging toy and a perfect one for a State banquet, and this occasion was further enlivened by the State band who at intervals marched round the table in truly Highland fashion.

This band, which played throughout the long banquet, ended with "God Save the King"—that is, King George V. In between, there were waltzes like "Sweet William"; a fox trot, "Now and Then," and a two-step, "Silver Heels"; as well as Gilbert's "The Lady of the Rose." Maharaja Scindia's guests—there were eighty-eight of them—were served the following courses: *Homard à la Russe, Consommé Strasbourgois, Flanc de Becti Maître d'Hotel* (that mainstay to this day of Indian hotel chefs), *Dindonneau au Vin Blanc, Jambon aux Cerises, Selle de Pré salé rôtie, Salade, Asperges Vinaigrette* (they would have been tinned in those days, from Fortnum and Mason probably), *Vacherin Chantilly,* as a savory *Anchois sur Canape, Bombe Napolitaine, Dessert,* and finally *Café.*

45

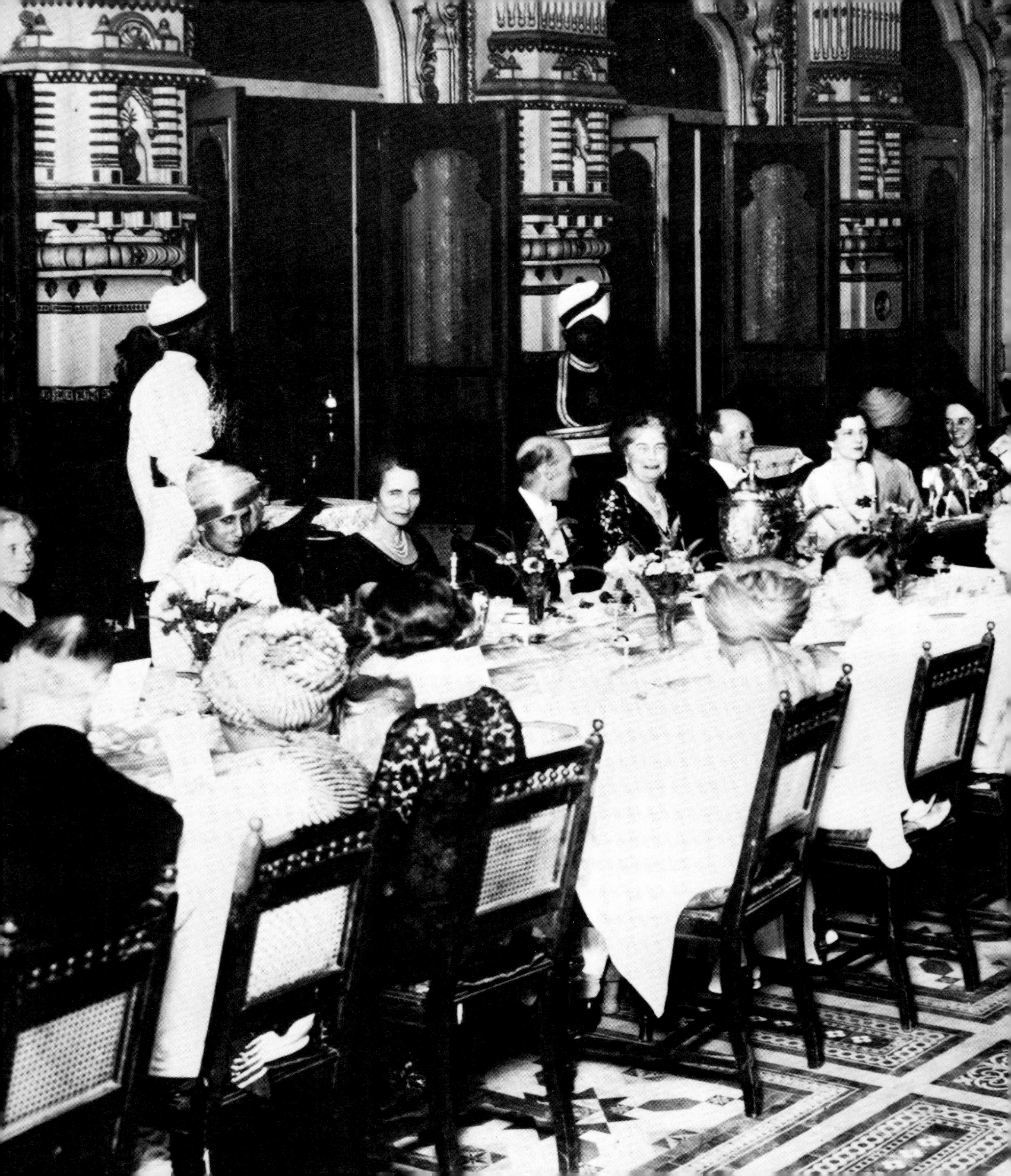

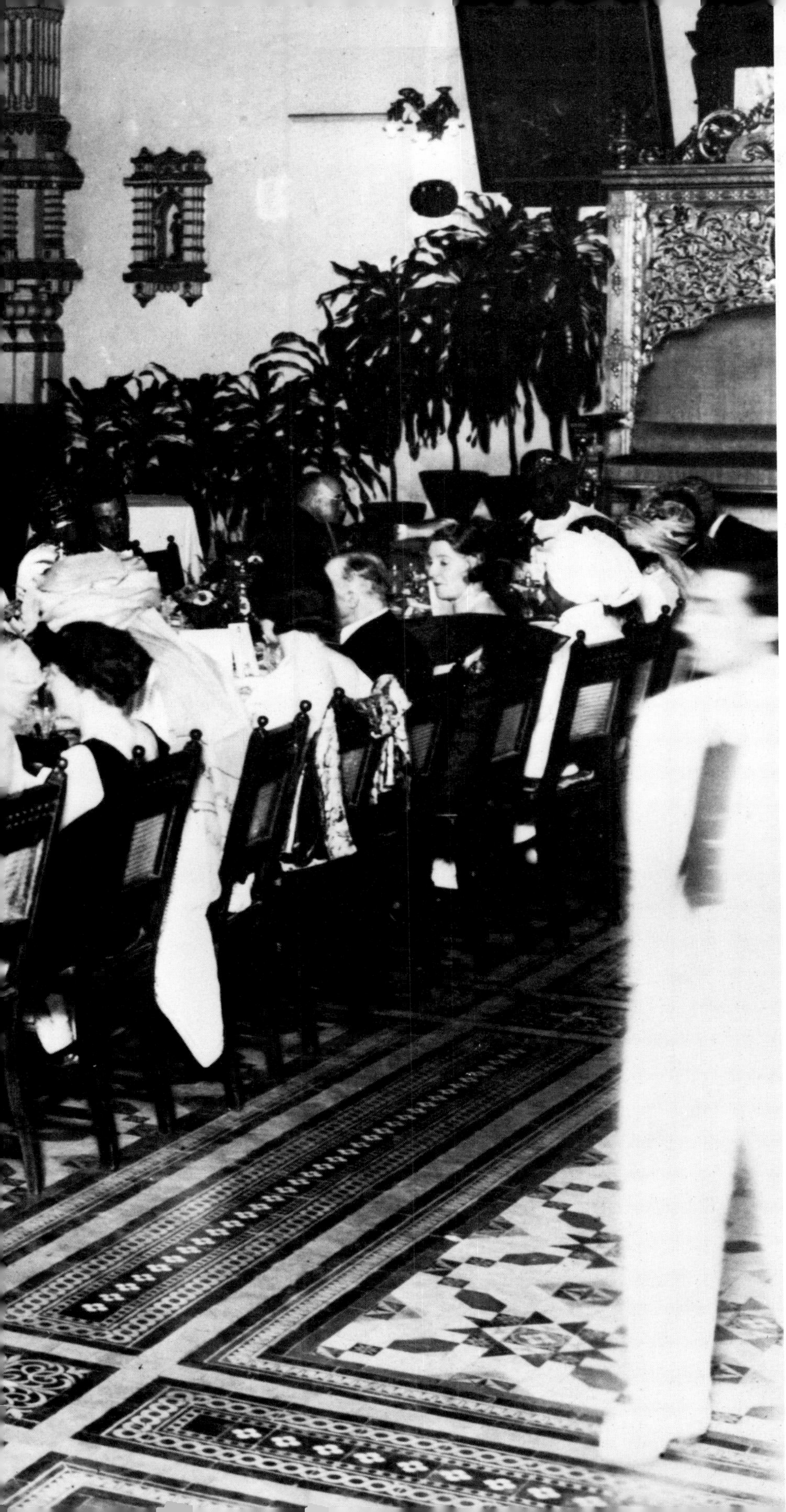

A Viceregal Tour, Kolhapur, 1933. The obligatory formal dinner. The dress was always very formal, the men in white tie. A banquet like this was completely outside Indian tradition. Note that there doesn't seem to be a single Indian woman present. These banquets were importations, as was much of the menu, as we have seen (page 45). Today only the recipes for the heavy English puddings that would have been served at such a dinner seem to have survived in India: cabinet pudding, tipsy pudding, Lady Smith pudding, Victorian bread pudding, steamed Spotted Dick. But, in spite of these names, Indian cooks have managed to Indianize them over the years, profusely decorating, coloring, and oversweetening them in the tradition of Indian sweetmeats. I was once served a delicious green trifle in Bombay, filled with fruit and topped with whipped cream and laced with *bhang*, (a derivative of marijuana).

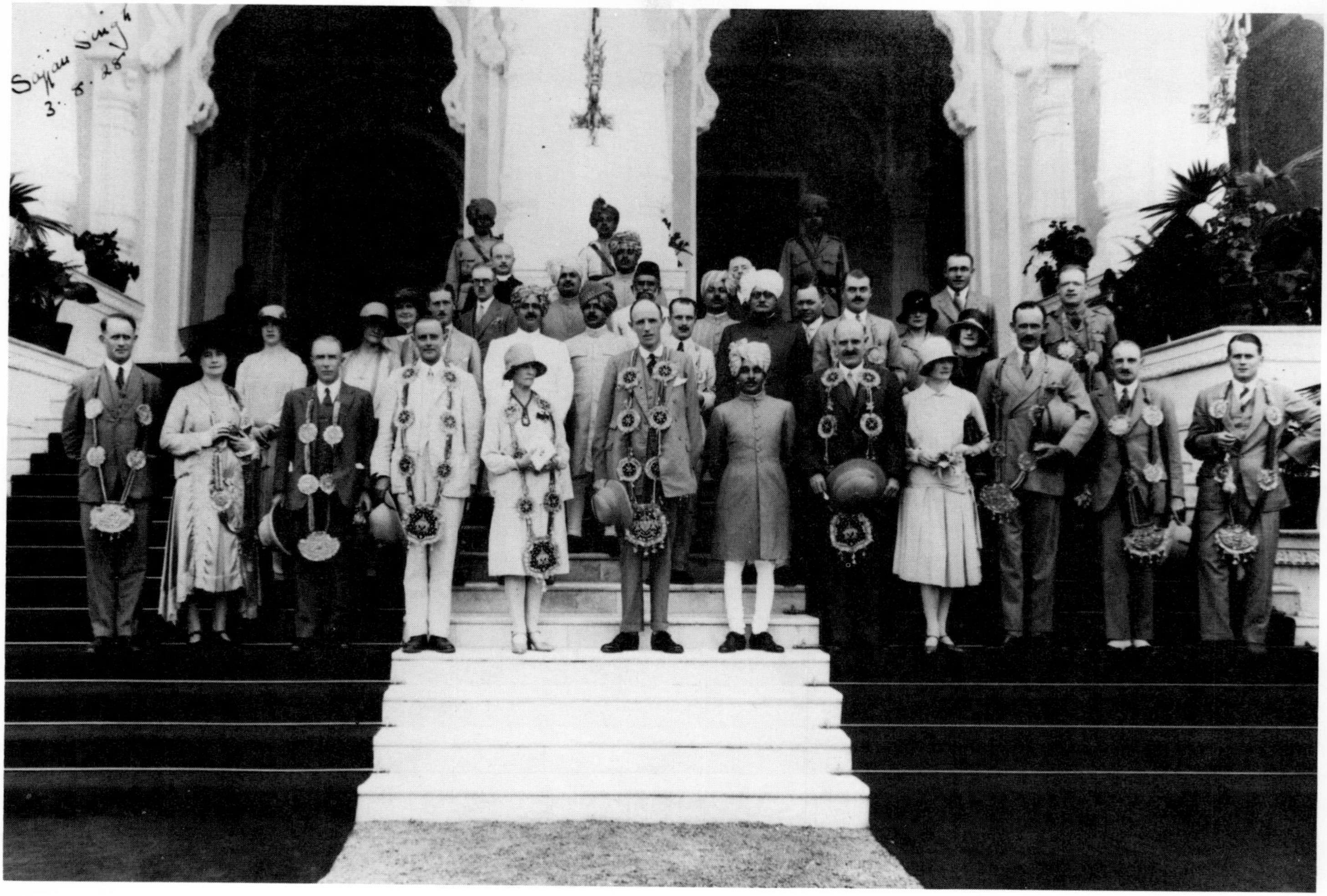
Sajjan Singh
3. 8. 28

A Viceregal Tour. Ratlam, 1928. The obligatory group photograph. The Maharaja, who is standing next to Lord Irwin, has presented his visitors with some rather grand garlands, made out of tinsel and gold thread. Etiquette normally requires the quick removal of the garlands from the recipient's neck. Foreigners in India often learn this too late, or not at all, and so end up looking a little foolish, like His Excellency's party here.

Miss Fitzroy's account of Gwalior ends with two incidents which shed light on differing aspects of her host's personality:

> I have already referred to his schoolboy delight in a practical joke; but though familiar enough with this, we had not bargained for the terrors the first of April might have in store! The ladies were, not unexpectedly, treated to a brackish concoction featuring as early morning tea, but the men fared worse. It was very hot, and they all departed to ride and bathe before breakfast; on returning they called loudly for lemon squash; lovely, bubbling glasses were brought to them, but, too late, were discovered to contain that healthgiving draught known as Mr. Eno's Fruit Salt! Our poached eggs were made of stone, our matches were duds, our cigarettes exploded, our ham sandwiches were lined with pink flannel, our chairs were uncertain, and when we came to play bridge in the evening our pencils boasted rubber points! The Maharaja's chuckles rested like a benediction on the distracted company, as he strolled, twinkling,

from group to group, but I believe he himself was caught at long last by some irreverent trap, prepared for him in his bed by A.D.C.s driven to retaliation!

The second incident was one of those strange, baffling, troubling experiences that happen to foreigners anywhere in India, though perhaps most frequently under the roofs of Maharajas. Miss Fitzroy writes that it left a deep impression on her, one difficult to express in words:

> . . . Last night we visited the Chattri raised by the Maharaja to the memory of his mother, who died some three years ago. As an orthodox Hindu her body was of course burnt, and the ashes thrown into the Ganges, but this memorial was erected on a spot for which, in her lifetime, she had great affection, and which she often visited. She was a lady of the old school, but her strict seclusion does not seem to have limited the scope of a very masterful and penetrating spirit. The veneration and affection in which her son held her, and which he has been at pains to establish for all time, are in themselves a remarkable tribute to the oft-told tale of the power behind the Purdah. We of Western emancipation commiserate the victims of the system, and often with reason enough, but it has little power to diminish, rather by respect and tradition would seem to accentuate, the influence of rare minds. And amongst such the Maharani must without doubt be numbered.
>
> Of the Chattri we had heard much, and we went in as skeptical a spirit as that with which you no doubt will listen to the story. We had heard of a pavilion where a life-size statue of the Maharani was attended night and day by a retinue of servants, was washed, dressed, jewelled, and had meals laid before it, with an electric fan to keep the image cool and a bed to rest on when tired. It smacked a trifle if not of bathos at least of a strangely perverse note; we were amazed, we were curious, we were doubtful, but we lived to appreciate its high sanity. Whether I can convey that appreciation to you is another matter, and if I fail it will be through no one's fault but my own, my excuse that the influences at work were so intangible. But it seems to me to-day that the Maharaja has amazingly made a joyous thing of death, has, with a courage and success that seems incredible to reason, swept away the bitterness of human defeat, by the simple power of human gaiety and affection. He has visualized memory, and this with no sacrifice either of dignity or regret.
>
> The Maharani was to hold her Durbar. The Chattri was lit and

carpeted, we drove up to the white gateway, an Indian band playing in the gallery overhead, and at the entrance the Sardars waiting to receive His Excellency. We walked down the paved and terraced avenue of the garden, a channel of water flowing down the centre, fountains playing and the path lit by stone lamps. On the left a bandstand, and the Maharaja's band playing "A Waltz Dream"! We grew increasingly bewildered, for were we not visiting a tomb or the next thing to it? On the right a pavilion for refreshments, a bungalow for the Maharaja, and farther, on our left, another pavilion for recreation. Here he comes with his friends and followers, here they work and play cards, eat and drink, enjoy concerts and roam in the garden; here parties are given, and every guest is the guest of a dead woman. Yet it is in no sense macabre but perfectly simple and sincere. The Chattri itself is a building of carved white stone standing above a big tank, there is a charming little pavilion in the centre, and on each side a temple, the one to Krishna, the other to Mahadeo. It was all brilliantly lit.

At the entrance to the courtyard we took off our shoes and skirted two sides of the tank till we reached the marble steps of the Chattri itself. These led to a miniature, but impressive, Durbar Hall, with brocade cushions lying ready for the guests between each pillar. At the farther end another flight of steps led to an open doorway and beyond, on a cushioned dais, in the orthodox attitude of the Hindu lady, sat the still white figure of the Maharani. I can think of no word but the French one *saissisant*. Behind her stood three women-servants, gorgeously dressed, fanning her with fans of silk and gold, and that quiet figure with the white, so intelligent face, was the presiding spirit both of the gaiety of the garden and of the grave dignity of the house.

We went up to the little room from which she looked down on her guests and then back to the Durbar Hall for the Ceremonial receiving of Itr and Pan, and to that figure each guest turned and bowed as he left, not so much, I think, because it was customary, as through the influence of a power stronger than himself.

More than fifty years have passed since this visit to Shivpura to see the *chattri* of Maharani Sankhyaraja Sahiba; she has been joined there by her son, Maharaja Madhava Rao, who has his own *chattri* now and his own effigy. The handsome buildings that house mother and son are of white marble inlaid in *pietra dura* reminiscent of the Taj Mahal. They are filled with the sound of beautiful music for hours every day: Gwalior is famous for its singers, and there are morning and evening concerts. The feasts still go on as they have for half a century (the food that is prepared for the effigies is given to the poor); there are still the frequent changes of clothing; electric fans blow in the summer to cool the figures, and electric heaters are turned on in the winter. American visitors to Shivpura say they find this not morbid or disturbing, but like Yvonne Fitzroy fifty years ago, they too describe it as restful, even beautiful. When Miss Fitzroy went there, the Maharani was only three years dead; now Sankhyaraja Sahiba and her son, the chuckling Maharaja who caused chocolate éclairs and iced tangerines to descend from heaven, have themselves become a goddess and a god.

Our greatest find of old footage from the Maharajas' golden days was in the cellar of the Umaid Bhavan Palace in Jodhpur, where we turned up quantities of deteriorating film. Most of it dated from the time of Maharaja Umaid Singh, who died in 1947. It really constitutes a pictorial record resembling the albums of miniatures the Moghul emperors commissioned in the late sixteenth and early seventeenth centuries to commemorate the high points of their reigns. There are no battle scenes—polo matches substitute for those—but there's just about everything else, including what appears to be the building of a city, the Umaid Bhavan Palace itself. And when the Maharaja died, there was a cameraman on hand to record his tremendous funeral procession.

These obsequies were shot in color (Ektachrome)—and very good color, too. We see a long, long column of people, perhaps ten abreast, coming toward the camera and then making a turn. The remains of the dead Maharaja are borne past, carried in a cloth box decorated with rosettes of tinsel. There is no weeping and wailing, just an army of men trudging by in the heat and dust, carrying out in an antlike way the prescribed duties of mourning. The cameraman repositioned his camera higher up, and now we see that the procession has reached a spot beneath the Jodhpur Fort near the palatial cenotaph of the previous Maharaja. The cloth box is set down, and the wrapped-up corpse is put on the funeral pyre. As the flames begin to consume it, the ant column far below continues its way upward.

From the dead ruler's funeral, the cameraman went on to shoot the first durbar of the heir, Maharaja Hanwant Singh. This footage is equally impressive, even gorgeous. The new ruler, seated in a *shamiana,* or tent, is receiving the respects of his people, the other princes, and the government of New Delhi. Hanwant Singh is quite a young man and gives an impression of physical power, of vigor and promise. He sits cross-legged on a raised marble platform, in profile, dressed in cloth of gold; he looks as if he is already used to presiding over such a scene, and has indeed been educated for it. The noblemen who present themselves are wearing bright orange turbans that move in a mass like an orange sea. Several European men in full morning dress appear. They come up to the new Maharaja, make little bows, and retire. Revolving electric fans are standing in corners. It must have been very hot there, with all those people, and everyone encased in his tight brocade coat buttoned up to the neck, with twenty yards of cloth wrapped around his head. (Moghul paintings, too, show us that it got very hot at these endless Indian functions: it was an artist's convention to paint in carefully the sweat stains under the arms of everybody present, even the emperors.)

Maharaja Hanwant Singh didn't live very long; he died in the crash of a light plane he was piloting. He is said to have shared his father Maharaja Umaid Singh's craze for airplanes. In the Jodhpur footage there is a delightful sequence from the early 1930s of the inauguration of Jodhpur's Flying Club. That must have been a great event. A Sir John Steel came from New Delhi to make a speech and pronounce the facilities officially open. He looks as though he is made of steel, too, with a long English face and long English teeth, and he has protected his hard English brains with a pith helmet. The Maharaja bounces around him like a happy puppy, shaking hands, hallooing to friends, seeing to it that everything is done just right. At the appointed moment Sir John takes a key out of a jeweler's box someone is holding (you expect to see a diamond bracelet), unlocks the hangar doors, and a plane is wheeled out. Afterwards there are loop-the-loops.

A big crowd of the Maharaja's guests is watching. Upholstered chairs have been arranged on carpets for them inside an enclosure, as at a race. The camera pans across the enclosure and ends up nicely on the rows of automobiles outside. And what automobiles! It is not possible to tell their makes from the footage, but they are all big and expensive and very well maintained—any dust that might have gotten on them on their way through the desert to the Flying Club has been wiped off. Something in the atmosphere of this sequence sums up that entire world. It all seems contained in one shot, across which a low sun is slanting: the desert, starting at the carpet's edge, stretches away into the distance; the little planes tumble about in the afternoon sky like gnats; the well-dressed people sit comfortably on their sofas, looking up; the shiny cars are standing ready with drivers and cleaners.

Most of the footage from Jodhpur is just as it came out of the camera—unedited, untouched except by what time and the Rajasthan climate have done to it. But the Flying Club sequence has been edited, so that the Maharaja could project it for his dinner guests; there are even title cards, so it is like a nice little silent-era comedy.

A Mighty Machine. The viceregal limousine, flying the Union Jack. Lord Reading lifts his solar topee.

III

Deposed and Dispossessed

Prince Bedar Bakht, Great-Grandson of Bahadur Shah Zafar, the Last King of Delhi. After the Indian Mutiny of 1857, the octogenarian descendant of the Great Moghul was exiled to Burma by the British. Bahadur Shah was allowed to take his last surviving son with him. That son married, and so did the son's son, but Bedar Bakht has remained a bachelor: he asked me, "What can I offer a woman?"

His whole life has been spent in obtaining official recognition of his claim of legitimate descent from Bahadur Shah, first from one government of India and then from another. The British, afraid nationalist forces might gather around him, maintained that his great-grandmother had been merely the old King's concubine and not one of the four official wives permitted by Islam. The new government of India under Pandit Nehru was kinder and gave him the benefit of the doubt, but they still refused his request for a stipend. After repeated submission of his case he was finally granted 250 rupees a month—at that time (1960) about $65. This last descendant of the House of Timur is looked after by the Calcutta Muslim community and spends his time writing melancholy verse in Urdu. He once took a job as a laborer in a Calcutta factory, until the manager called him in and asked him if the rumors that he was the Emperor Akbar's descendant were true; whereupon he quit. His privy purse—i.e., the $65—has presumably been suspended along with those of all the other Indian princes, whom, it could be argued, he vastly outranks.

*T*HE interviews that follow were recorded by us for *Autobiography of a Princess* at the time the princes were fighting the de-recognition decree. In the election of 1972 the decree was made an important campaign issue by the Congress Party. The party won a resounding victory, and the Indian Constitution was amended to take away the princes' privileges—including the royal allowances the Indian government had been paying them. Their titles have also been abolished.

FROM AN INTERVIEW WITH GAYATRI DEVI, AN OPPOSITION MEMBER
OF PARLIAMENT AND FORMER MAHARANI OF JAIPUR

. . . I used to be very idealistic. . . . The main thing is that one wants to do something for the people. You want to bring their grievances to the notice of the authorities. But I find it extremely difficult because unfortunately in our country, the authorities take very little notice of the grievances of opposition constituents. In fact, the Congress candidates go to these constituencies and say that, because you haven't voted for the ruling party, such and such thing hasn't been done in your district.

About ten or twelve years ago a whole lot of us were sitting together, a whole lot of friends, and we were grumbling about the government of India and how this hadn't happened and that hadn't happened, and how this should happen and that should happen, and I suddenly said, "Instead of grumbling we ought to *do* something about it!" And they said, "What sort of thing?" and I said, "Why don't we just try to get into Parliament and have a say somewhere?" They all said it was a very good idea. But of course I was the only sucker that did it, and they all stayed out of it.

Gayatri Devi, Former Maharani of Jaipur. For the last few decades Jaipur has been considered the most *social* of the Indian states. This was because of the personalities of the late Maharaja, Jai Singh, and his Maharani, Gayatri Devi: they were *the* beautiful people on the Indian royal scene for visiting celebrities doing the princely states. The Jaipurs were also well known in Europe and England—they had a large house at Ascot—and their appearances there were always welcomed by hostesses, society reporters, and fashion photographers.

The late Maharaja is seen in the portrait above the fireplace. The Viceroy's wife, Lady Reading, gives us our first glimpse of him, in 1922, at age eleven: "March 22nd: a very thrilling week this, starting with the visit to Jaipur, which we did through the night as heat was so great. We arrived at 8:30 in the morning, were received informally by all the court officials on a lovely carpet, 300 years old, which I coveted! The heir, a boy of 11, was there to greet us. He has only just been made heir, H.E. [His Excellency, the Viceroy] settled the claim in his favour to the everlasting gratitude of the Maharajah who is an old man, paralysed in his legs. We had a marvellous reception all through the streets and bazaars. . . . Every few yards a guard in brightest orange yellow with crimson turban. When we reached the old Palace a crowd of nobles and a scarlet and gold palanquin awaited me where I had to lie at full length and be bumped and shaken till we reached the Maharajah's private apartments. I was not going, but he expressed a wish to see me so I was 'swung' in on the palanquin.

"Imagine a very dirty gilded room, the walls covered with oleographs, conspicuous among them a coloured one of the old Empress William, Königin Louise. Big pieces of furniture swathed in dust sheets, dozens of early Victorian gas chandeliers the colour of dust and only one beautiful thing in the room, another priceless century-old carpet; and on it you came upon—as if by chance—a figure seated cross-legged on the carpet, no cushions, leaning against a bolster—the Maharajah!

"A splendid man with magnificent head and straight features, olive-skinned with a mane of grey hair and dark, flashing eyes. He looked every inch a Rajput Chief, but a dying one. The heir sat drowsing cross-legged as H.E. and the Maharajah had an interesting talk (interpreted). The boy was hung with emeralds and pearls, and half-a-dozen little sons all about the same age, with *kohl*-darkened eyes, stared at us as hard as they could stare. . . ."

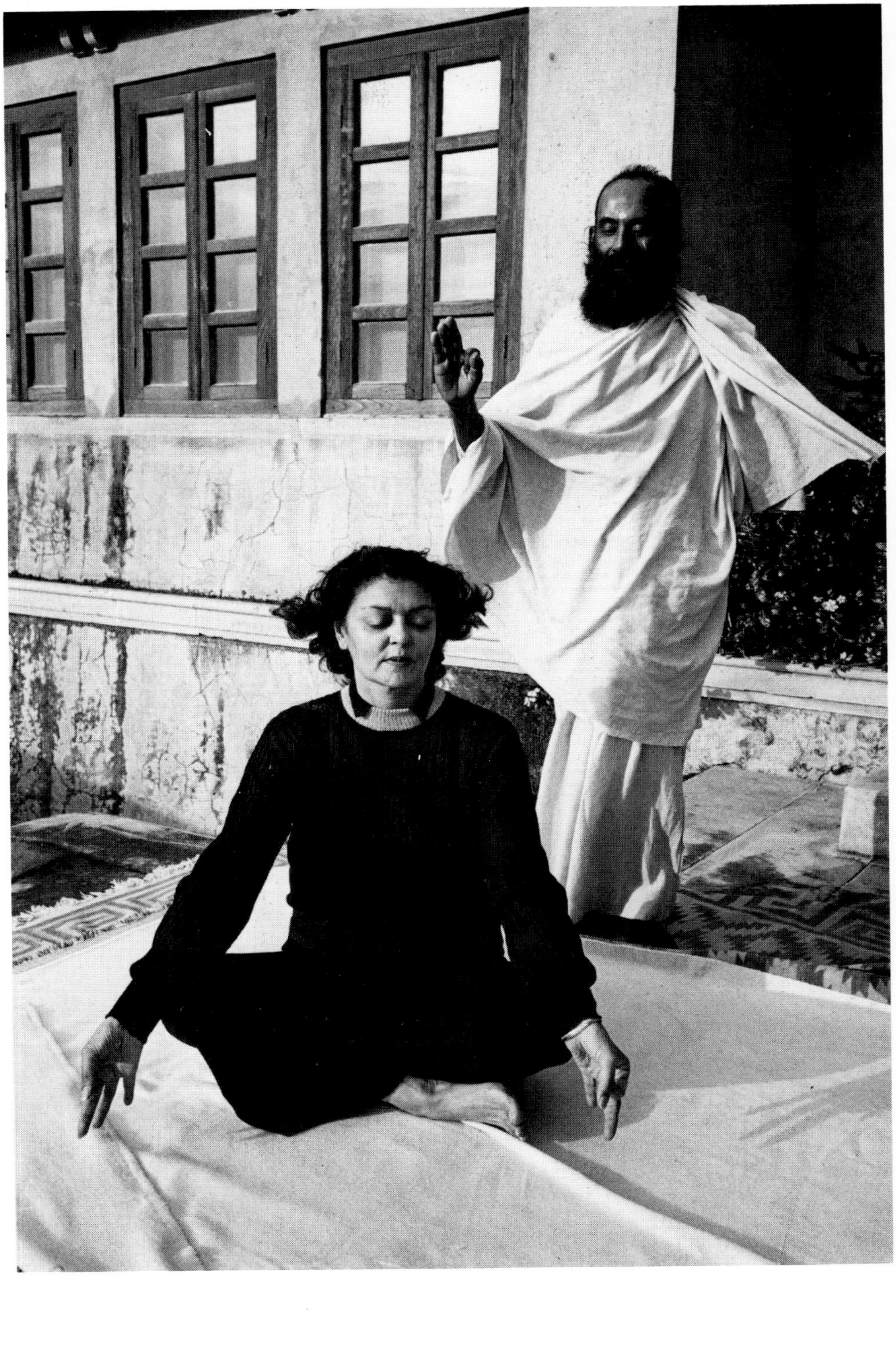

Gayatri Devi with Her Yoga Teacher.

All the same I keep on trying to help in any way I possibly can. When I first got married most of the women in Jaipur were in purdah and my husband said that he would like me to try and bring them out. I thought about it and I said that if you let me start a girl's school, where all these girls in purdah would come, then in ten years time I could guarantee that purdah would be finished in Jaipur. That is something we *did* do, and today it is one of the biggest public girls schools in India. We get Indian girls from all over the world, even from Africa, coming to it.

As far as the poor are concerned, we help by doing social work. My husband started a fund called the Benevolent Fund, to which we used to give about one lakh from his Privy purse. We've helped the poor and needy in many, many ways. For instance, we give them medical assistance in hospital and things like that. . . .

. . . When I'm not in India, I travel a lot. You see, my husband used to play polo regularly, right up to the last minute. That took us to England every summer and, before that, to Deauville. And through polo naturally we made many, many friends all over the world. I went to school in Europe and in England, so I like going to see our friends and to be among them. I remember when I was eighteen I used to think to myself that I would work very hard all year round if only I could have six weeks of skiing in the winter and six weeks by the sea, completely relaxed. That is my dream today, also. Unfortunately, nowadays going abroad means London, New York and Paris. But it's not the cities I seek. If only I could get away I would go to the resorts. With all my friends of course. . . .

. . . Jaipur was always a seat of learning and culture. In the City Palace there were painters and the people who made the medicines, there were singers and there were sitar players; fabrics and carpets were woven. It was a place where you could learn all these arts and crafts. And all these maestros had their *chelas* who learnt under them. It was all done in the City Palace. My grandfather-in-law, Maharaja Swaran Singh-ji, started a School of Arts and Crafts—I think it was in 1857. It was going to have its centenary celebrations when the government decided that it was unnecessary to keep this institution up, so they did away with it. I was so unhappy when I heard this. I was determined to revive the School of Arts and Crafts because I think that there is a great need for it; otherwise we will lose all our traditional arts. We started in a modest way, with the traditional Jaipur blue pottery. We do a little tapestry work. The students are taught fresco painting. I hope that gradually all these will be incorporated in the school again, that the

The Unfinished Cenotaph Outside Jaipur of the Late Maharaja Jai Singh.
In the old footage we discovered at the outset of *Autobiography of a Princess,* Jai Singh appears again and again and always most attractively. It is easy to see why he had so many foreign friends; there was certainly star quality there. In that footage he is first seen as a very young man officiating at a solemn ceremony of the Sawai Manguards at the Amber Fort; afterward, he kids with his brother officers in a friendly, easy way. He was a great polo player, riding right down to the last day of his life, so there is a lot of film showing him in that aspect. In England in 1933 after a polo match which Jaipur won, he is there to accept a silver cup from Queen Mary on behalf of his team. He turns up at weddings—as a bridegroom at his own marriage in Jodhpur to a Jodhpur princess, where he can be seen being lifted in a silver palanquin onto the back of an elephant; and as a guest at the wedding of Hanwant Singh, who shortly became Maharaja of Jodhpur, at which he appears as a dashing and trim figure in black military dress, contrasting with the gaudy silks of the other (mostly corpulent) Indian princes. His handsome face smiles out at the camera from the door of the wedding train taking the big wedding party from Jaisalmer to Jodhpur. In these shots he seems to be something of a loner, or at any rate a bit aloof from the others. Later on, we see him at a campsite in a jungle with the young and beautiful Gayatri Devi, his third wife. He was ambassador to Spain toward the end of his life.

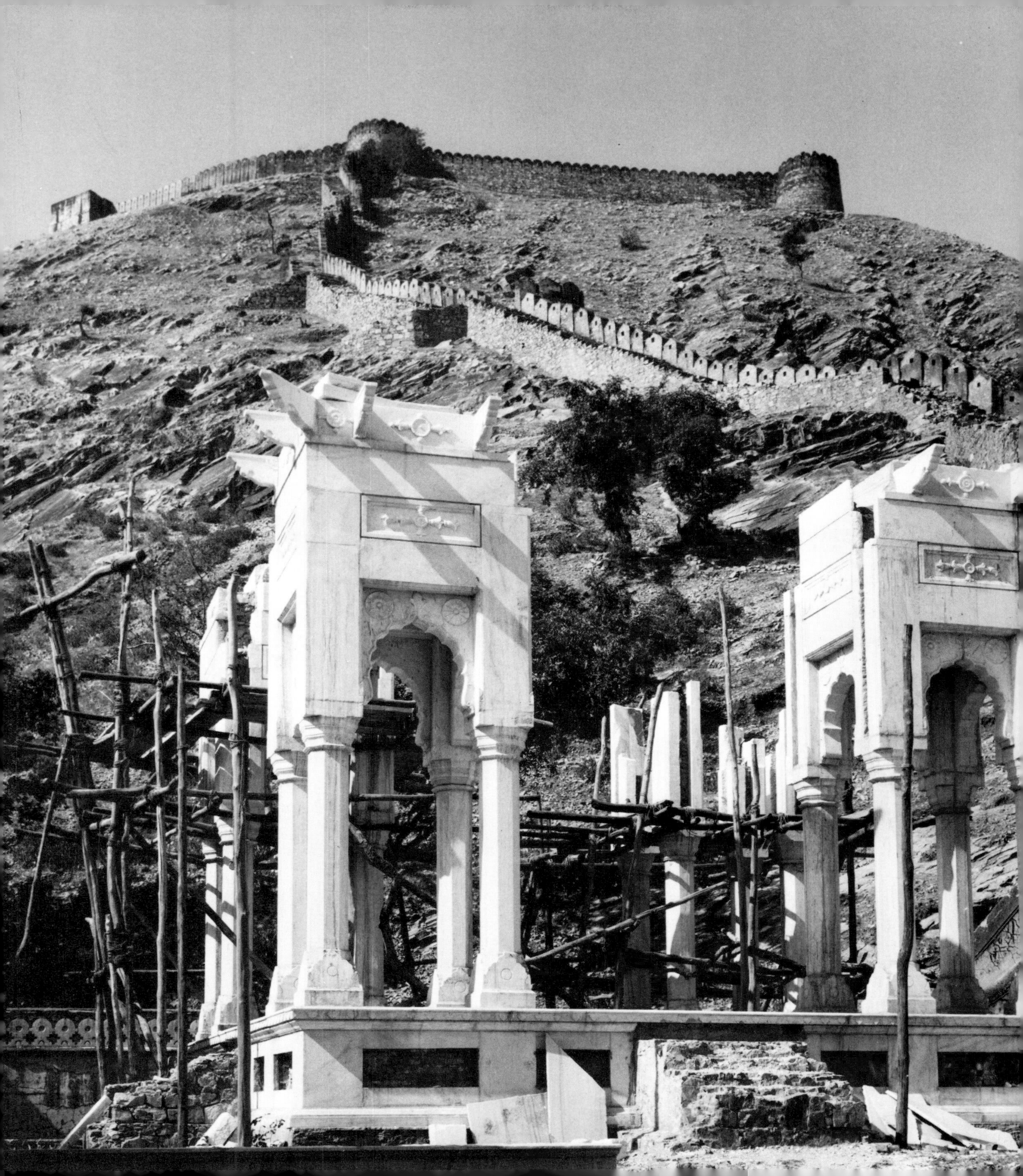

A Proud Old Queen. "Ma" Cooch Behar, the dowager Maharani of Cooch Behar, in her flat in Bombay, 1955. She was Gayatri Devi's mother. The Maharajas kept luxurious flats in Bombay, where they went for the racing. The decoration of these flats, however, often seems influenced by the exuberant taste of the set designers of Bombay films.

students will come and learn these old arts and crafts. . . .

. . . When I first got married and came to Jaipur I thought it was the most beautiful place I had ever been to in my life. My ambition is to give Jaipur back the beauty that is hers. Unfortunately, over the years Jaipur has gone into hands that have not cared for her. Before, in the olden days, the façades were maintained, they were painted every year. And the white work and all that, the trellises looked after. But today, as you can see, nothing is maintained; Jaipur is getting uglier and uglier every day. Advertisements up everywhere and also electric poles. And today it is not the "Pink City" anymore, because everybody puts up any color they like: if somebody thinks that green looks nicer, then he puts up a green house and no one stops him. They think modernisation means square blocks of concrete, any old color, and masses of advertisements in neon lights. . . .

62

"Bubbles" Jaipur, Gayatri Devi's Stepson. He succeeded in 1970—but succeeded mostly to a lot of trouble in the final breakup of the world of the Indian princes, which included the systematic stripping of his family's possessions and treasures. These latter were so great that they were kept hidden in a secret place, guarded by a fierce tribal chief. Even the ruler was never allowed in there unless blindfolded. But in 1975 that did not prevent the income tax officers from breaking in and bringing a charge against the royal family for "nondisclosure of income."

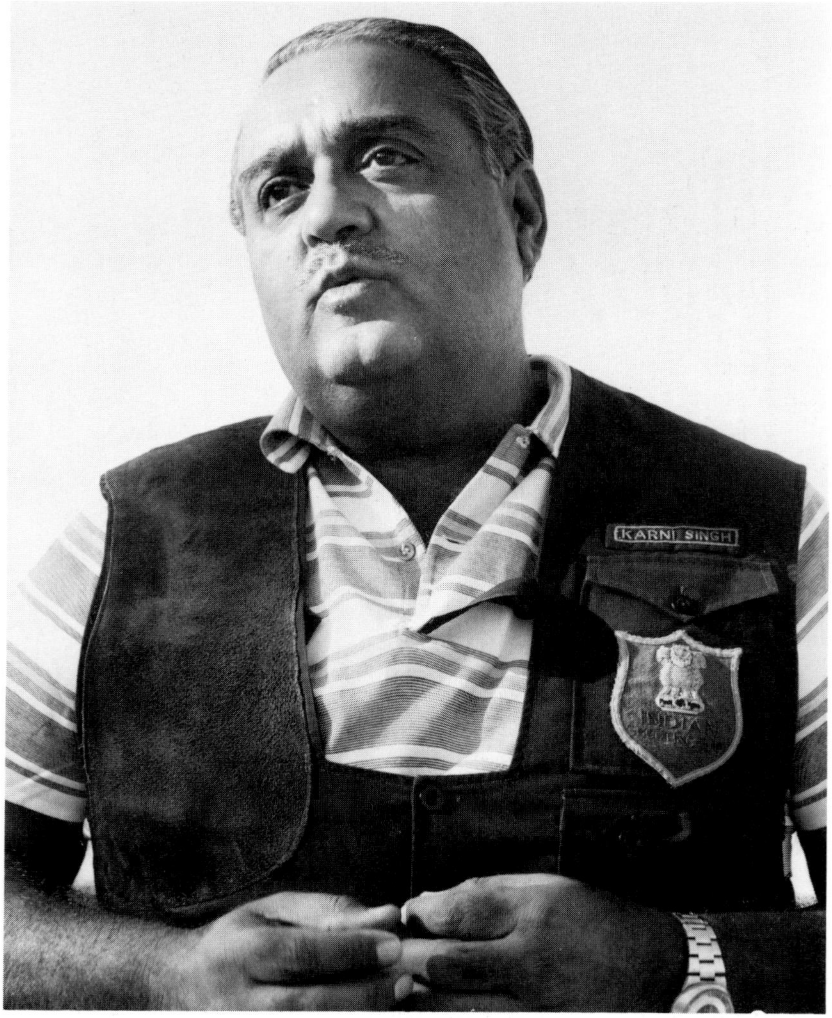

Karni Singh, Former Maharaja of Bikaner. (*left and right*)

FROM AN INTERVIEW WITH DR. KARNI SINGH,
FORMER MAHARAJA OF BIKANER

. . . I will be quite candid and frank. . . . I have been in Parliament twenty years now; I have seen the kaleidoscopic changes that my country has gone through; I would quite honestly say I do not derive any satisfaction from being in politics today. But I did twenty years ago. And the reason candidly is that I find too much

(*overleaf*)
The Cenotaphs of the Bikaner Rulers in the Thar Desert.

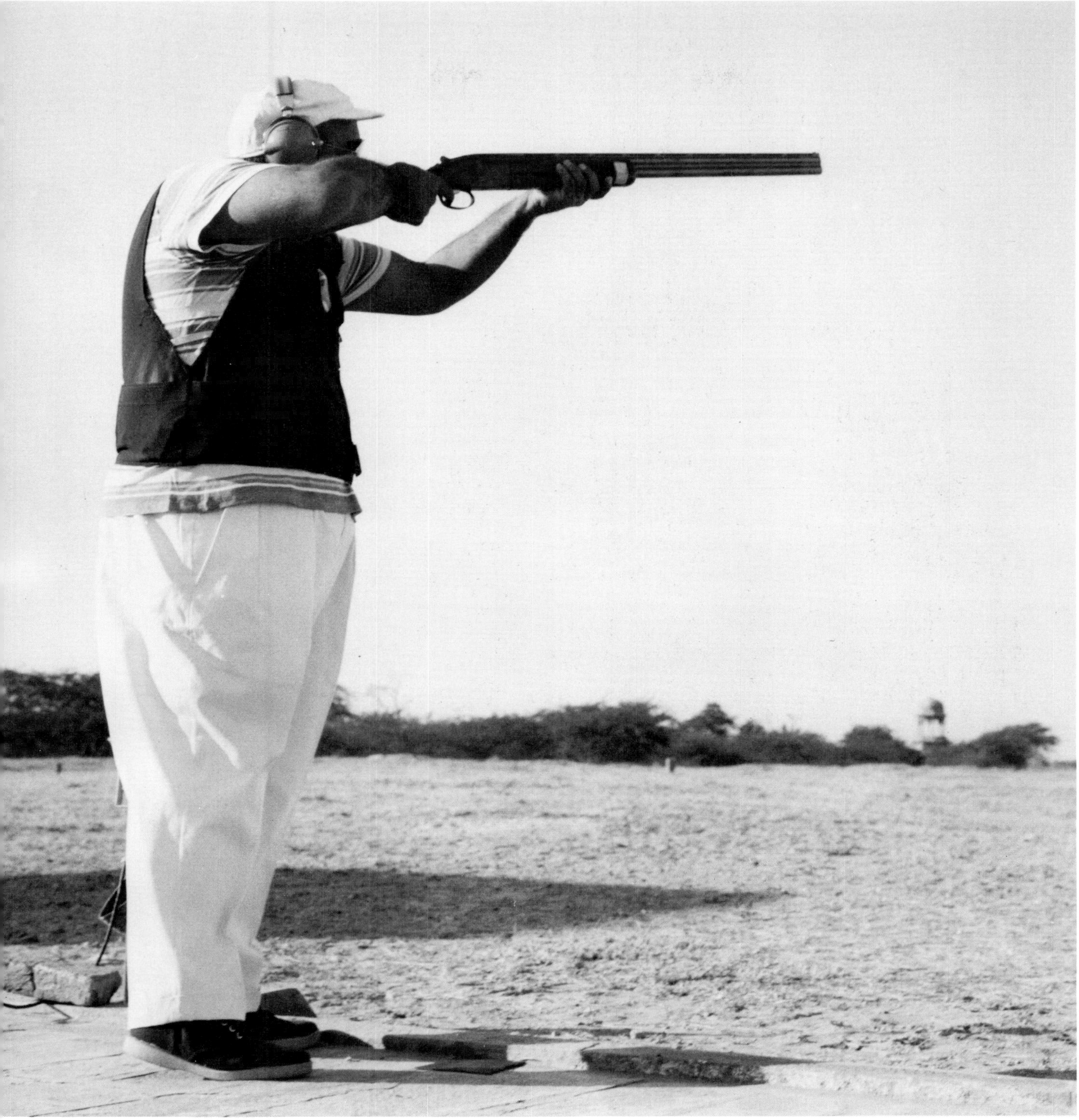

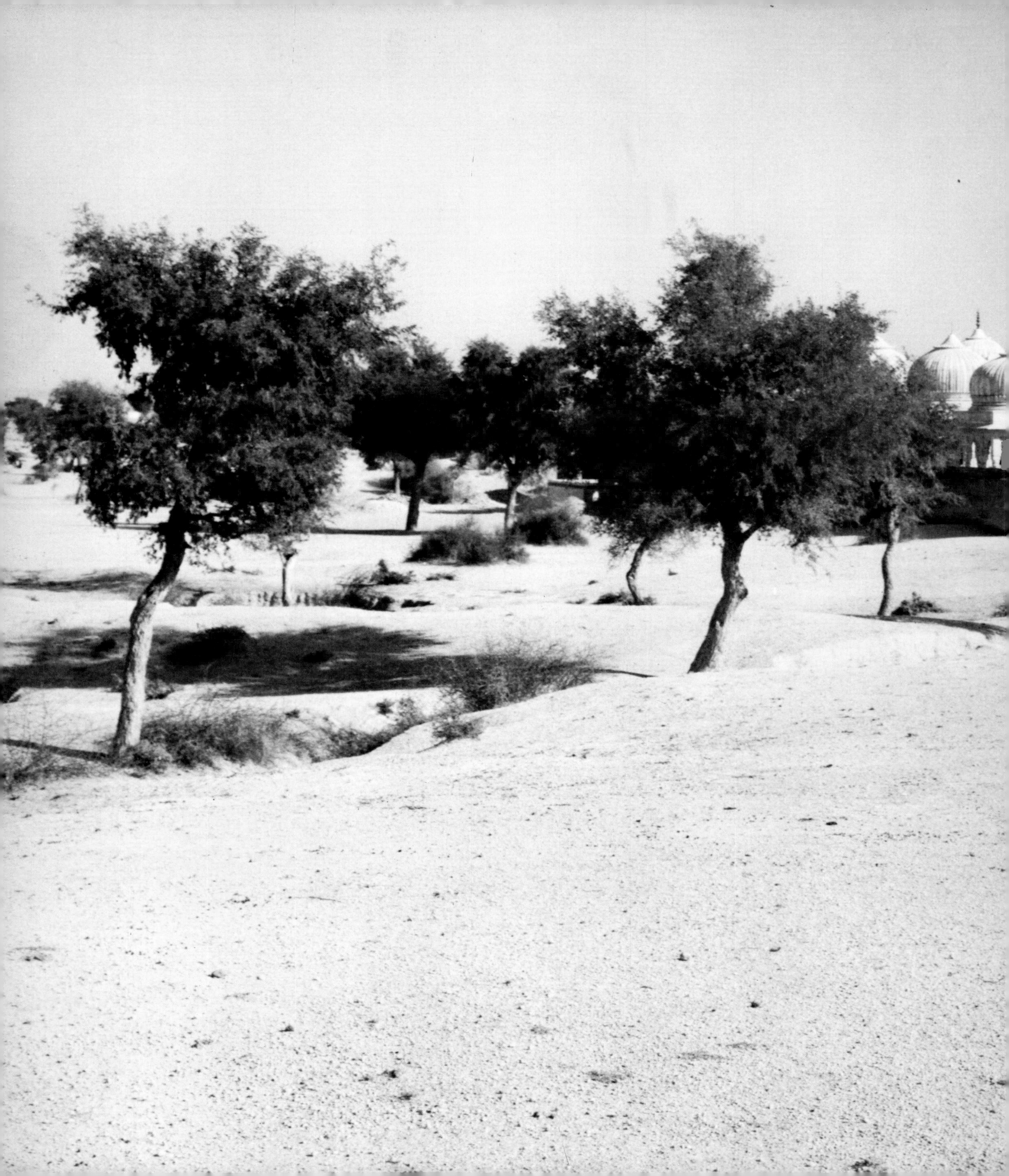

selfishness injected in politics. I find, that while using the name of the people, we are thinking all the time more of ourselves and our parties. As for the . . . satisfaction of being a ruler: I've never ruled once. My father was the last ruler; he signed the merger agreements. I've always considered myself the same as any other citizen, having gone to colleges at Delhi and Bombay and rubbed my shoulders with 'most anybody. I feel happier when I'm allowed to live like any average citizen.

I feel a complete misfit today, both occupying the position of the Maharaja as well as a Member of Parliament. My mind works more in line with the average citizen; I cannot quite fit myself into the title I have inherited. At the same time I can also say, quite frankly, that I feel unhappy sitting in Parliament House. I find that far too much egotism and selfishness are being projected by politicians. And because of this I sometimes do find myself at a loss as to how I should lead the rest of my life. I have traveled in many, many parts of the world and I enjoyed most of all meeting people at hamburger stalls, in small cafés in England, in France, in the United States, and in many other parts of the world where I had the opportunity to mix as man to man. And for me that type of relationship is far more interesting than the titles and the fact that I happen to be an M.P. . . .

. . . I've been interested of late in clay pigeon shooting, in painting and playing golf; all of these have been a challenge. I've enjoyed making movie films—putting in my own soundtrack—but when one looks at the number of years that a man has to live, you realize that all these interests are very hard to attend to. But I have divided my life in such a way that I can attend to all of them. If I were to spend, say, six hours a day in Parliament, half-hour to an hour once a week in painting, a couple of hours most afternoons playing golf, and two days a week for clay pigeon shooting— be able to concentrate, think only of that thing when I'm doing a particular activity—then I find it's possible to reach a certain standard of proficiency. But I find that my time is more and more taken up with politics. I enjoy being a sportsman and an outdoor man much more than I do a politician. . . .

. . . I think the fact that my father sent me to universities in India and my education has been wholly Indian has been an advantage to me today. Being educated in a foreign country, seeing

Bikaner, Lalgarh. Most of these palaces have their busts and full-length portraits of Queen Victoria and their inscribed, silver-framed photographs of King George V and Queen Mary. The statues of former British rulers and administrators have been toppled all over India now, and the streets and institutions formerly bearing their names now bear those of Indian leaders and patriots. In Bombay, the British Raj statues have been put in the zoo.

all the glittering skyscrapers and high standards of living, many young people of my country come back and find themselves misfits. For this reason I have insisted on my children being educated in India also: I think they fit in better. We have three children. My boy is twenty-six, a girl eighteen—Rajishri. She shares the same interests that I do. We paint together, we shoot together, and she was eighth in the world in the Ladies' Shooting at San Sebastian two years ago when she was only sixteen. I feel that education to education there is not a great deal of difference between one country and another. But with the India that is developing today, with all our socialist thinking, it is important that the education be imparted locally, so that the young people feel themselves having their grass roots in the soil here. . . .

69

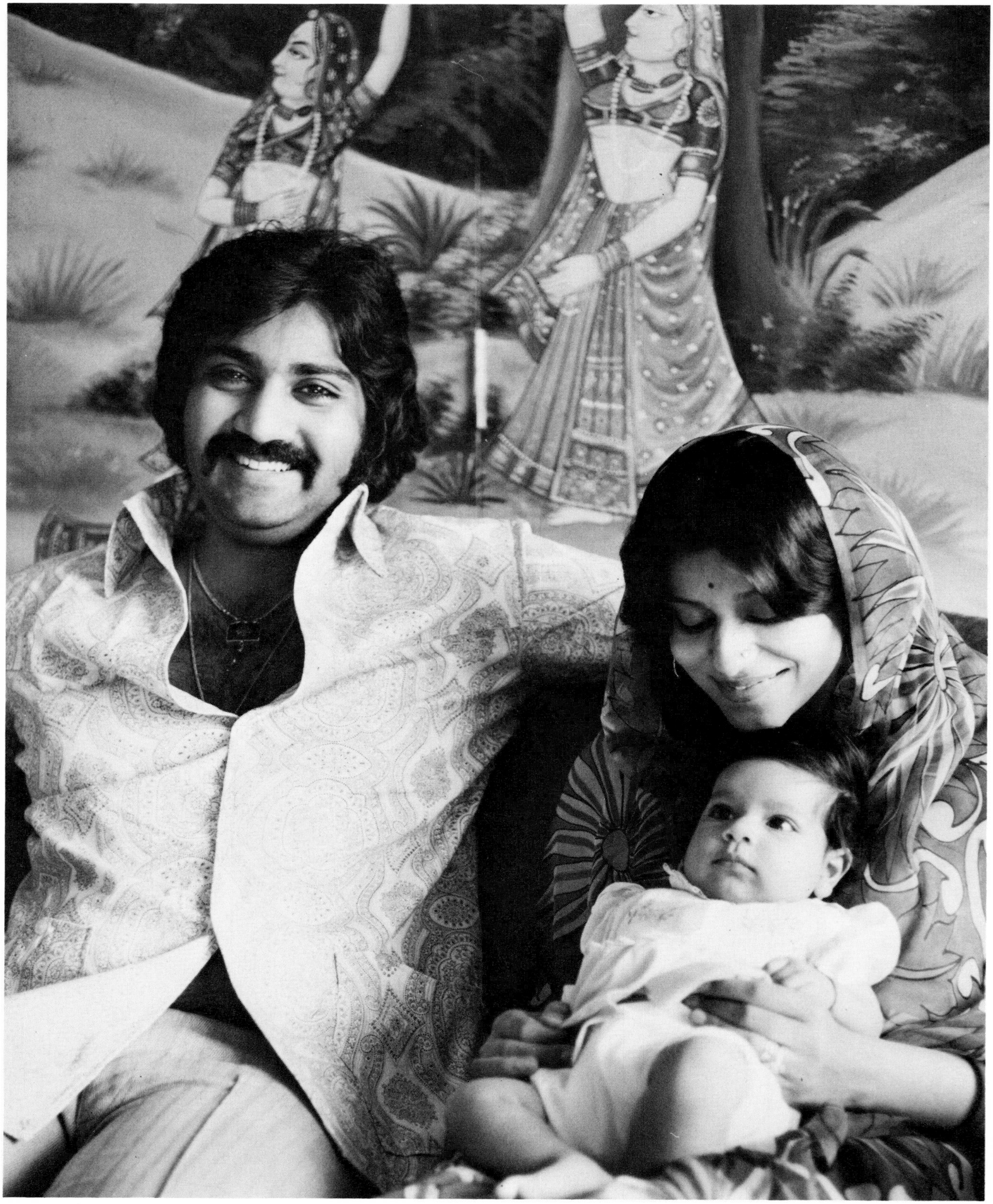

FROM AN INTERVIEW WITH GAJ-SINGH, FORMER MAHARAJA OF JODHPUR

. . . The way things are moving in this country, I'm very un-certain as to our future role. On the one hand, we Princes are Public Enemy Number One. On the other hand, we still have our traditional support; the local people look up to you for some kind of lead, some kind of assistance. I have to find some way to justify this support, this loyalty; to do something for the people. If one were a "real" politician, then one could exploit this support and use it to the benefit of one's party. But I am not a party man. I feel that I have to be honest with myself as well as with the people.

When I became Maharaja of Jodhpur I was very young. My father had just died in a very tragic plane crash; he was about twenty-eight and at the peak of his career. He was the first prince to contest an election and, in fact, he died the day before the results were announced. He had contested for the local seats and when the results—which he never heard—came out, he'd won thirty-two out of thirty-six seats. This was just after Independence, so it was quite a major feat. I was about four then. . . . From that age I began to be geared to this kind of life—towards tradition and things like that. It was decided by my mother and various others that if I stayed in India I would probably get spoiled or something. . . . I went to England in about 1956 to prep school, [then] to public school, and then to Oxford. It was a good period of my life, being abroad, because there I could be free. At the same time I used to come back every year, so I kept in touch with India as well. It was really much of a game, going abroad and coming back; somewhere on the plane on the way back here I did a sort of switch in my mind: I became Indian. And when I returned, again the same thing, I did a switch and became English. It was a good game while it lasted, but as I grew older it began to dawn on me that I had to make a choice of what I wanted to retain: what was good of one system and what was good of the other. And I'm still in that position now.

As soon as I returned from university I was expected to get involved in politics and at that time I felt I didn't want to. . . . It was felt by most of us here that we had to do something . . . to be left out of it would not be doing our duty. Being too young

◄ Gaj-Singh, Former Maharaja of Jodhpur, With His Family.

myself, I persuaded my mother to stand for elections against the Congress Party. My mother stood from Jodhpur, and in all we supported five candidates in the five Parliamentary constituencies. In spite of our expectations, we lost four out of five seats; the only person who won was my mother. . . .

. . . As you know, today India is really the thing for tourists; there is now a great deal of interest in Rajasthan. I think that with the coming of the airline, we can provide a focal point for Rajasthan here in Jodhpur. As I can't continue to live in a palace which is this large, I think the most practical thing is to convert it into a hotel and provide all kinds of facilities. Not being over-ambitious, just giving the tourist what we have to offer—clothes, food, music, whatever it is—saying this is what we have to offer and what we show the tourist whether he likes it or not. If he likes it, he will come back; if he doesn't, he won't come. This is a desert area, as you know; we want to put across an image of an unspoilt Rajasthan, where village life and so on is very much as it was a hundred years ago. . . .

. . . You see, I don't have many friends here, just a few relations —though I do have some friends coming from Europe occasionally. But I can occupy myself because I have such a backlog of adjusting properties and so forth. That takes up most of the morning's work. Then meeting people takes up the afternoon. And then I play golf or squash. I have to get out of here eventually to get some fresh air. . . .

FROM AN INTERVIEW WITH SHOBHA KANWAR BAI-JI, GRANDDAUGHTER OF SIR PERTAB SINGH

Pertab Singh was one of the great Rajput leaders of his day (he died in 1922) and, like Maharaja Ganga Singh of Bikaner, was a progressive, forward-looking statesman. He was much admired by the British and is still deeply revered by the people of Jodhpur. His personality dominates the modern history of his state. But in spite of his progressive policies, the life of his womenfolk remained essentially traditional.

Shobha Kanwar Bai-ji. She sits ► in a palanquin and seems to be making a beckoning gesture to us—into the purdah palace, into a life of seclusion. In fact, though, her story is a repudiation of all that, of the immurement that is the traditional lot of aristocratic Rajput ladies.

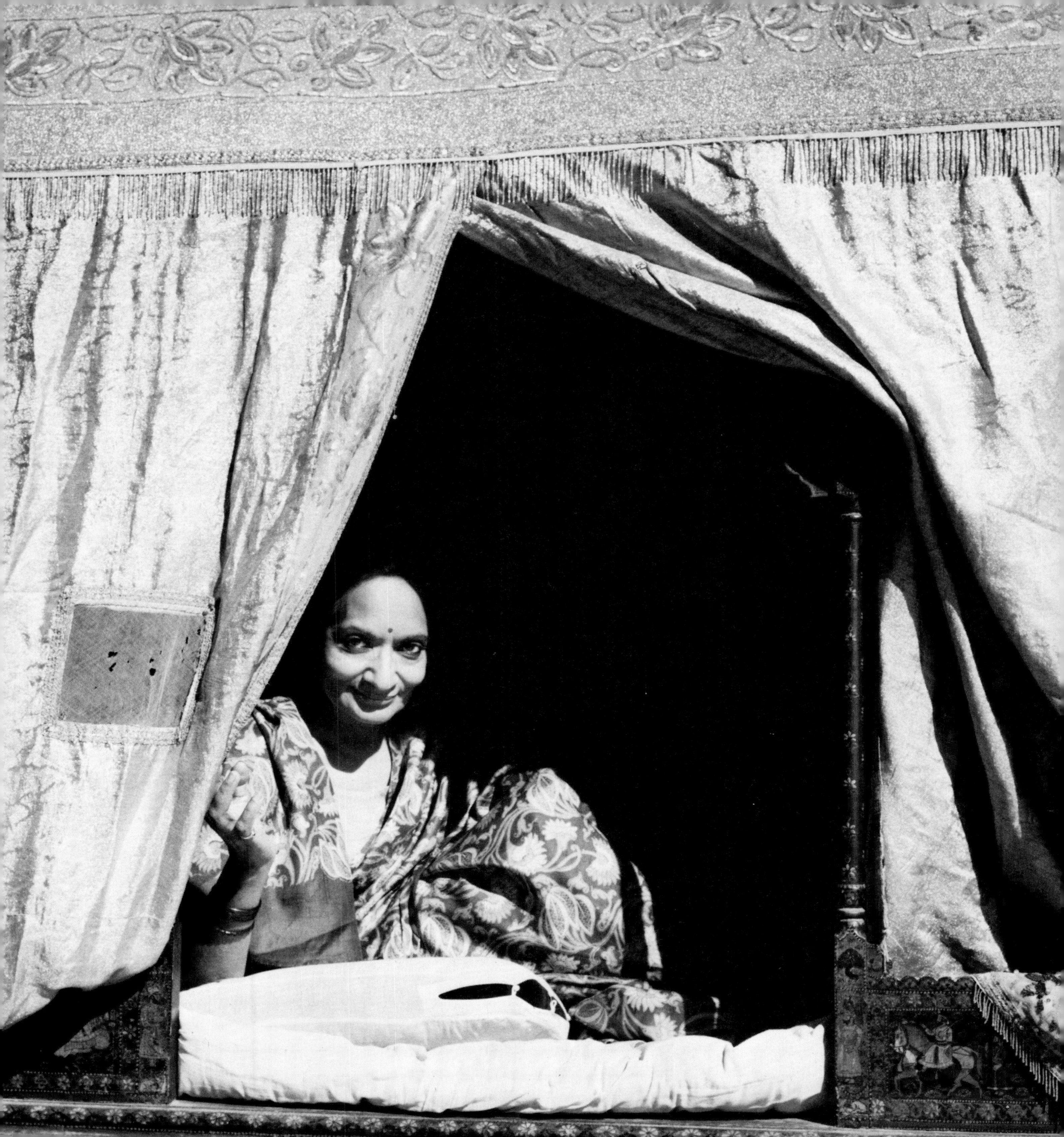

. . . The zenana quarter was guarded by two men in relays: it was only maidservants who were allowed upstairs. You could not go anywhere, except to certain houses of relations. If I went there I had to go in a purdah car, with the driver and one of my *doridars* sitting in front. After being able to go about wherever I liked in Europe, to have that kind of restriction was very, very difficult. . . .

. . . My father had been sent over to England for eleven years by my grandfather. He was brought up in a Vicar's family in Sussex. I think he owed everything to his background there. He brought us up in the same way. I had an Italian governess: because of health reasons of my younger brother, we were in Switzerland for seven years, where I learned French and Italian and a little German. I think that I can claim that I was the first girl in Rajasthan, of our family and status, who had an education. The bitterest fight I had was when I found that even though I *had* an education, still I was being brought back to this—to *this*, which was for me literally an imprisonment. I remember my thoughts in those days were: if only I could lead a suffragette movement over here. But the women would have been the last people to have followed me. . . .

. . . I had nothing in common with anyone: nothing and no one. Because no one had my education and without the same level of education you cannot have the same level of understanding. I was the most outrageous and the most criticized person in the whole of Jodhpur in those days. My father was very much criticized because he had had me educated. I was never told why purdah was necessary. It was the custom. Everything was always the custom. And because of my father's position in Jodhpur, I had to obey it. Otherwise, his position would have become incredibly difficult. Now, being much more mature, you realize what your family background means, what your name means. I think it's a lot of family pride or egotism to be known as my father's daughter or my grandfather's granddaughter. . . .

. . . My grandfather! I can remember, as a very small person, being taken to pay my respects every day. He used to get up at crack of dawn and ride every morning; my elder brother and I would go in the dark to see him. When we got there we were so frightened we used to hide behind the servant, who was much more frightened than we were. My grandfather, rather as he fed his horses I think, would take out a biscuit from his pocket. We used to rush out, take whatever he offered us, grab it, and rush behind the servant. And that is as we remember him. But he was a fantastic administrator. I think Jodhpur to this day owes everything to his administration. He is the person who brought free education. . . .

. . . He had an idea that he would send one of his own daughters over to become a lady doctor, because he considered that in the zenana a lady doctor would be of much more use than just getting her married off. And in fact, that particular daughter he brought up as a boy. Up to the time that she was nine she had only worn jodhpur breeches; she had her hair cropped like a boy and was a very, very good rider, on equal status I'm told with her two brothers. My grandfather ruled my father with a hand of iron, as he ruled the rest of the state. I remember my father used to tell me tales of when he came back from England and was put into administrative service. My father would be told, "We will be going to such and such village." So, getting on a horse, one blanket, and off tomorrow. That's what they had to do. If they got to a village they might get a bed to sleep on, otherwise it was under the stars, under a shrub, or a bush, or a tree. I can well believe how my father must have suffered. He was a person who loved his comforts.

. . . I am contented here. Here you are a personality. You've got so much to be proud of, so much to live for. After all these years you find that you still count in spite of giving nothing, that they still look up to you. I would certainly not live anywhere outside our own, not only India, but Jodhpur. . . .

A Silver Bed on Which Royalty Slept, Watched over by European Nudes. Would they have been insulated, inside that bed, against the rest of India? The Begum of Rampur doesn't think so: ". . . I wouldn't say we're unfamiliar with the life of the common people. How can that be, when we had thousands of servants living with us? Our servants used to live with us like our own children. Might be we had a different approach— we were better dressed, we had a silver bed—you know, we had the more expensive things. But they shared our home. If we slept on the bed, they slept on the carpet just near us. It's not like we had a very aloof life from the common man—ever." [In an interview with Granada Television in 1972]

The Chattris at Mandor, Outside ► Jodhpur. These cenotaphs of former Maharanis were customarily erected on the spots where the funeral pyres consumed their remains. "It was more quiet and empty and lonely than any other place I know on earth . . . Nothing there except a few vultures . . . I thought the cenotaphs themselves resembled vultures. Or some extinct species of bird come to roost in the desert . . ." [Cyril Sahib, in *Autobiography of a Princess*]

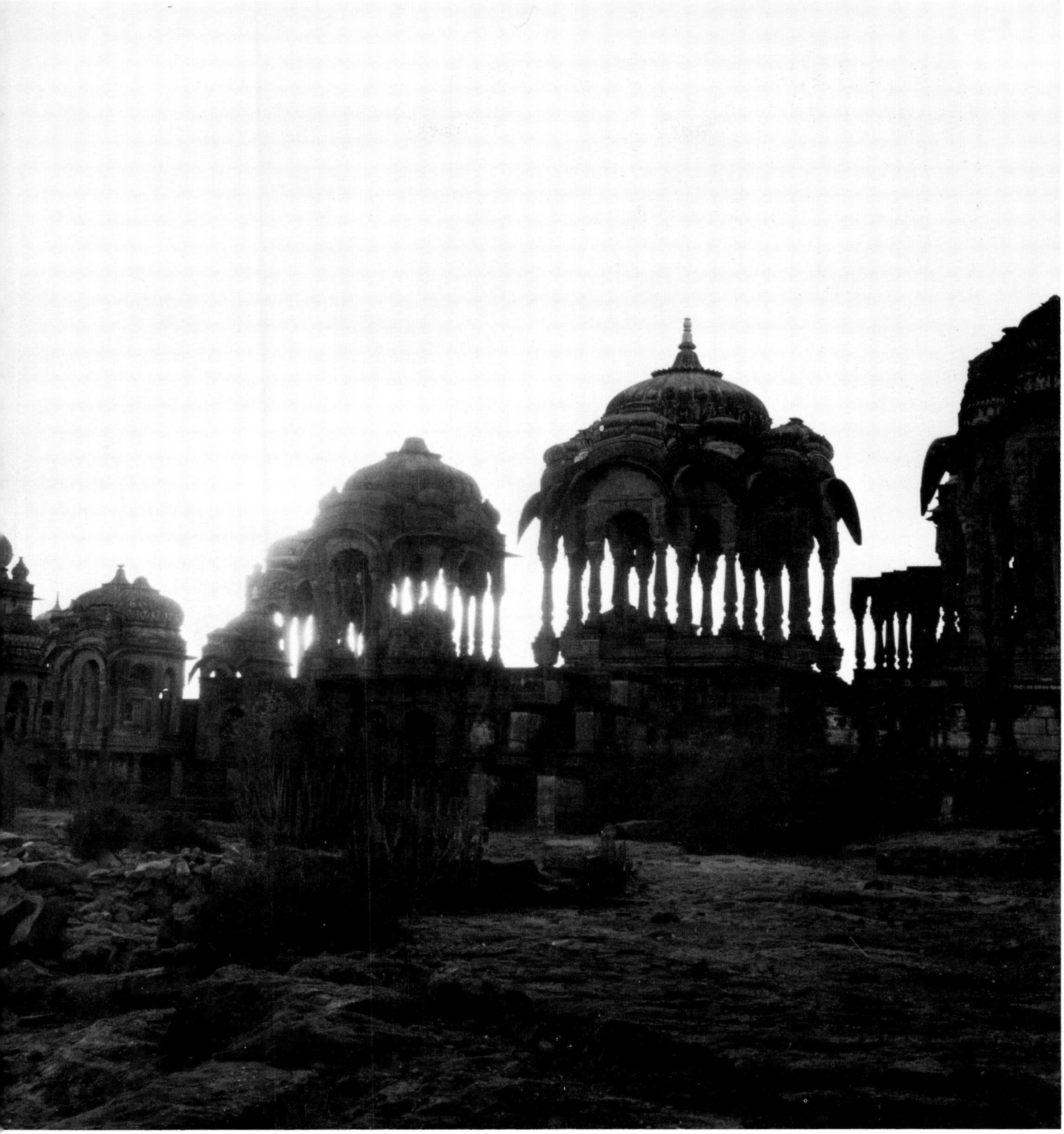

IV

The Land of Death

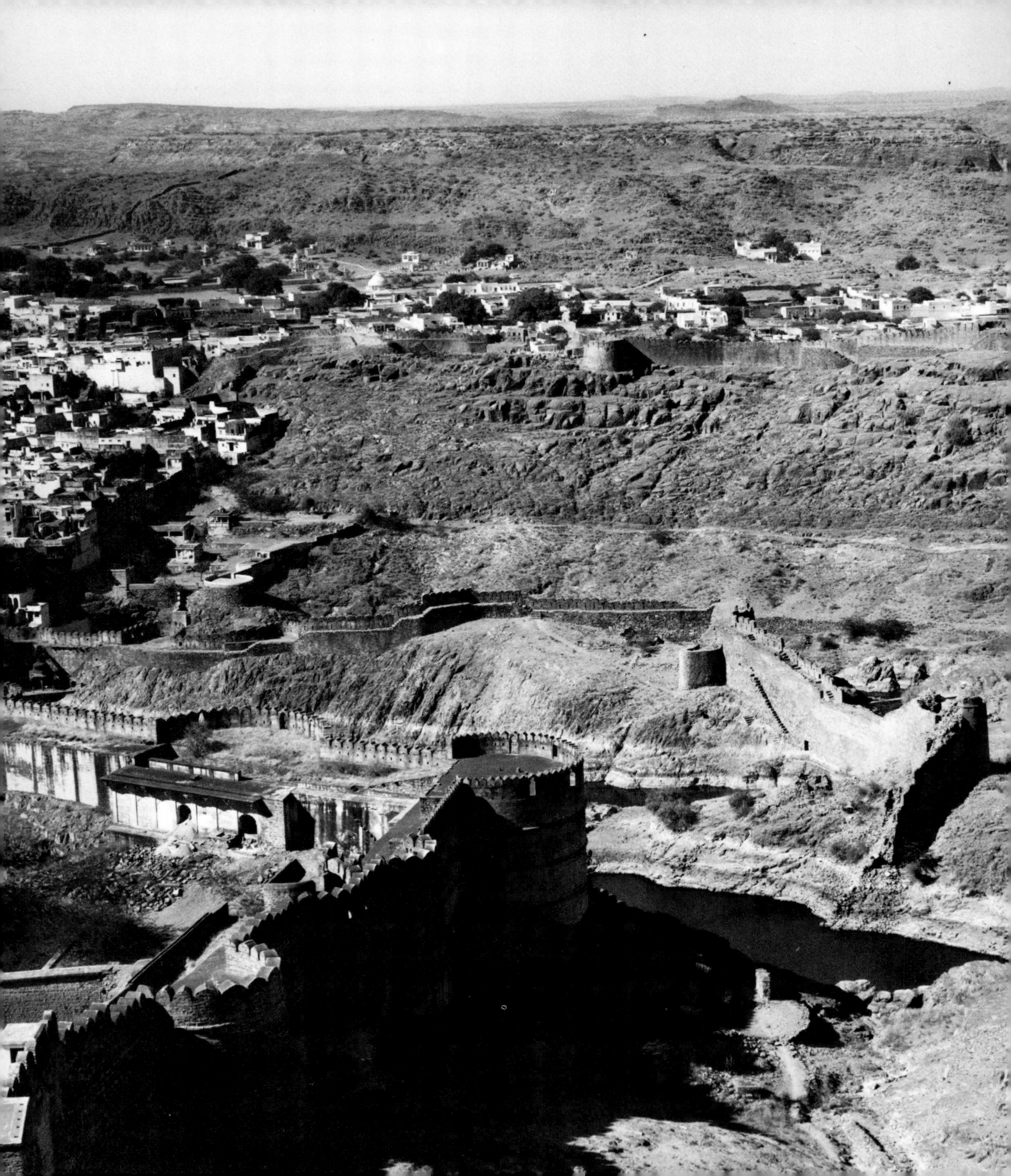

$\mathcal{T}$HE state of Jodhpur used to be called Marwar. In his *Annals and Antiquities of Rajasthan*, published in 1832, James Tod gives the origin of the name: "Marwar is a corruption of Maroo-war, classically Maroost'hali or Maroost'han, 'the region of death' . . ."

A brief glimpse over the Table of Contents gives a good idea of the history of a typical Rajput state:

> Seoji massacres the Dabeys of Mehwo, and the Gohils of Kherdur—Massacres the Brahmins and usurps their lands . . . Doohur succeeds —Slain— Leaves seven sons—Raepal succeeds—Revenges his father's death . . . Rape of the Rahtore virgins—Accession of Rao Maldeo—Witnesses the subjection of his kingdom—His death—His twelve sons . . . Installation of Raja Oodi Sing—The name, Oodi Sing, fatal to Rajpootana—Numerous progeny of Oodi Sing—Remarkable death of Raja Oodi Sing . . .

This last event must be related in full from Tod's text:

> . . . The manner of his death . . . affords such a specimen of superstition and of Rajpoot manners that it would be improper to omit it. The narrative is preceded by some reflections on the moral education of the Rahtore princes, and the wise restraints imposed upon them under the vigilant control of chiefs of approved worth and fidelity; so that, to use the words of the text, " they often passed their twentieth year, ignorant of women." If the "fat raja" had ever known this moral restraint, in his riper years he forgot it; for although he had no less than twenty-seven queens, he cast the eye of desire on the virgin-daughter of a subject, and that subject a Brahmin.
>
> . . . As there was no other course by which the father could save her from pollution but by her death, he resolved to make it one of vengeance and horror. He dug a sacrificial pit, and having slain his daughter, cut her into fragments, and mingling therewith pieces of flesh from his own person, made the "homa," or burnt sacrifice to Aya Mata, and as the smoke and flames ascended he pronounced an imprecation on the raja: "Let peace be a stranger to him! And in three hours, three days, and three years, let me have revenge! . . ." [then sprang] into the flaming pit. The horrid tale was related to the raja, whose imagination was haunted by the shade of the Brahmin; and he expired at the assigned period, a prey to unceasing remorse. . . .

(*page 79*) **Jodhpur.** A royal bus used for pig-sticking excursions into the desert.

◄ **Jodhpur. View from the Fort over the Land of Death.**

(*overleaf, left*)
Jodhpur. The Fort.

(*overleaf, right*)
Jodhpur. The Ascent to the Fort.

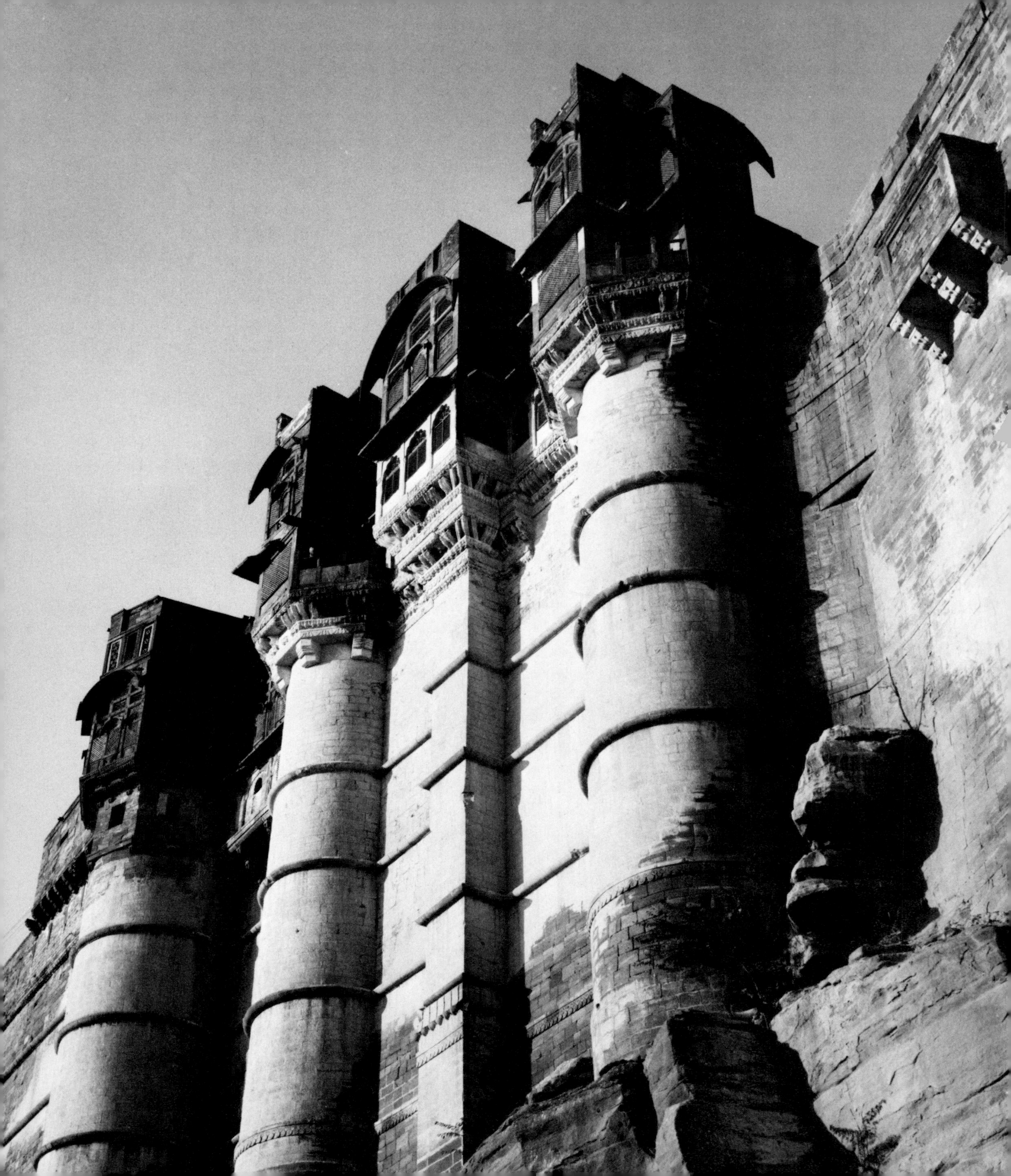

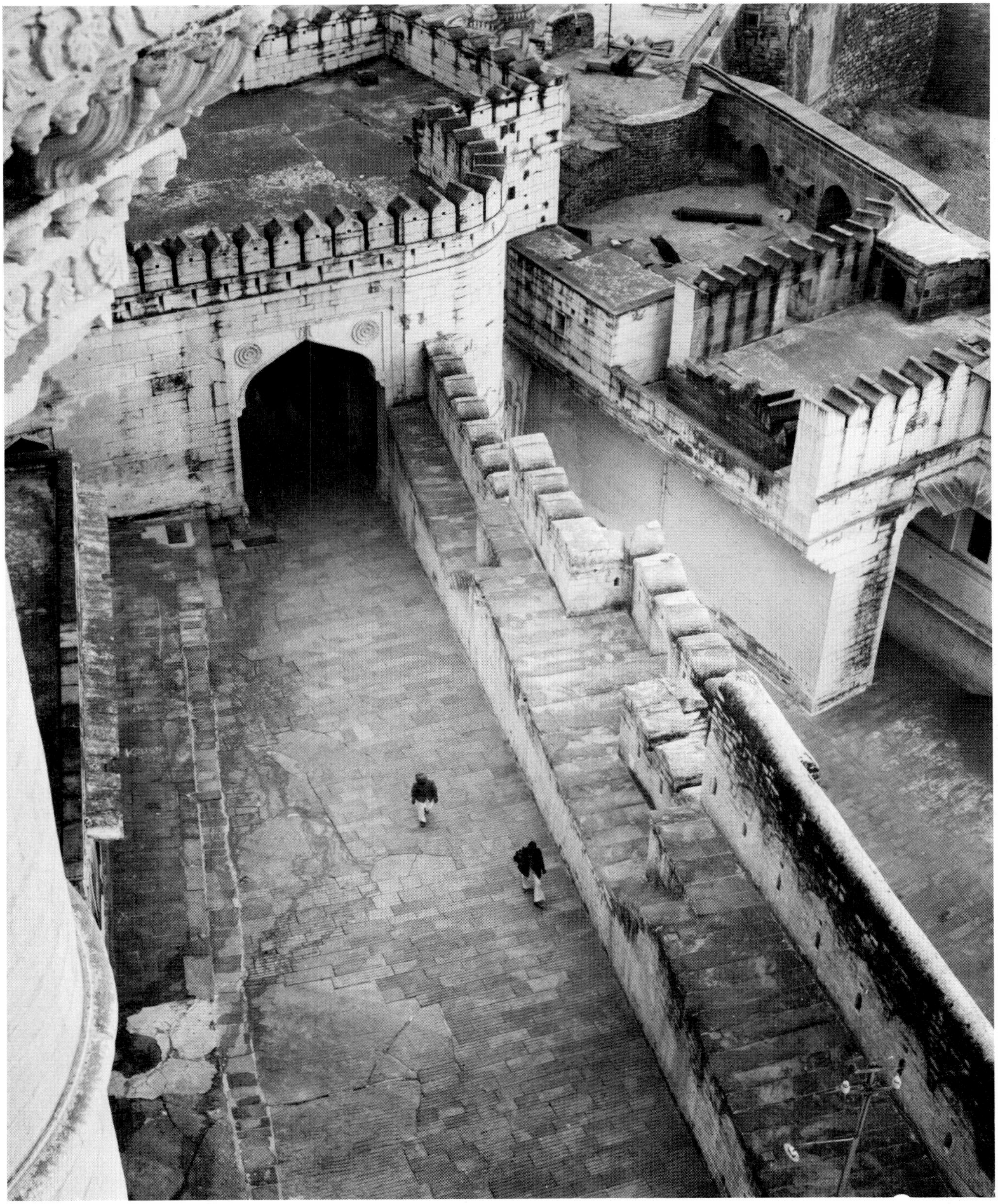

Jodhpur. Exteriors of Private ►
Apartments at the Fort.

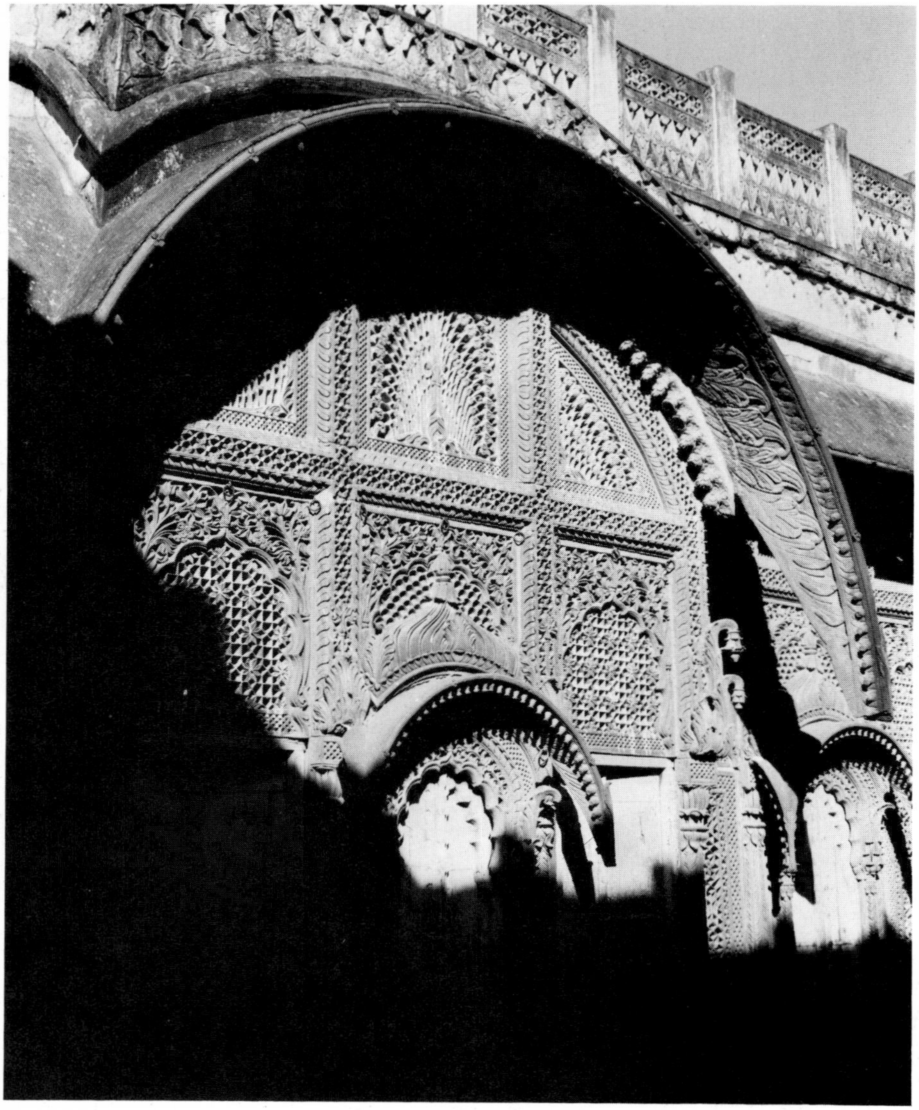

◄ **Jodhpur. The Fort.** Detail of the *jalis*—pierced stone screens that are a feature of Indian architecture in every period. Here they have reached a point of delicate perfection almost unimaginable.

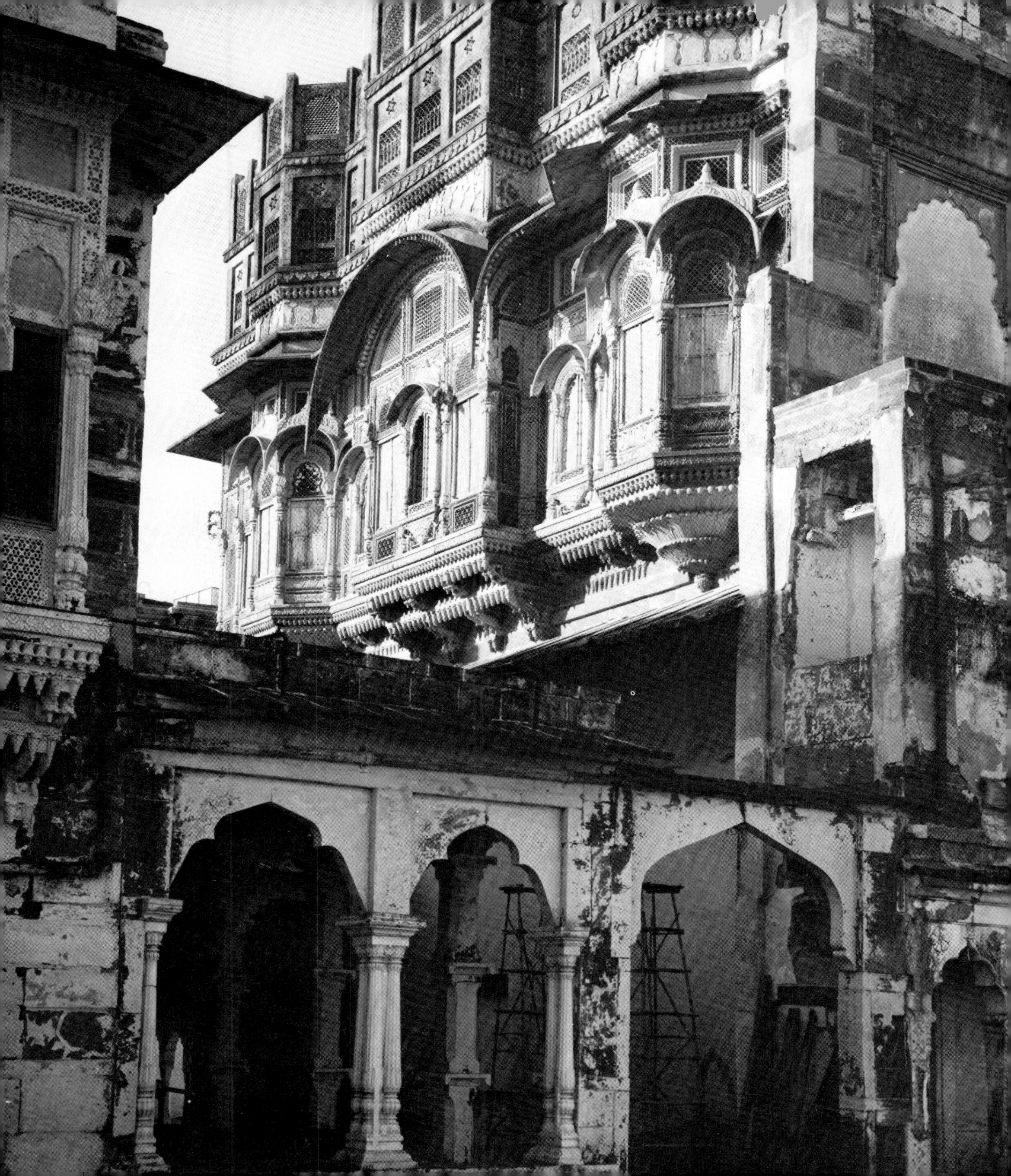

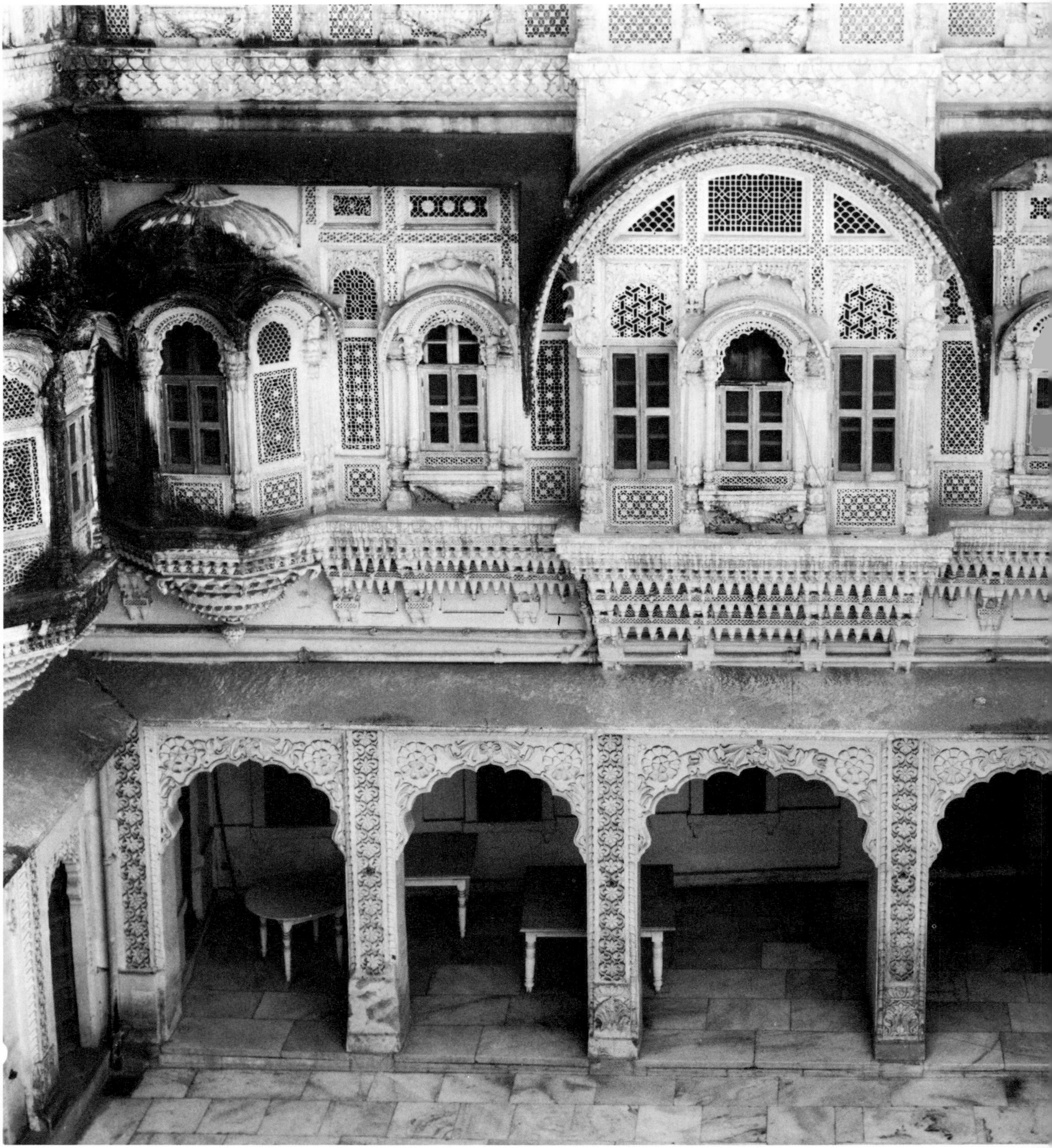

Jodhpur. The Purdah Palace in the Fort. Lady Reading went to Jodhpur in 1922 for the investiture of the young Maharaja, Umaid Singh. His sixteen-year-old Maharani gave up her private rooms for her guest, who later made a visit to the Fort and to the purdah ladies there. She describes those borrowed rooms and her visit in a letter to her family:
". . . pale blue silk hangings with lovely dressing and bathrooms with every known bath salt and perfume from the Rue de la Paix. Next day we visited the Fort which is perfect; high up, carved out of the rocks. We motored part of the way and then were carried in red velvet and gold chairs. Up top I was met by the chief European ladies in Jodhpur and conducted to four more Maharanis, widow and sisters of the predecessor. I wish you could have seen the Purdah Courtyard, all carved in white marble like alabaster, a circle of chairs, an arm chair in the middle for me, round me the Maharanis and ladies. An outer circle of retainers, some young with wonderful nose rings, some old, all wrapt in saris of orange, yellow, gold, all alive with curiosity. . . ."

Jodhpur. The *Gadi*, or Throne, in the Fort. Indian rulers by tradition sat cross-legged against a bolster like this one; that is how they were always painted in miniatures. Throne chairs were an importation from the West.

Jodhpur. The Fort. Guns on the ramparts overlooking the town.

Is it any wonder the Rajput forts and palaces we visit today as tourists seem sinister to us, despite the pretty rooms we pass through, painted with gilt flowers and colored by rainbow glass? In Jodhpur two mighty monuments recall these generations of intense living and dying: the old Fort, and the Umaid Bhavan Palace.

The Fort is the citadel of Marwar and seems to have been carved out of the mountain it stands on. One approaches through a massive gateway of Victory, the first of seven barriers thrown across the steep zigzag ascent. On the wall by the last of these are the handprints of fifteen widows of Maharajas, the commemoration of their becoming *sati*; the prints are painted silver. At the top of the rock are the palaces: courtyards within courtyards surrounded by beautiful lattice windows.

It was in this honeycomb of carved stone that the purdah ladies, sometimes as many as a hundred at a time, lived their little, useless lives. Each had her own flat of about three rooms, with her own servant to prepare her food, as each was afraid of being poisoned by the others. And when those lives were over—cut short in childbirth or by smallpox or the cholera morbus—they were rushed down the mountainside to the cremation grounds. It is hard to go through the *zenana* of the Jodhpur Fort without thinking of funeral pyres—and of all those poor women who waited there for their hour to come, when they would show everybody how resolutely they could climb on the pyre with their dead husbands and not move even a muscle.

When we were in the Jodhpur Fort to shoot some footage for *Autobiography of a Princess*, a religious event was in progress involving a crowd of women from the town below, and the Rajmata, or Queen Mother, and the young Maharani were present. No one was able to explain to us what was going on, and I don't think anyone really knew any more: it was what was done. A silver doll, dressed in gaudy clothes, was carried about the palace and finally stood up in front of a shrine. The women from the town sang and sang, but a bit listlessly; they were more interested in the filming. There were many little bits of temple stage business, and some of these were repeated by the priests for the benefit of the cameraman: the doll was fed sweetmeats, was fanned, was sprinkled. We were told that the Rajmata and the Maharani had gone away in a huff because of this intrusion; probably they were relieved to have gotten out early that year. Our shoes had been left at the door of the shrine, and when we came out again a pair was missing. One of our party, a European lady, made the long zigzag descent barefoot, watched by everyone. We wondered whether the stealing of the shoes and the barefoot descent would be incorporated into next year's ceremony as one more ritual that no one knew why it was done except that it had been done the year before.

We came back to the Fort the next day for more shooting. We wanted to film some typical nautch girls, so it was arranged that they would be there with their musicians to perform in the durbar hall for us. Two girls arrived in the morning with their pimp, who played the *tabla*, and a harmonium player. They were accompanied by a sort of duenna/manageress, who was also the mother of the prettier of the two dancers—a girl of about sixteen who had the luscious figure, round face, and big eyes so prized in Indian ingénues. She was put forward by her mother and the pimp as a kind of star attraction. After we described what we wanted to film —a real old-time Rajasthani nautch—she began to dance for us. She threw coquettish glances as she stamped and whirled around the red and gold room, her ankle bells jingling. But it was all

(overleaf)
Jodhpur. Façade of the Umaid Bhavan Palace Overlooking the Gardens.

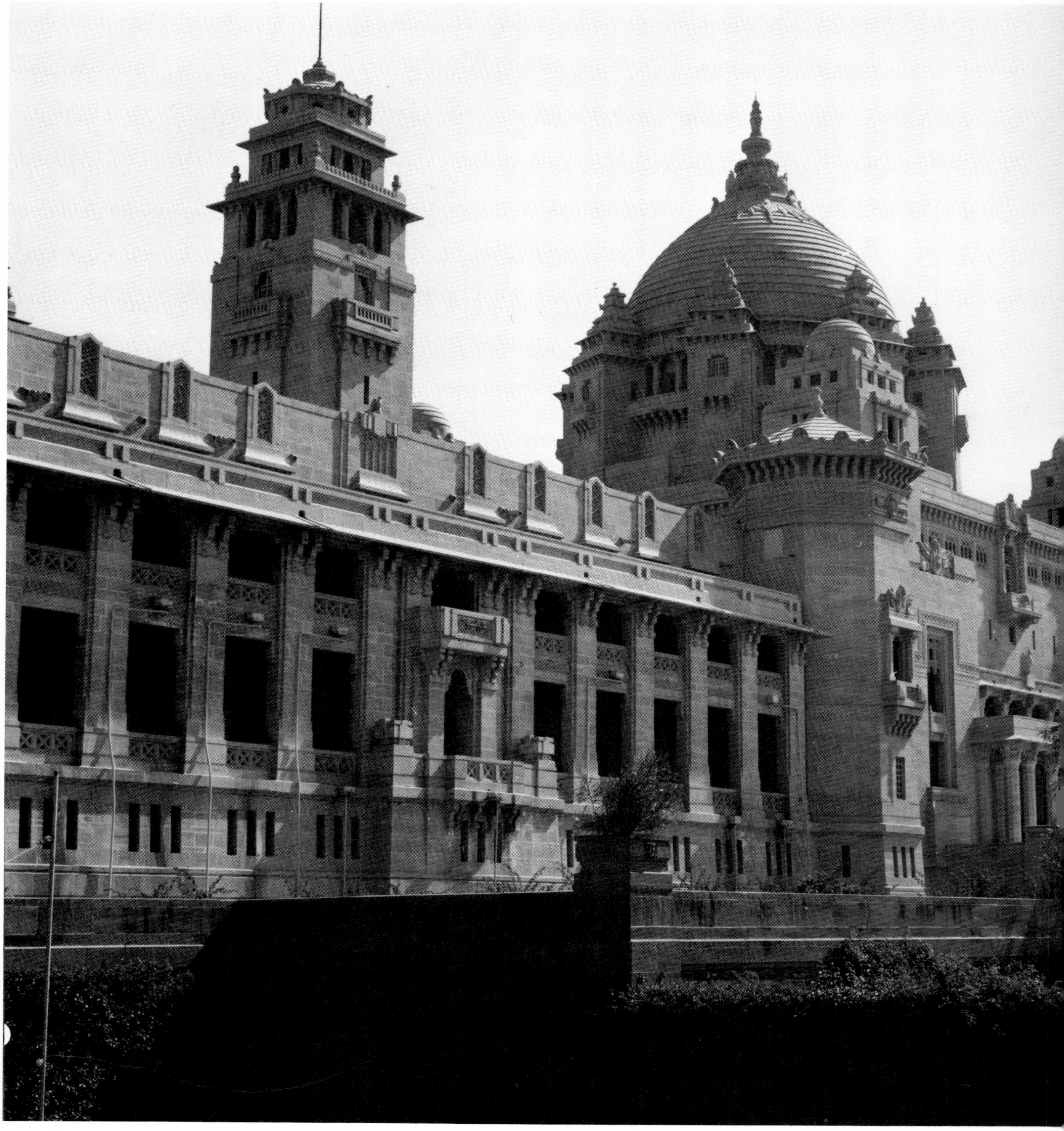

for nothing: her dance was a sad copy of a musical number from some Bombay movie, full of mannerisms and gestures which are modern, even Western. We told her to stop, and through the manageress we asked for something more traditional. The girl grew sulky and tossed her head, and her mother muttered to the pimp. Then the other girl spoke up: she would dance for us and try to give us what we wanted. This girl was no longer young; she looked worn and her face was pockmarked. She wasn't a very good dancer, but she was very touching as well as graceful. While she danced she sang a sad little song in a high-pitched, quavering voice. She was sweet and childlike; the words of her song were about a lover with very fair skin who had gone away.

The other grand monument the Rajput feudal system produced in Jodhpur is the Umaid Bhavan Palace. I think this must be to Rajasthan what the château at Chambord is to the Loire Valley. In a few hundred years—probably much sooner—it will have become one of the great Indian ruins, like Fatehpur Sikri or Mandu. It is one of the very best Indian buildings, but much underrated. "Ashokan Art Deco" perhaps describes the style of its embellishments. As an architectural conception, however, it is in direct descent from the Taj Mahal, via the Victoria Memorial in Calcutta: basically a big, domed building with a rectangular plan and a tall tower at each of the four corners—counterparts of the minarets of famous Moghul tombs, such as Humayun's and the Taj. It is one of those heavy, rather brutal public buildings that can be found in many parts of the world dating from the 1930s. It was started in 1929 by Maharaja Umaid Singh as a public works program during a famine.

We found some footage shot during construction of this last of the great Indian palaces. The Maharaja is assisting at the corner-stone-laying ceremony, wearing high boots and a knit shirt. The English contractor is down in the hole dug for the foundation of the palace, or, more likely, blasted out by dynamite: the site is on a great escarpment of stone. There are shots of workmen carrying blocks of it up to the roof. When it was completed, the palace was intended to be as self-sufficient, as self-contained, as any luxury liner: there were the same luxurious and impersonal public rooms and first-class suites, inhabited by people who didn't know each

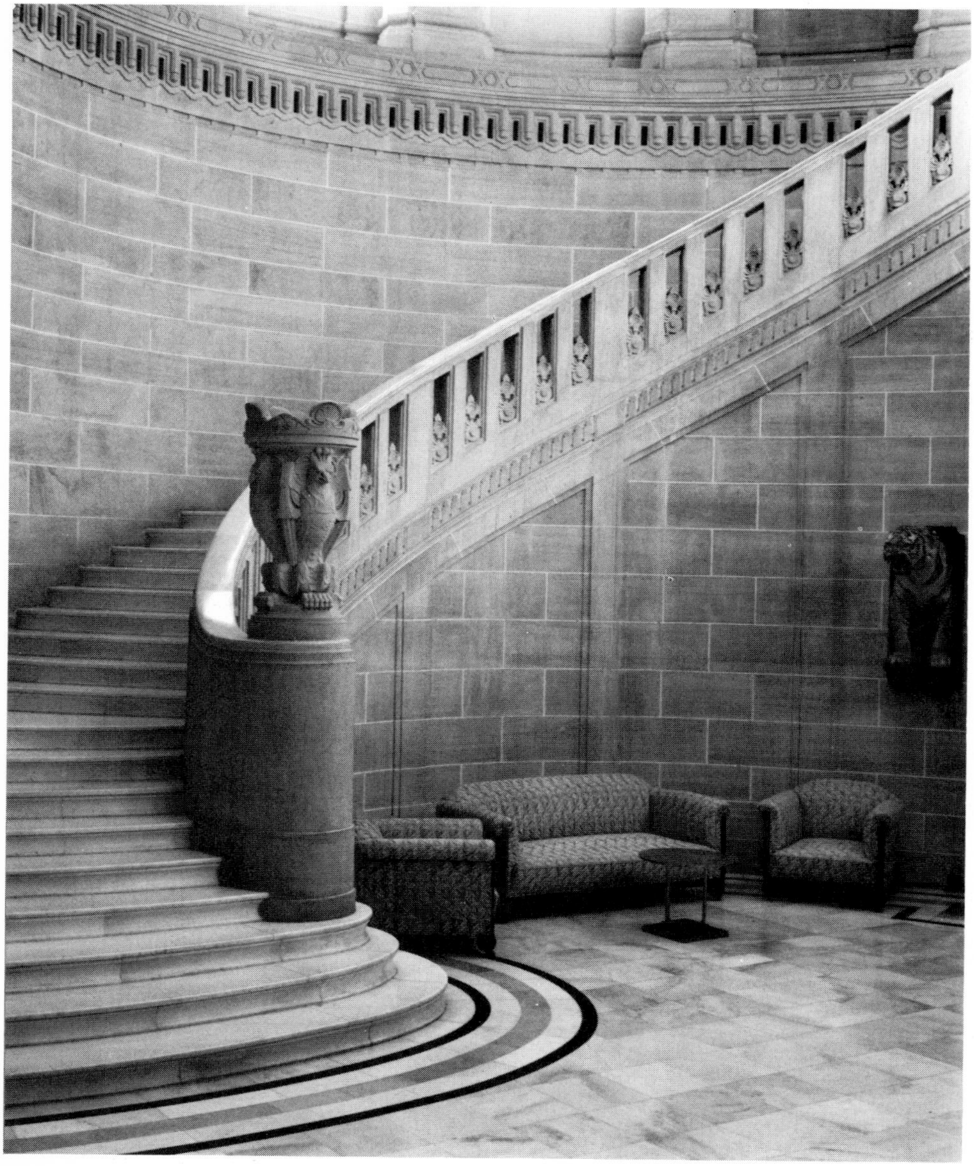

▲ Jodhpur. The Grand Staircase in the Umaid Bhavan Palace.

Jodhpur. Reception Room in the ► Umaid Bhavan Palace.

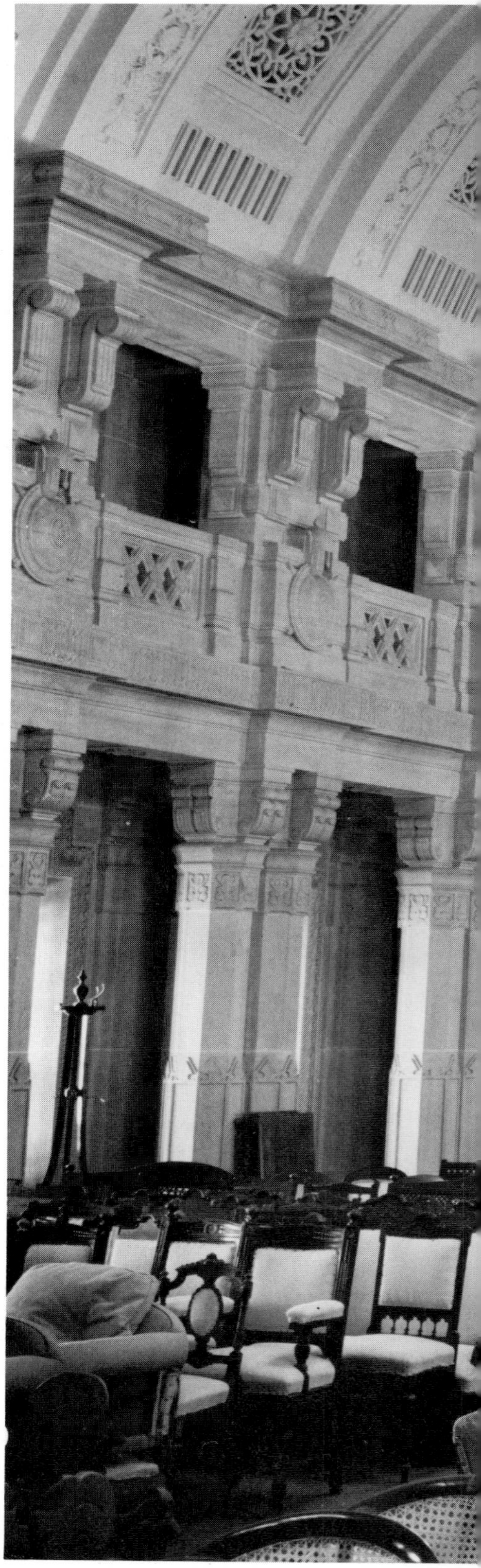

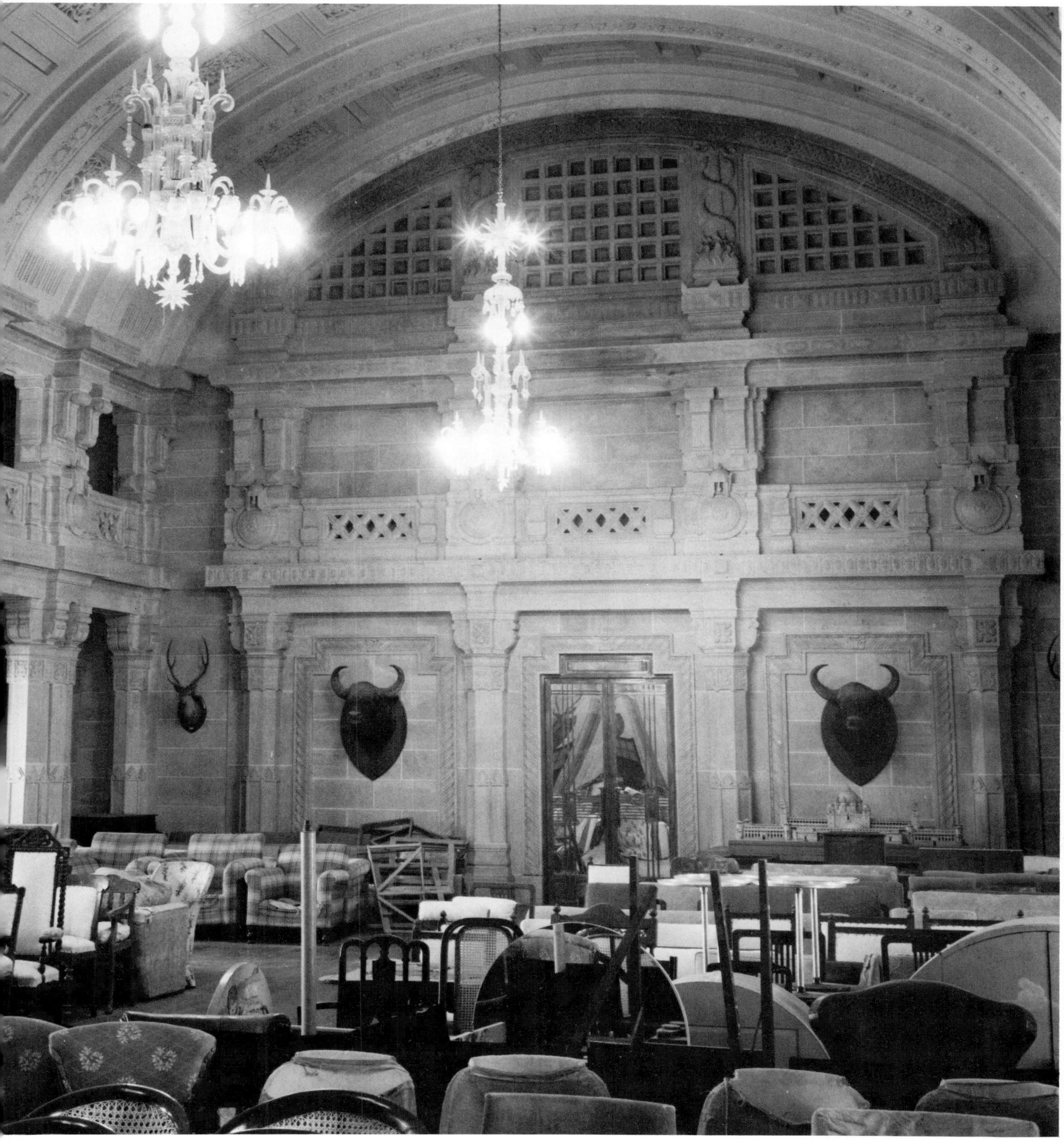

**Jodhpur. Hallway Outside the ►
Suites of Guest Bedrooms in the
Umaid Bhavan Palace.**

Jodhpur. Umaid Bhavan Palace.

**Jodhpur. Door Handles on
Screen Doors at the Umaid
Bhavan Palace.**

94

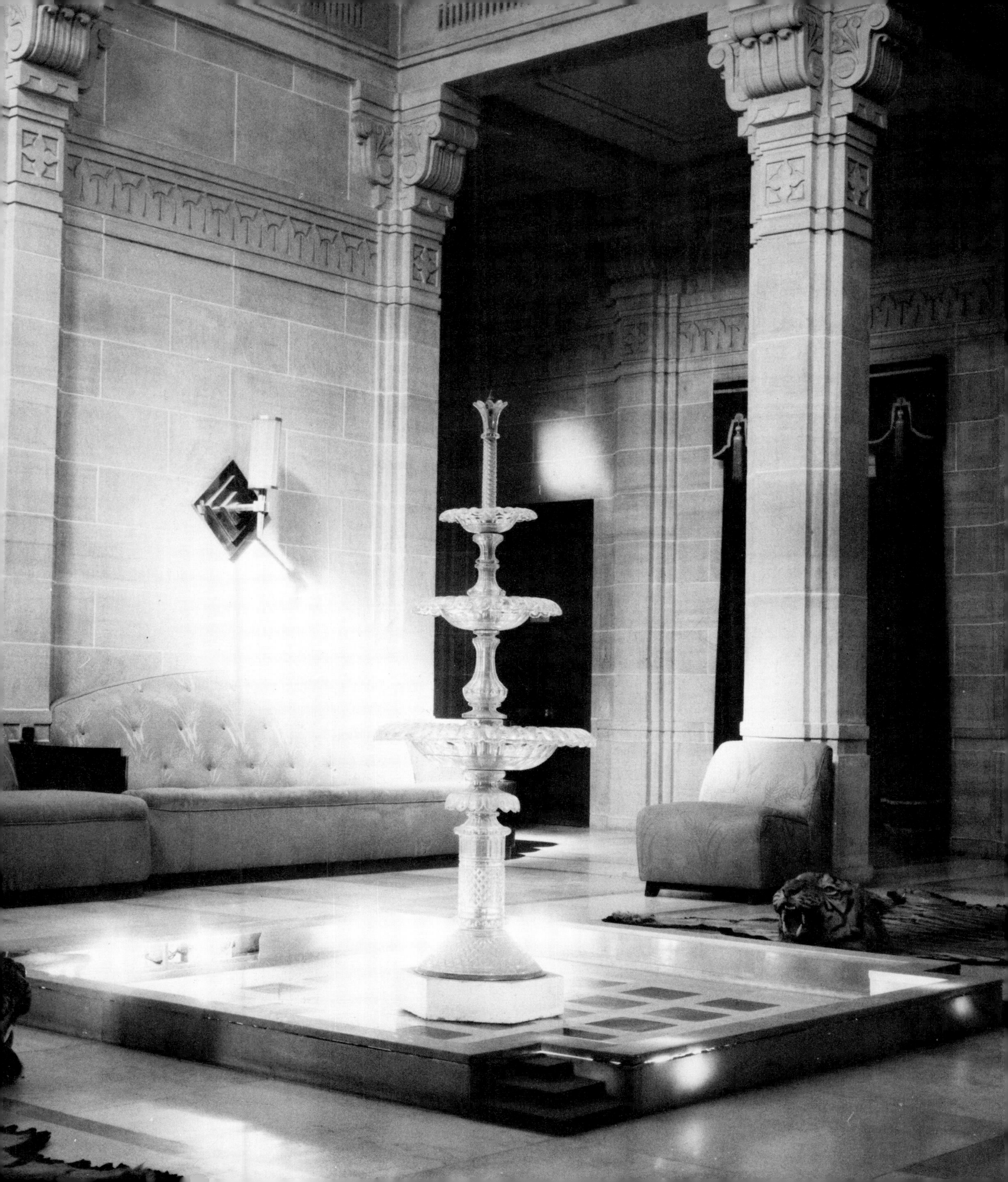

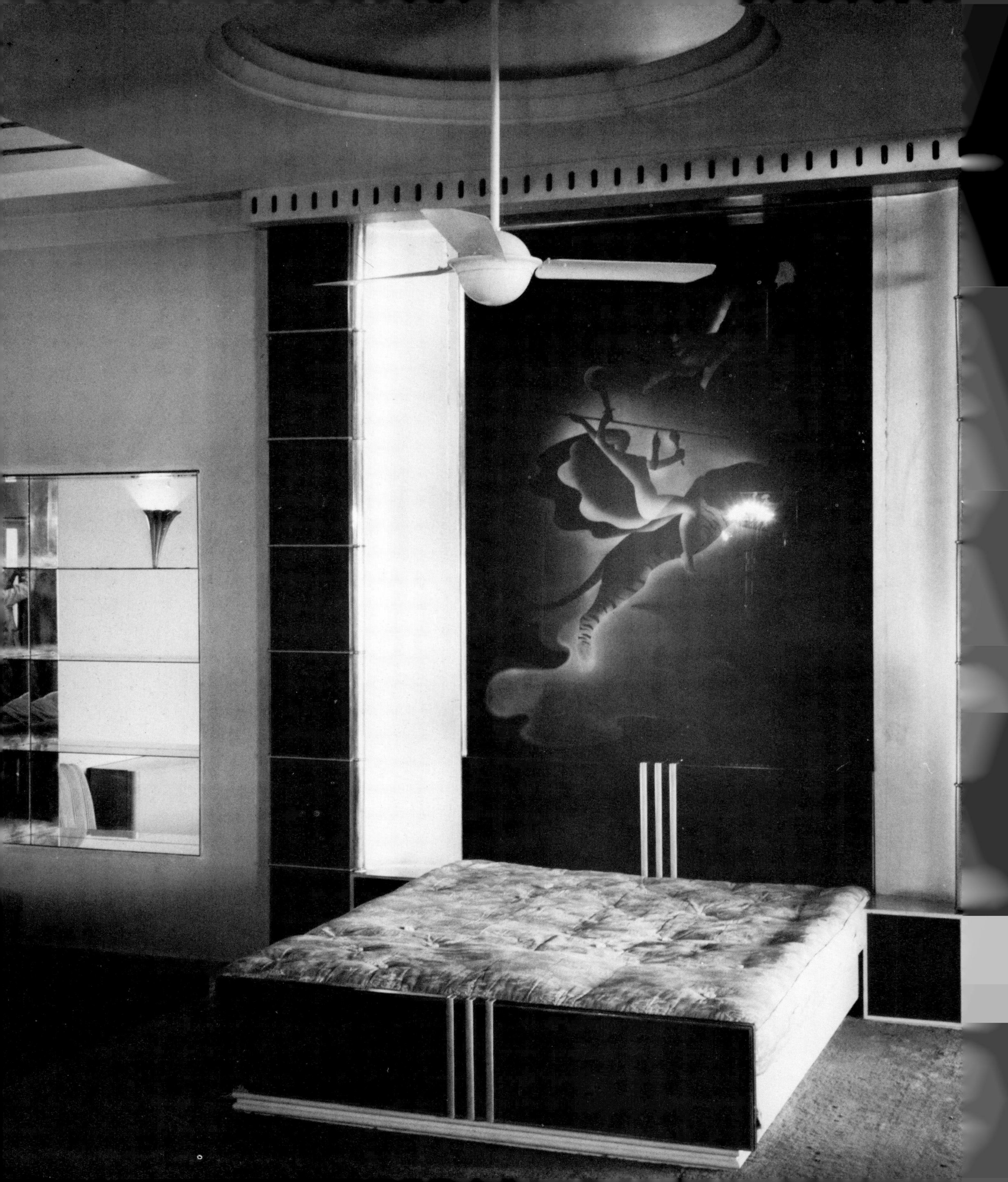

◄ **Jodhpur. Guest Bedroom in the Umaid Bhavan Palace.** The guest staying here would most likely have been a relative, possibly another Maharaja. Humbler visitors were put up in another wing. English officials who stayed with the Maharaja in the old days had rooms at the opposite end of the palace. These suites corresponded in size with the royal ones—but not in decoration, which was dry and formal.

Jodhpur. The Swimming Pool in ► the Umaid Bhavan Palace.

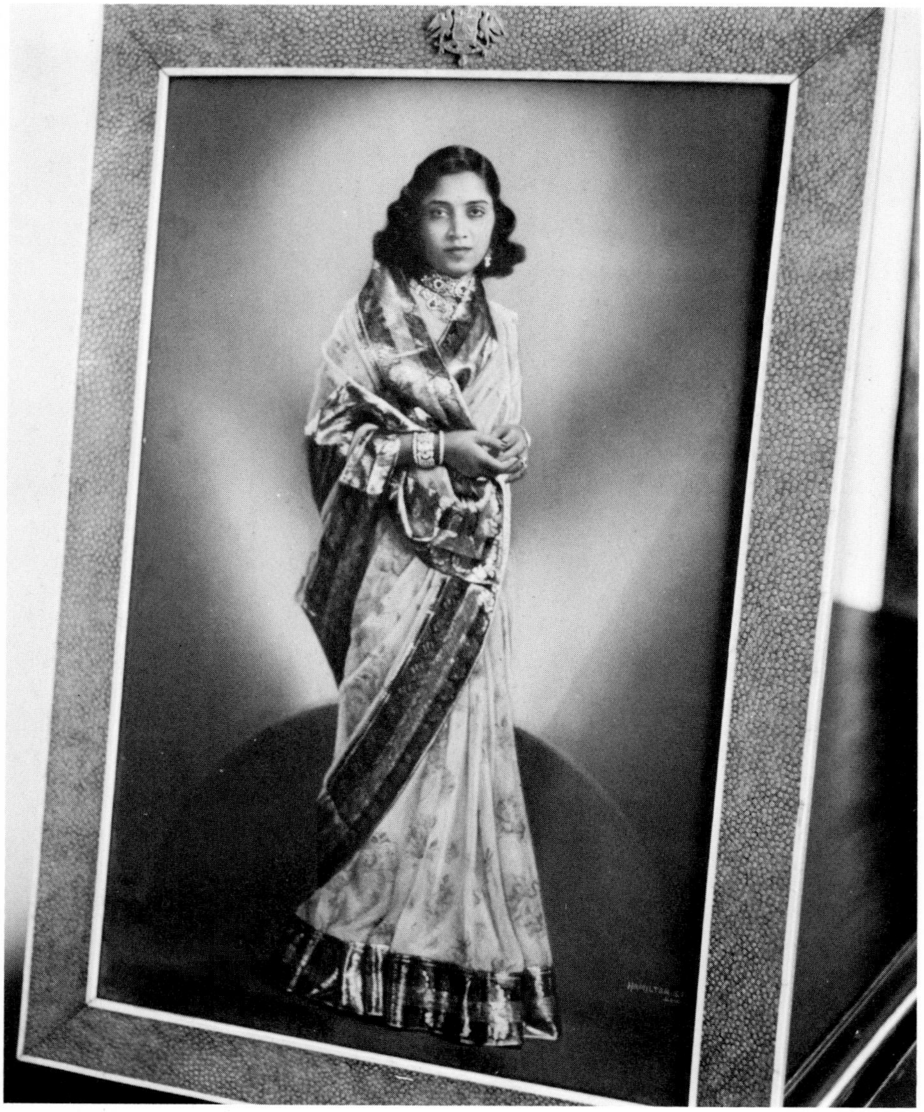

▲
Jodhpur. Photograph in the Umaid Bhavan Palace.

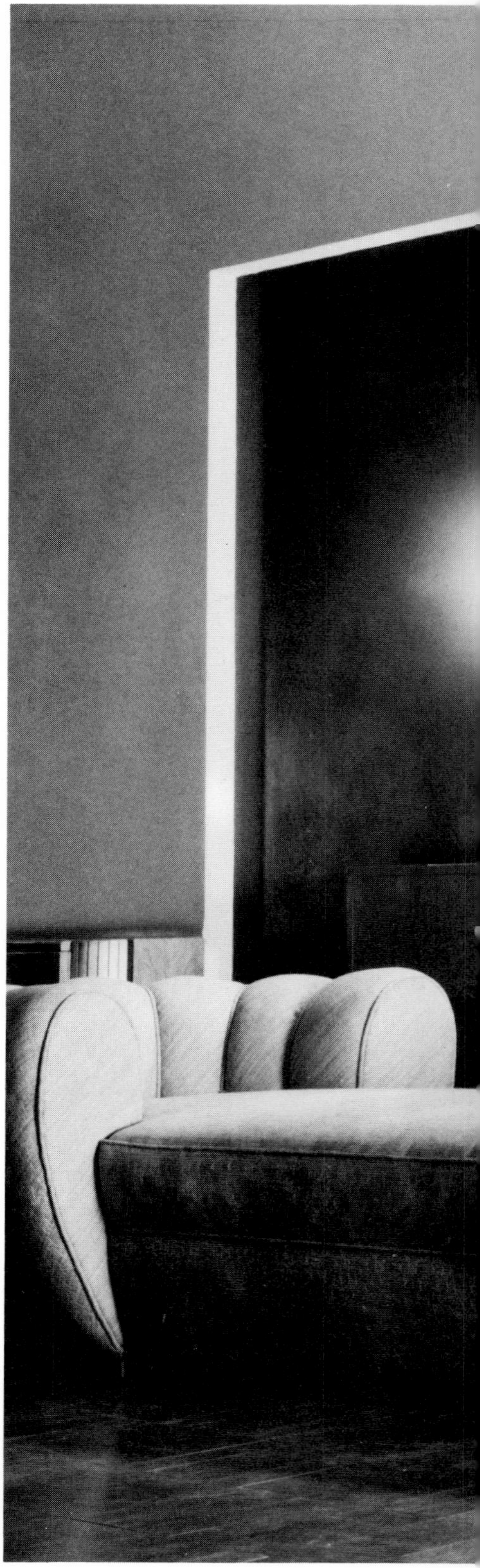

Jodhpur. Guest Bedroom in the Umaid Bhavan Palace. ►

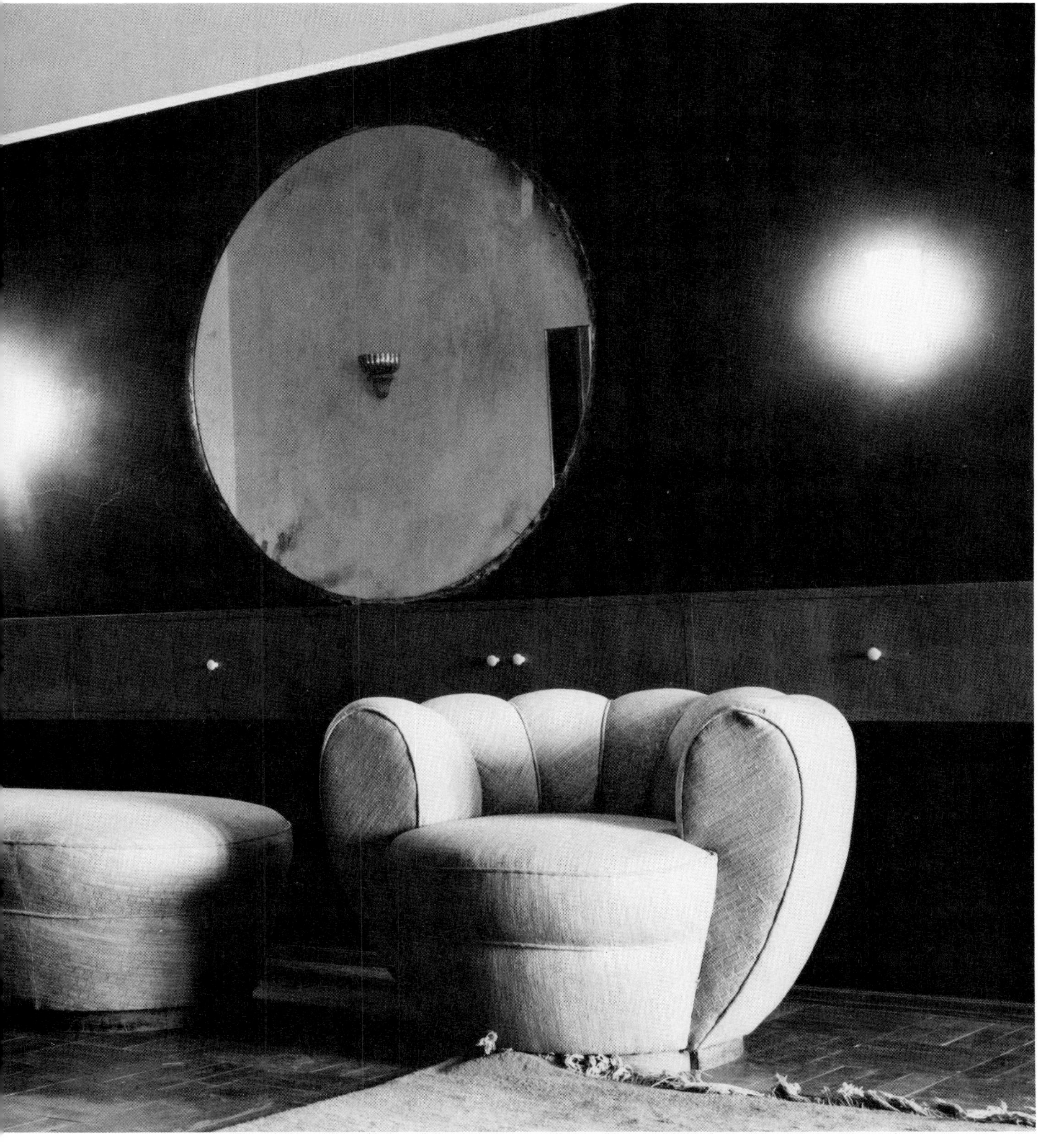

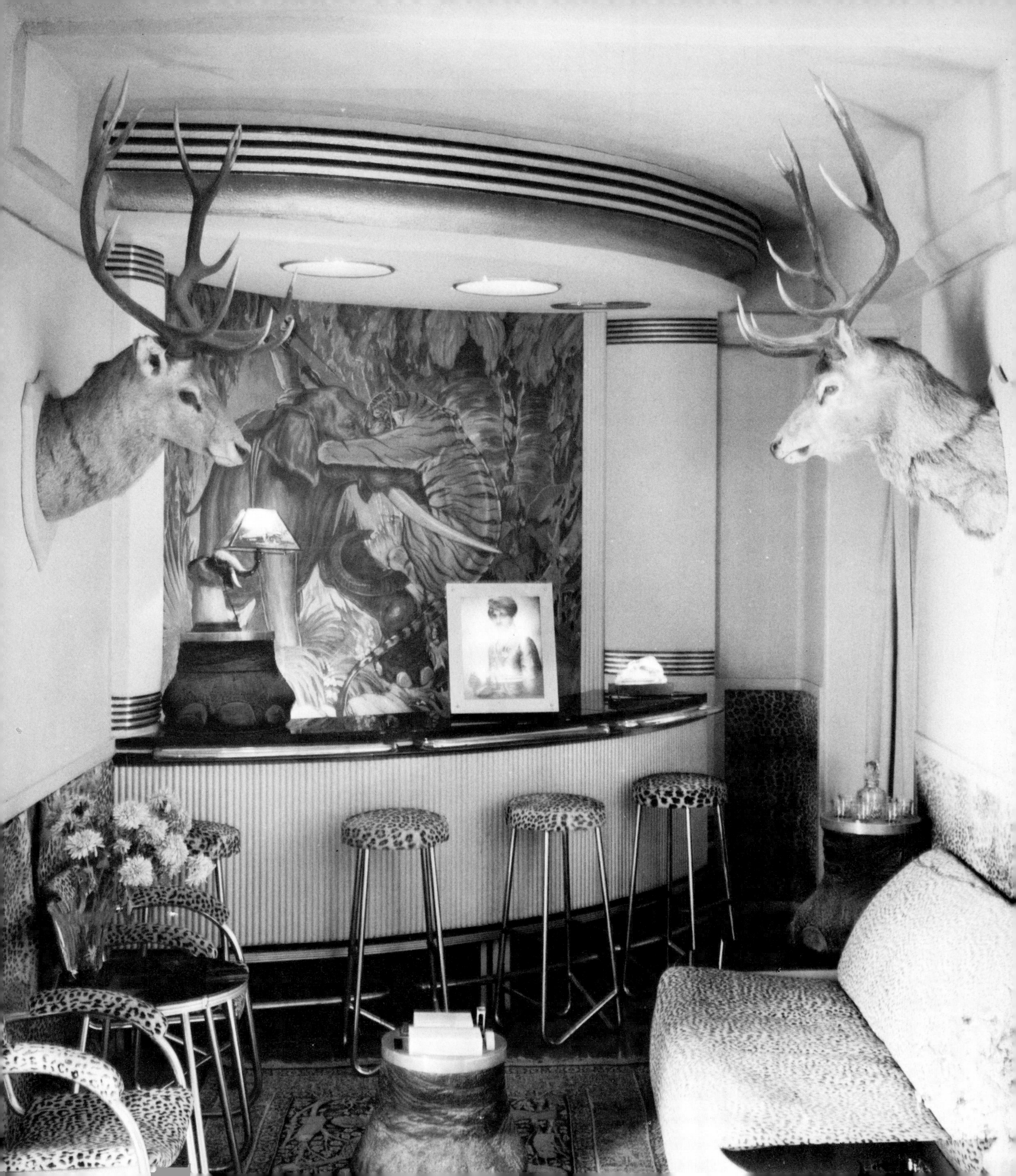

other very well; there was a lot of feasting, a lot of drinking; there were games of all kinds to fill up the long hours; there were dancing and theatricals to take part in, films to watch; there was such interesting etiquette to learn and observe; there was the glamour of arrivals and departures; and there was—best of all, for some—the excitement of the passenger list. The difference is that the palace ship lay becalmed in a dead sea of sand and hot rock.

In the past, before there was air service, few sightseeing parties came to Jodhpur. One had to travel over terrible roads, eating dust for days and putting up at night—if one were lucky and timed it right—in Circuit Houses or Dak Bungalows. Or one came by slow train and ate soot. It was an adventure getting there, all right; and if one weren't invited to stay with a Maharaja, finding accommodation in Jodhpur City was another. Now the Umaid Bhavan Palace itself is being turned into a hotel, and the present Maharaja and his family have moved into an apartment in the old guest wing.

A Hide-away Bar in a Hide-away House. Maharaja Umaid Singh's retreat at Sada Samand, twenty miles from Jodhpur. The house stands above a little lake inhabited by flamingoes; from the ramparts, the view of the desert stretching away makes the eyes ache. There is a swimming pool and pastel-painted guest bedrooms that look like motel accommodations in the American Southwest thirty years ago. The narrow bar, except for the hunting trophies, reminds one of those on the old transcontinental trains. It would take many drinks to make this seem as nice a place as a transcontinental train, yet people must have had fun here in the old days. At Sada Samand I felt as if I had arrived at the farthest edge of civilization. Below those ramparts there was nothing, a soundless void.

There are also plans to set the Royal Train steaming again to carry tourists on overnight trips to even more remote desert states. This train was built in England fifty years ago, and it is very luxurious, a miniature rolling palace. But traveling in it may not be such a luxury after all. Yvonne Fitzroy tells of her experience of traveling on a private train in India:

We had heard much of the Viceregal train, even the Russian Imperial train could not compete with it for luxury, we were told, and were not disappointed. But all the luxury in the world cannot defeat this climate. . . . No screen was the least use against the dust—the fans merely circulated a hot, exhausted wind—door-handles nearly too hot to touch—beds far too hot to lie on—clothes, a literally painful necessity—and the hopeful rush to the cold water tap greeted by a flow of nicely boiled water.

All the luxury in the world cannot defeat this climate. . . . Still, if the Royal Train fails as a tourist attraction, perhaps I could use it as a set. If it has no further destiny except to stand in the train shed in Jodhpur, no further destinations except ones I might find for it, perhaps it is up to me to set it rolling again: we were probably meant for each other, that train and I.

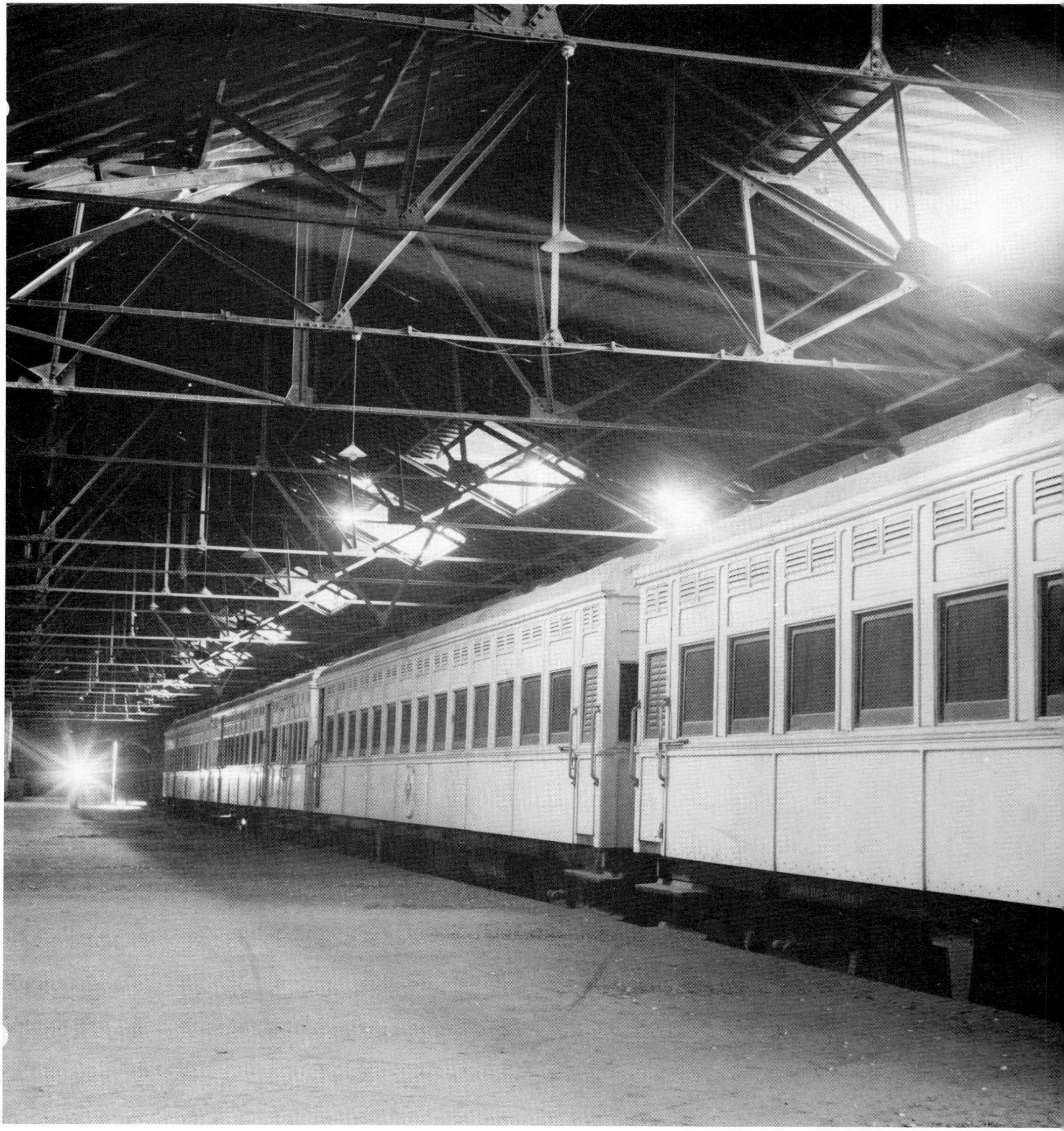

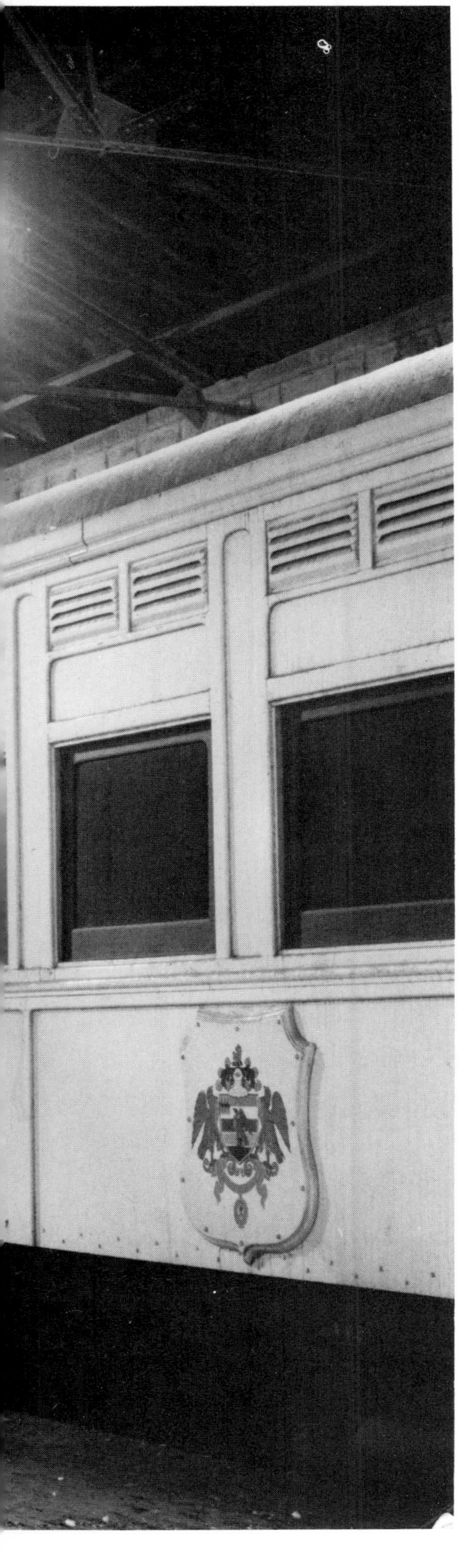

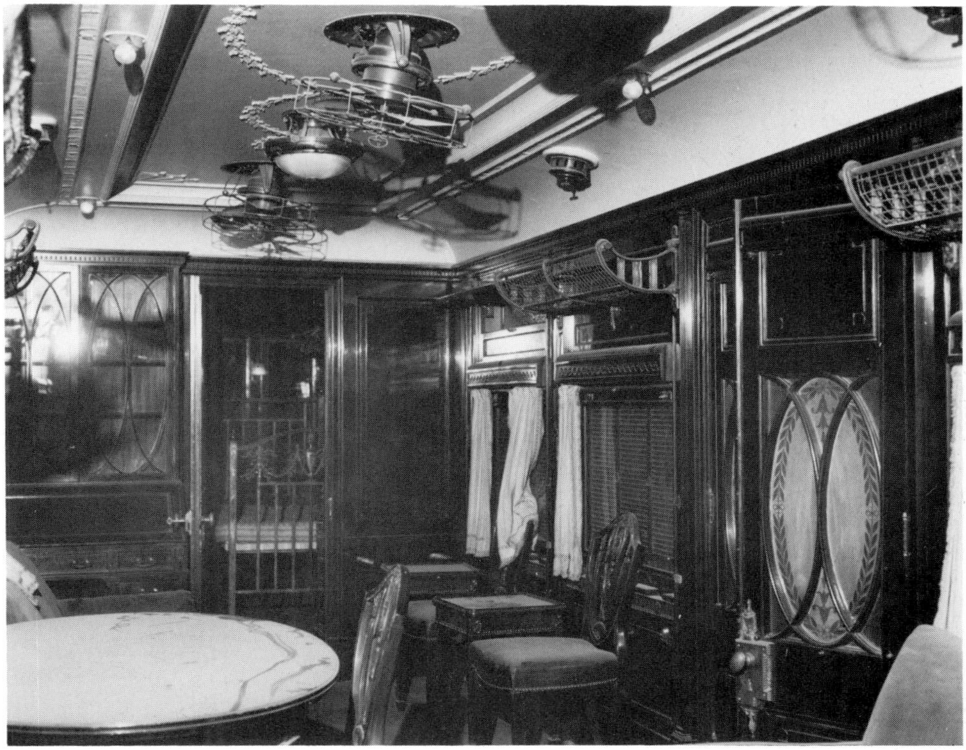

Jodhpur. Interior of the Royal Train.

Jodhpur. The Royal Train.

V

Palaces as Sets

Alwar and Bikaner

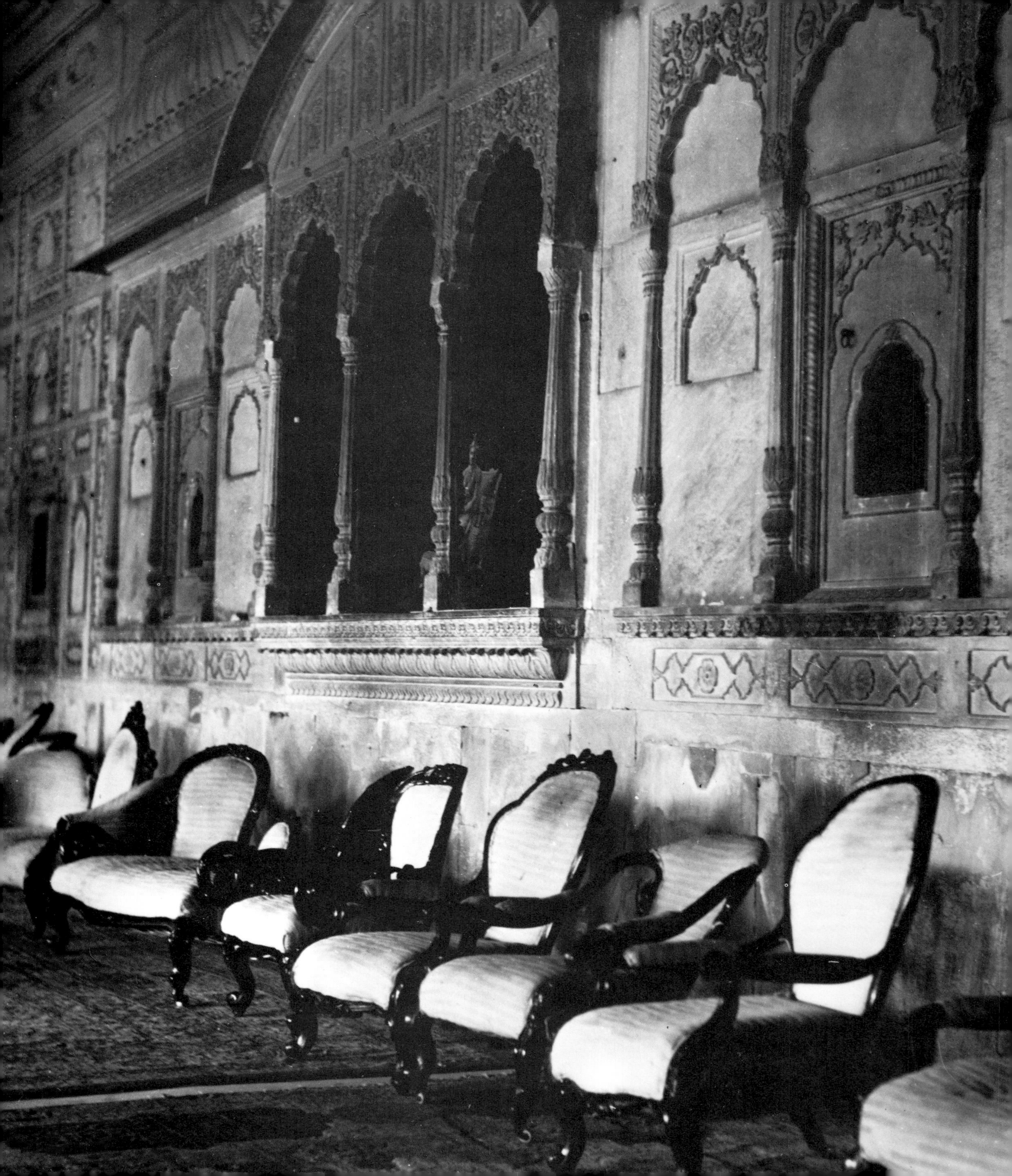

(*page 105*) **Alwar. The Old Palace.** On the swing, Ismail Merchant.

◄ **Deeg. The Diwan-i-Khas.** The old eighteenth-century palaces were outfitted in Victorian times with suites of furniture like this. It was part of the modernization which led the richer states to build palaces like the Rambagh in Jaipur.

THE first film of ours to present Royal India—or a glimpse of it—was *Shakespeare Wallah*, made in 1964. This is the story of some strolling English actors who go about India presenting Shakespeare's plays wherever and however they can. We called our troupe the Buckingham Players, but in fact their adventures were based on those of a real troupe called Shakespeareana, who for many years had traveled all over India presenting Shakespeare's plays in schools and colleges and convents and palaces. They were led by an English actor couple named the Kendals, with their two daughters and whatever English actors they could attract from England, or occasional Indian enthusiasts who joined them in their pilgrimage across India. They toured with all their sets and costumes in every conceivable mode of transport from one out-of the-way place to the other, having to make do on very little money. When we came to make the film—in which the Kendals played their own roles—we were as impecunious as they and had to shift in the same kind of way. Unable to afford sets and studios, we shot everything on location—in Simla, the old English summer capital; in a misty hill station in the Punjab called Kasauli; in a school in Lucknow founded by an eighteenth-century French merchant-adventurer.

We also had to find a palace, for it seemed appropriate that our English actors should at some stage of their wanderings perform for a Maharaja: the representative of one dying order saluting that of another. There are many splendid rooms to be found, in many splendid palaces. There are rooms in the Indian classical style, like the backgrounds of miniature paintings, with walls inlaid with little mirrors and colored glass, and enchanting stone trellises. Or there are wonderful, muffled-up rooms with lots of massive furniture and giant chandeliers hanging in cloth bags.

Deeg. The Diwan-i-Khas. The arches, which have been closed in with modern doors, would once have had beautiful painted and embroidered curtains of canvas rolling down from above to keep out the cold in winter; in summer there were screens made of split reed, which were periodically sprinkled with water to cool the hot winds blowing in.

But neither kind was what we wanted. We needed something more intimate, more attractively human, perhaps with a few pieces of tatty European furniture; yet the background, the actual palace, should suggest something noble, from a finer, better past.

The place that seemed just right for us was the *Diwan-i-Khas*, or private audience hall, at Deeg: a grand, typically Indian pillared hall, of very good proportions and very fine workmanship, dating from the early eighteenth century (a vintage period for palaces in Rajasthan). It contained a lot of attractive Victorian furniture in the French Rococo style, with the stuffing coming out a bit here and there. But we couldn't get permission to shoot there. A pity: I've seldom seen a palace interior that I liked more than the one I chose at Deeg.

Finally we went to Alwar for our palace. Alwar is on the road between Delhi and Jaipur and, as far as I knew, was supposed to be the archetype of a dusty, derelict Indian state. Actually, the town itself was rather like that, but the palace suited our needs and everything turned out well. We made a theater for the Buckinghams' performance in one of the interior courtyards in the *zenana*. As the play that they were staging for the Maharaja in the film was *Antony and Cleopatra*, it was possible to have the actors appear on various levels: in the little domed boxes and trellised windows, and on the balconies that grace these Rajput palaces. We put our Maharaja under a canopy held up by silver posts— all lent to us by the real Maharaja—and that was how the scene was staged.

Deeg. The Diwan-i-Khas in the Old Palace. In the background is the "window of appearance," where the ruler sat in state before his assembled courtiers.

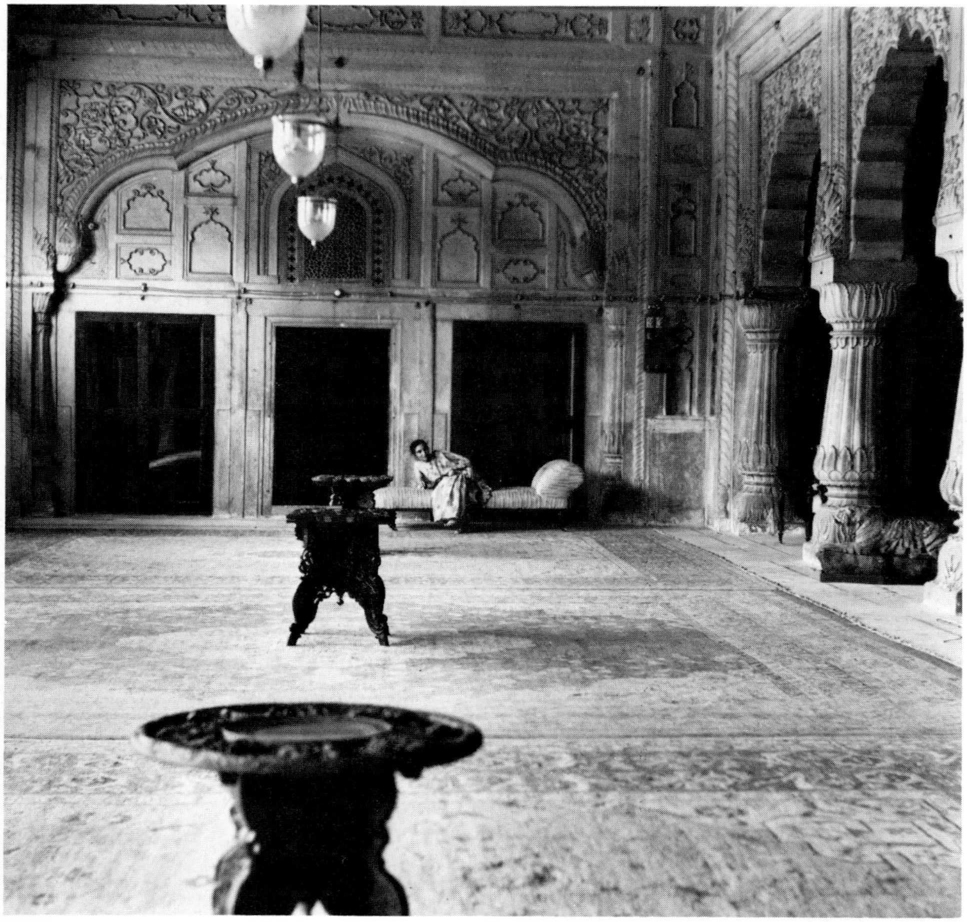

◄ **Deeg. The Diwan-i-Khas.** On the couch, Ruth Jhabvala.

While we were shooting, a crowd of peasant women gathered at the gate below and began to sing a doleful song. It was explained to me that they had come because they had heard the *zenana* was again occupied. A purdah car which had brought some ladies to see the shooting had been there; all that activity must mean that the Maharani had returned.

There were two aspects of this shooting at Alwar I never got used to: the place was full of squeaking bats, which also made it stink; and there was a sinister well, very deep, full of slime way down, without any railing, which we had to walk past. I used to worry about people falling in. I thought a lot about myself falling in, and how no one would hear my cries. In these kinds of places in Rajasthan, ideas like that get hold of you.

Alwar. The City Palace, Built in the Early to Mid-Nineteenth Century. ►

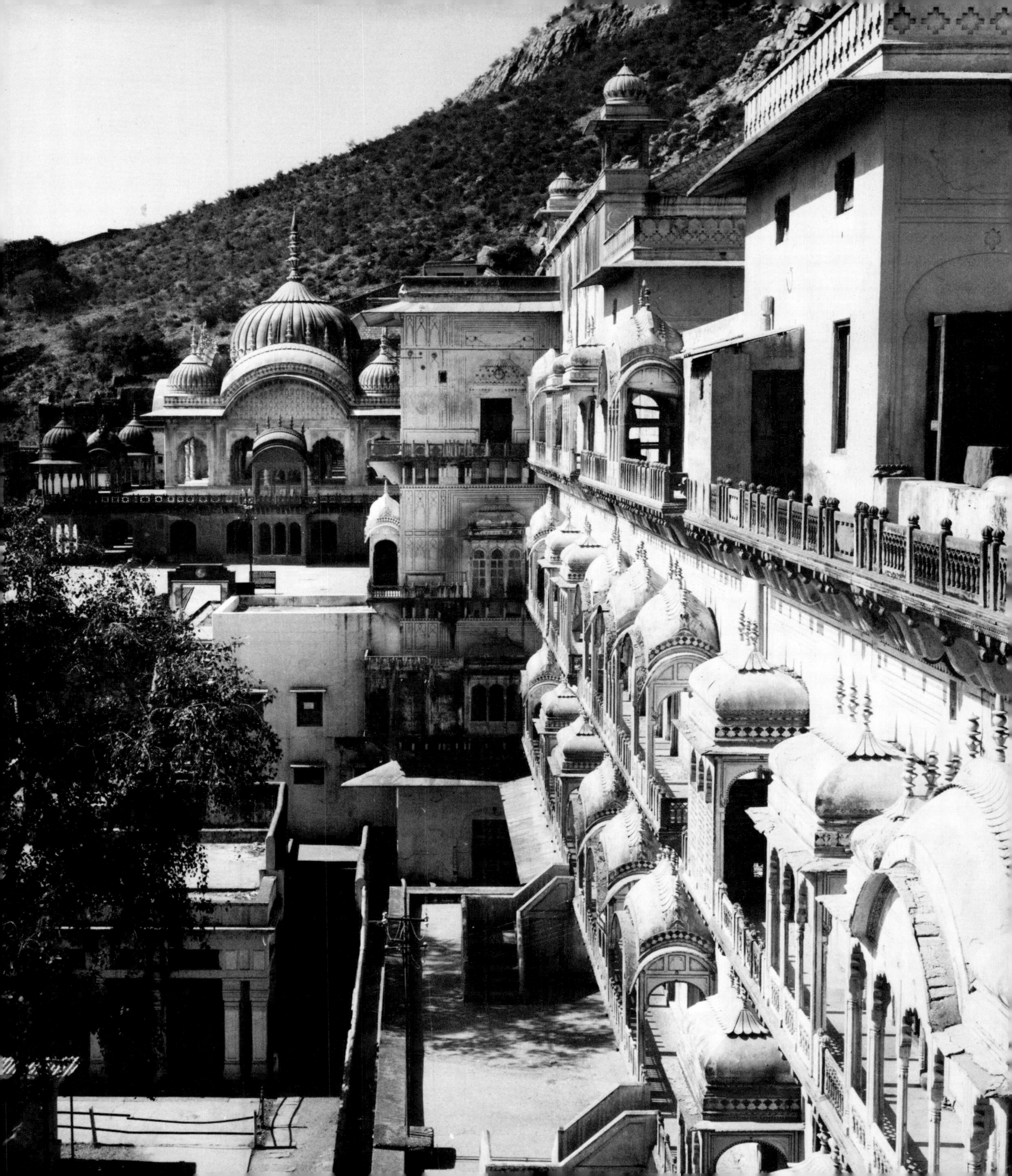

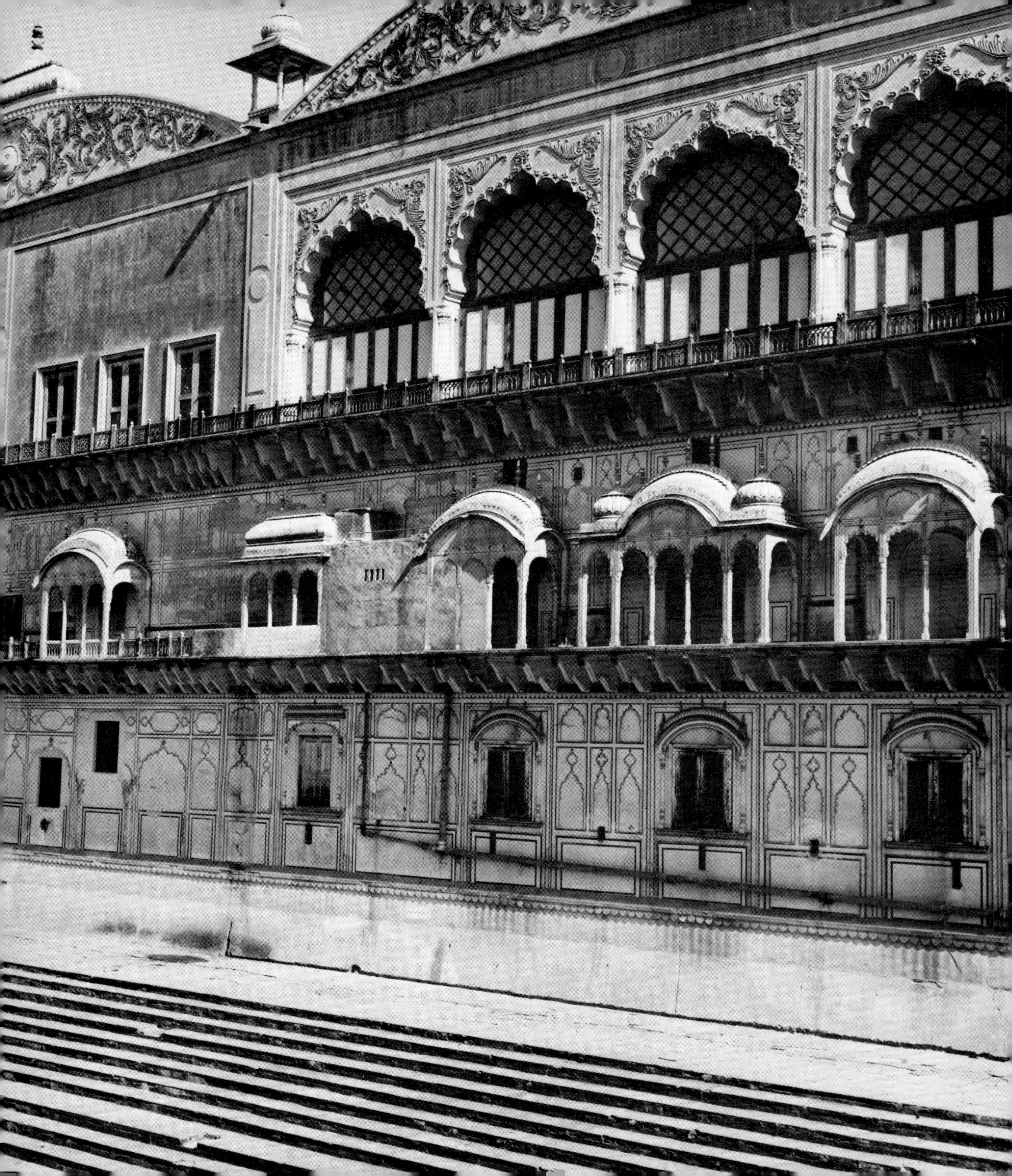

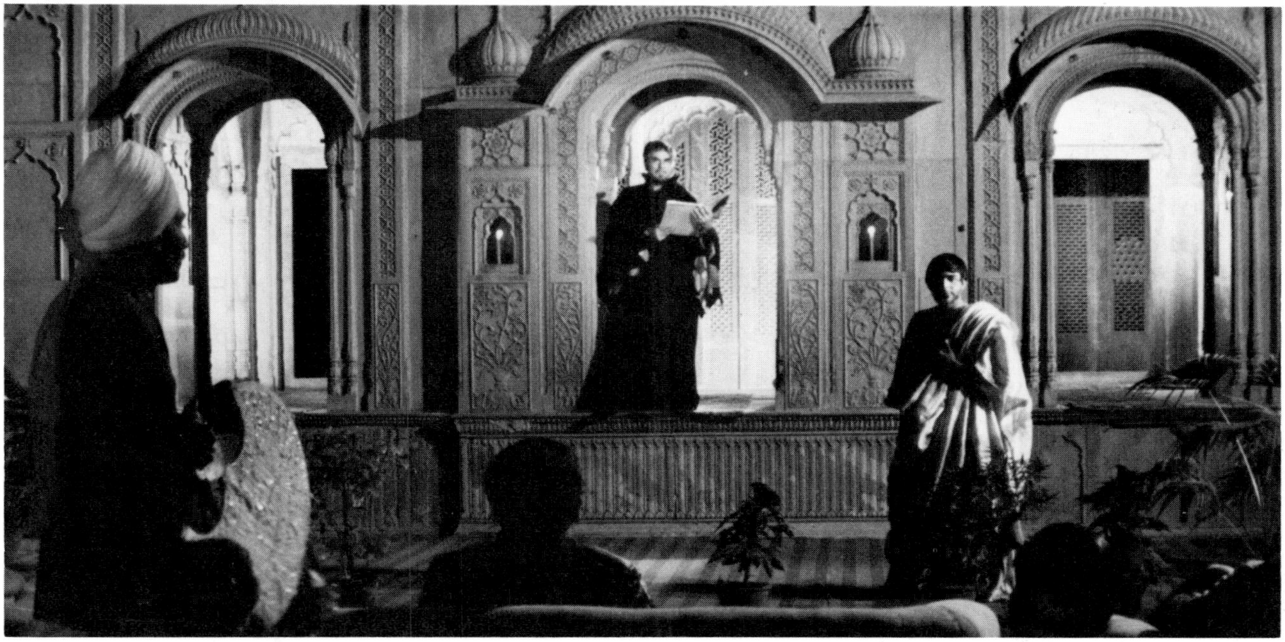

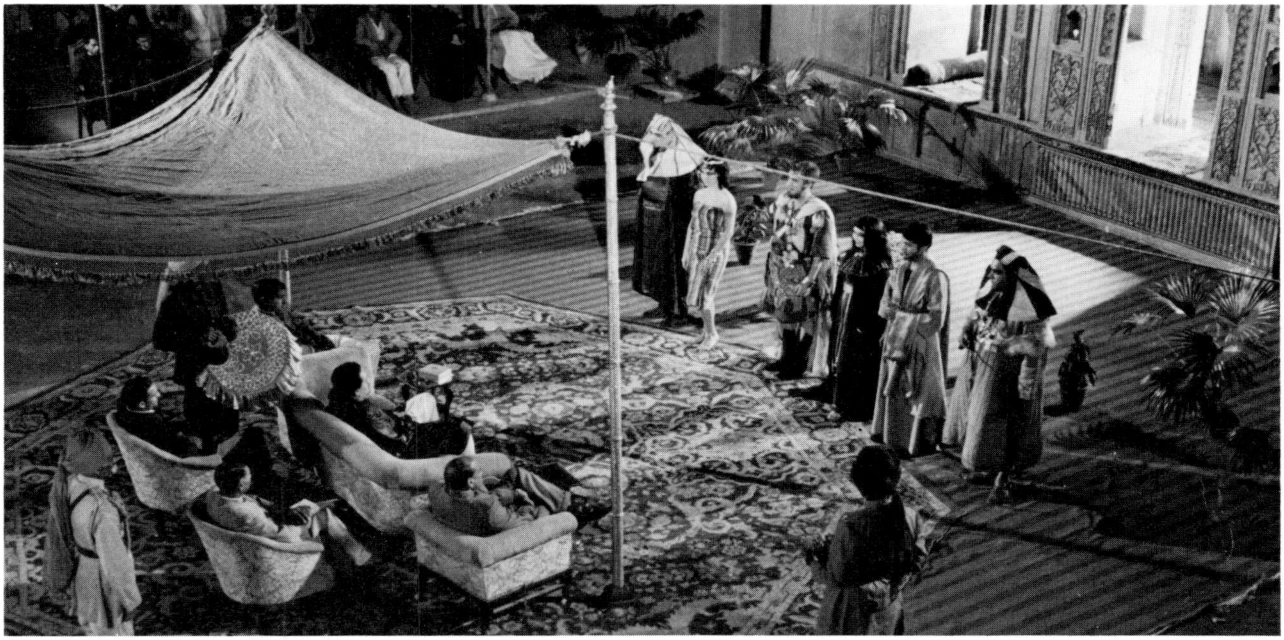

◄ **Alwar. The City Palace.** There's something of the Victorian merry-go-round suggested by the gilded scrolls around the arched windows and at the top of the building.

Alwar. The Buckingham Players performing *Antony and Cleopatra* in the purdah palace (above), and taking their curtain call before a Maharaja (below), in two scenes from *Shakespeare Wallah.*

The first time I went to Bikaner it was again to go palace hunting—we needed a large set for several sequences in *The Guru*. But I had an ulterior motive for going there: I wanted to meet a dealer in Indian miniature paintings whose collection of pictures was supposed to be very good. I went there by train with my collaborators, Ruth Jhabvala and Ismail Merchant. The trip from Delhi to Bikaner is, as Yvonne Fitzroy wrote in 1922, not an alluring journey:

> . . . by morning the greater part of the desert is deposited on the top of you, not to mention in your eyes and up your nose and down your throat. . . . By 7 a.m. your temper is hideous . . . your appearance past all praying for and certainly beyond all hope of reconstruction!

Nothing had changed in forty-five years. She went in January and froze, while we went in September, our sweat mingling with the soot and dust. For all I know, we traveled over the same bumpy tracks. We stayed at the Circuit House, a kind of state-run hotel, from where I called the picture dealer. As soon as possible—pushing *The Guru* to the back of my mind—I went around to see him at his house in the old section of town. The streets I passed through to get there were quite wonderful. The houses were built of stone and were beautifully proportioned, with carved doorways and cornices, also of stone; they were like the representations of houses in sculptured reliefs—simple and cubelike. One steps down into the ground-floor room from the street, which in that quarter of the town was mostly inhabited by bony-looking cows and pariah dogs sniffing at refuse.

But the picture dealer's house was different from the others. It was as old, but it had been redone, and instead of stepping down into it, I had to climb a flight of smooth marble stairs. Everything was scrubbed clean, and the walls had been freshly painted in brilliant ugly colors. As usual in middle-class Indian homes, the lights were fluorescent tubes. My host greeted me and called for a Coca-Cola. While I drank it, we made polite conversation before the pictures were brought out. There is always a certain amount of testing each other at this time: veiled references to paintings one has heard about and hopes to see, references to other collectors and what they may have bought from this or that source and for how much. It is a way of presenting one's credentials as a buyer, to induce the dealer to come out with some of his choicer items. You still may not be shown what you came to see, but nice things get dislodged by this method. The most interesting ones I saw there that day were not paintings but a pair of extraordinary Indian metal chairs in the Empire style, painted all over with a tiny floral pattern in gold on black. The seats were of gold chain mesh. Those chairs were something; the price was something, too: 40,000 rupees, or nearly $5,000. That was a lot for a pair of Indian chairs in 1967.

Since then, the Maharajas—the sources of such treasures— have been turning their palaces inside out. First they sold their showy, campy Victorian things—the silver beds and carrying chairs and gilt thrones set with mirrors; then, as they became more knowing, they moved on to their Art Nouveau glass and china and their Art Deco dressing-table sets from Cartier and other such knick-knacks brought back by their fathers and grandfathers from their buying sprees in the great days of princely spending. As a rule, however, the Maharajas have held on to their choicest possessions, those made in India, or else brought to India, centuries ago: Moghul paintings and the best pictures painted in their own states; Moghul weapons and jades and carpets; collections of valuable textiles and clothing. It can be maddeningly hard to view some of these treasures, particularly the Moghul pictures. I asked a princeling once where his family kept a famous album: Was it true that his father had it in his airplane? It wasn't true, he said; he had it at home under his bed.

Our search for locations in Bikaner took us to Gajner, the royal shooting lodge built by Maharaja Ganga Singh twenty miles outside the city. It seems to have been a tradition among the Maharajas to maintain an intimate, private pleasure palace of this kind, a retreat where the ruler and his guests could go and enjoy themselves. There is an air of fantasy about these places, built out in the desert, peeling under the blazing sun, but fully staffed and provisioned and decorated in the latest style of the day. One can't help wondering who would have ever wanted to go and stay there, even overnight, to sit at the little bars the Maharajas built or in the private cabarets they maintained, while outside jackals bayed at the moon.

Gajner, however, is not depressing in that way. We were urged

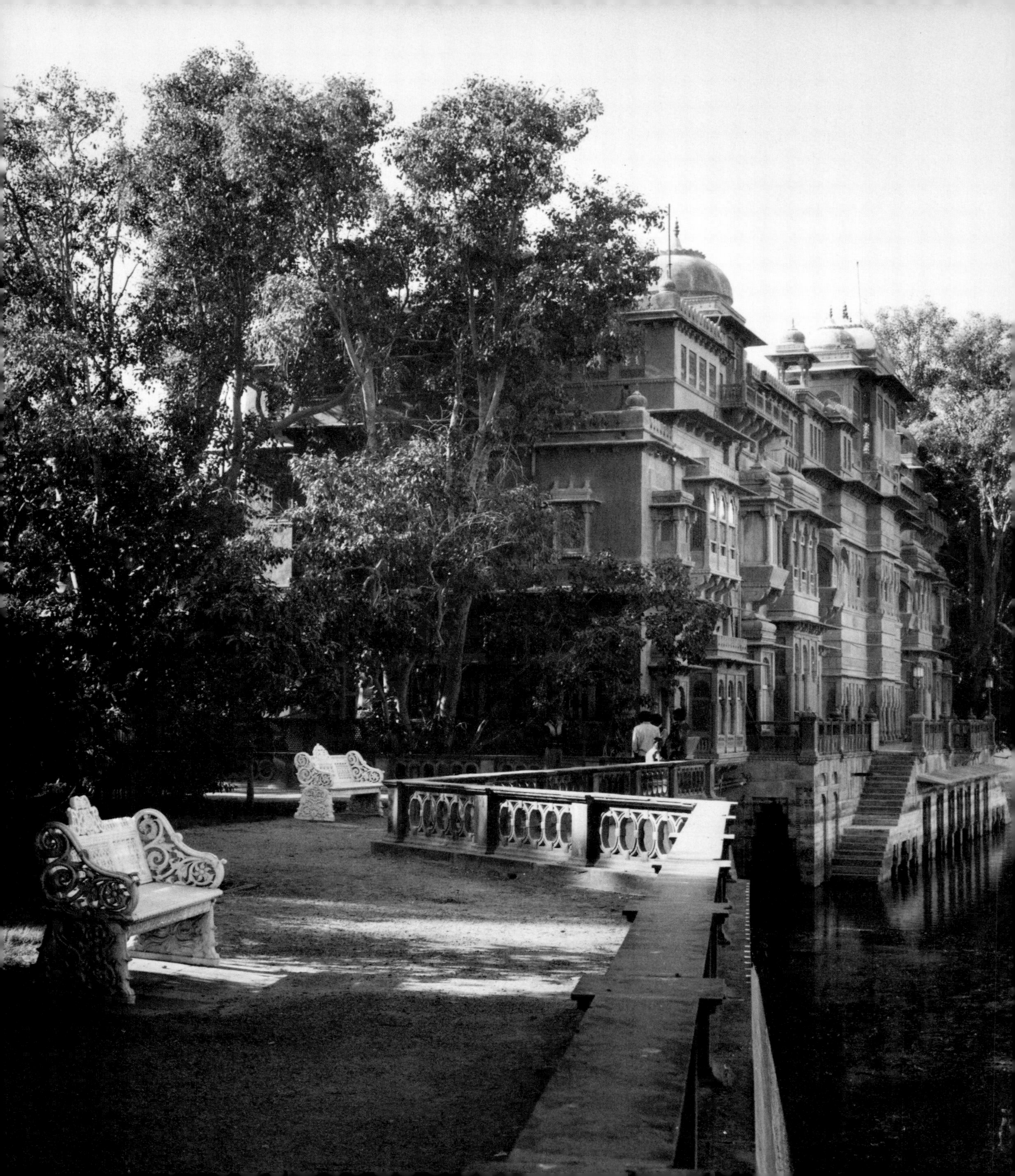

Gajner. A Corridor Giving ►
Access to Guest Bedrooms.

◄ The Shooting Lodge at Gajner,
near Bikaner (*page 40*).

(*overleaf*)

Bikaner. The Private Apartments
at the Fort.

to see it, so we went, but it turned out that the place, lovely as it was, didn't suit our story.

The story of *The Guru* is the reverse of *Shakespeare Wallah*: the English are no longer coming to India to offer their own culture but to immerse themselves in India's. It is the story of two young English people who follow a famous Indian musician as his disciples. Their quest leads them deeper and deeper into India, until they end up in a place called Bajapur in the Rajasthan desert. For "Bajapur" read Bikaner: it is just the sort of place where English enthusiasm for India and things Indian might be expected to founder. And such a sensation might well come to its climax in the old Bikaner Fort.

A massive, looming structure, it is the work of successive rulers, begun in 1600. It is empty now. At the turn of the century Maharaja Ganga Singh, like many other Rajput rulers at that time, felt the need of a more up-to-date, comfortable palace; he built himself a new Edwardian one called Largarh outside the town and went to live there. In the deserted old Fort the gardens have all blown away and the little pleasure pavilions that were spotted around them have begun to fall down. But the main building is well maintained, and it offered us many possibilities. A quarter of *The Guru* takes place in it. It is here that the heroine decides that home is best. Her gradual disenchantment with her guru, and with India itself, culminates in the Bikaner Fort.

The set needed to be both menacing and beautiful: menacing for a frightened European girl who feels she has had enough of India, beautiful for the Indians who belong naturally to this world she wants to escape from. We needed a set suggestive of a very strange, alien place—which a Maharaja's palace often tends to be. Although the older ones have an ambiguous beauty about them that is seductive, the atmosphere seems ultimately sinister and disturbing—particularly in a dead palace like the Bikaner Fort. So much has happened in these places. Nearly every story told by a guide has violent death as its theme; there are terrible tales of revenge, poisonings, parricides, mass widow burnings. Finally it is all—well, just weird and unnerving. One does want to go home.

What is it like when an Indian palace gets turned into a set? The biggest problem is always electricity. During shooting of *The*

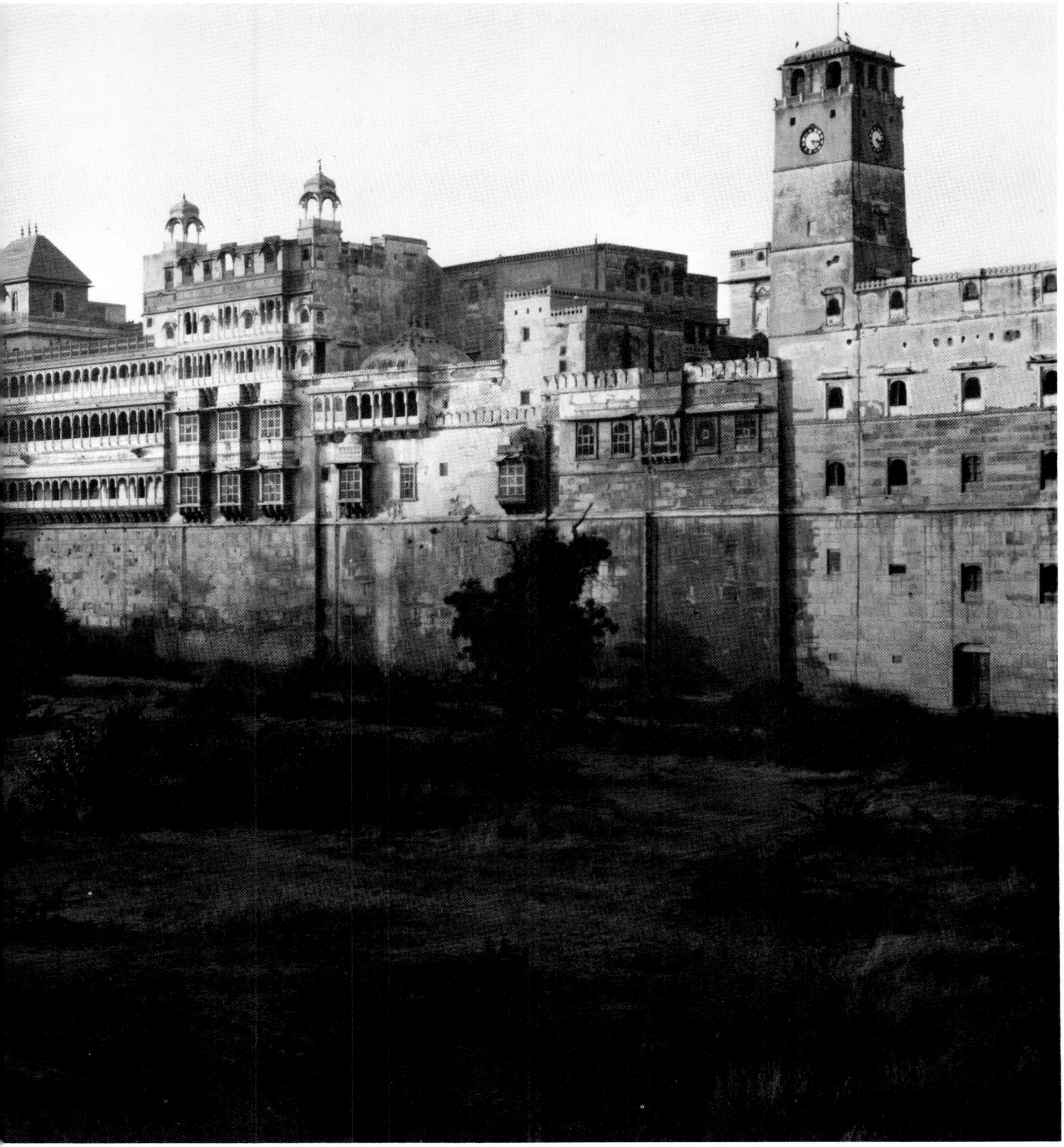

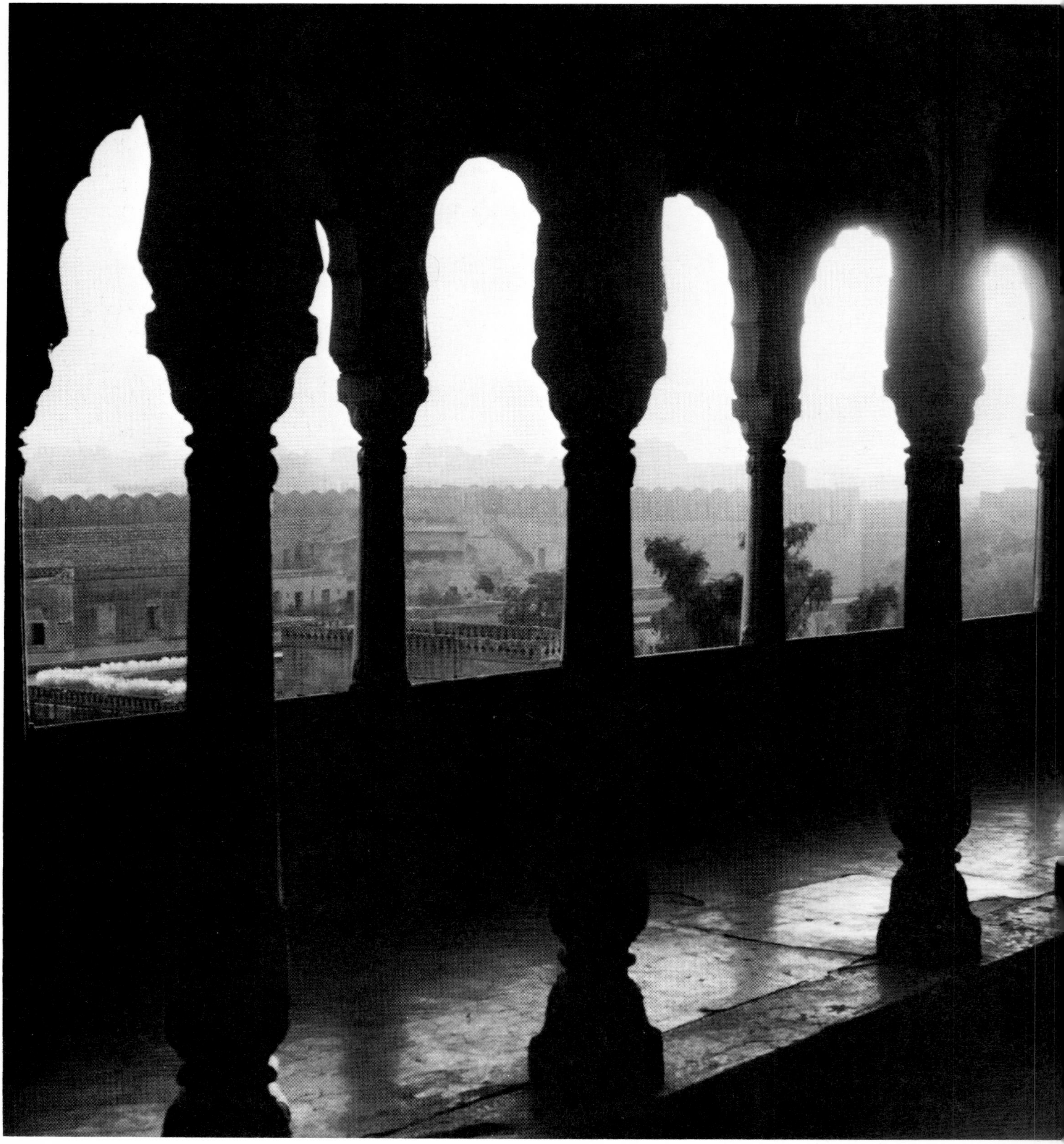

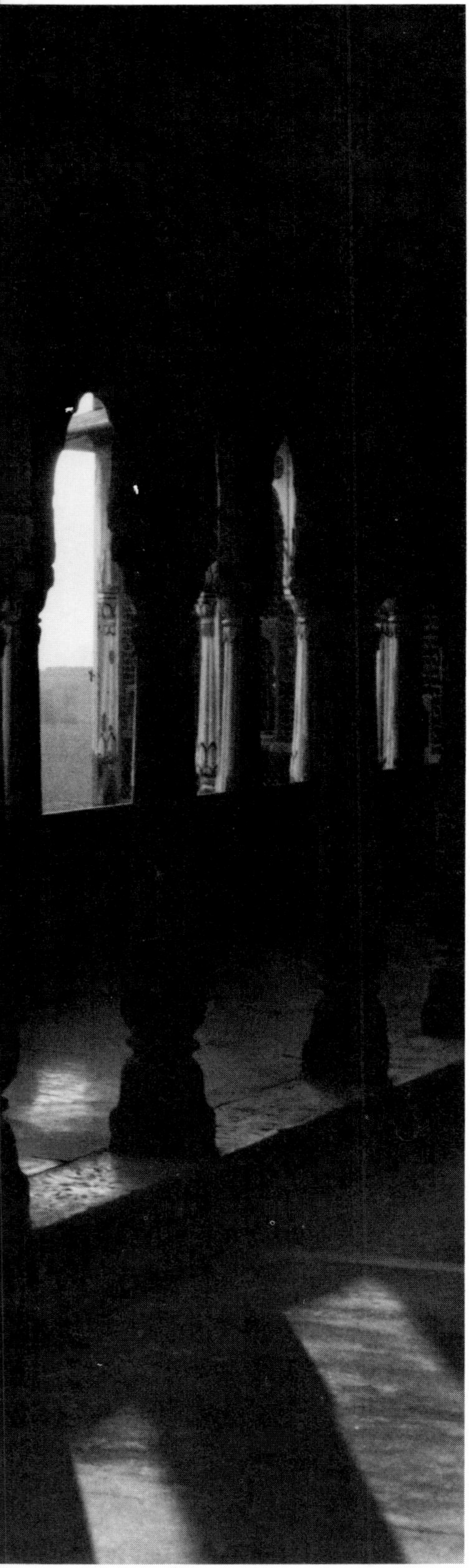

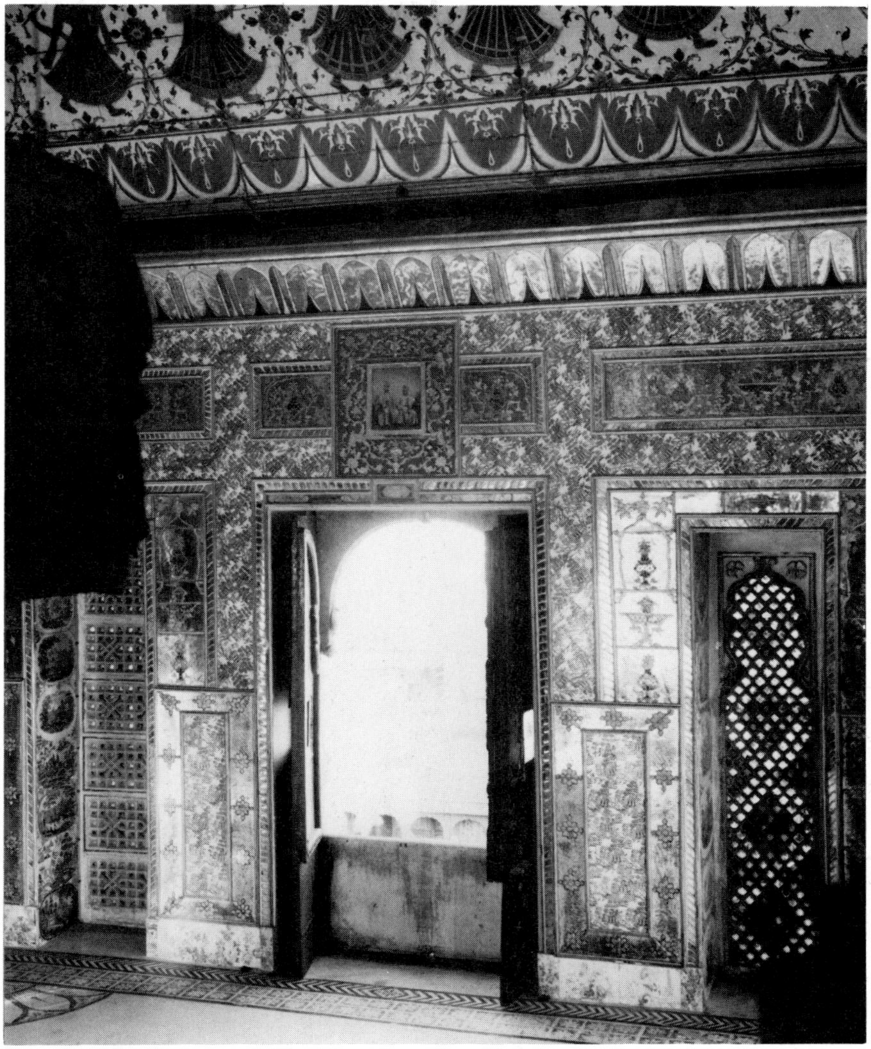

▲
Bikaner. A Painted Room in the Purdah Palace Within the Fort.

◄ Bikaner. From the Fort, Looking over the Ruined Gardens Toward the Town.

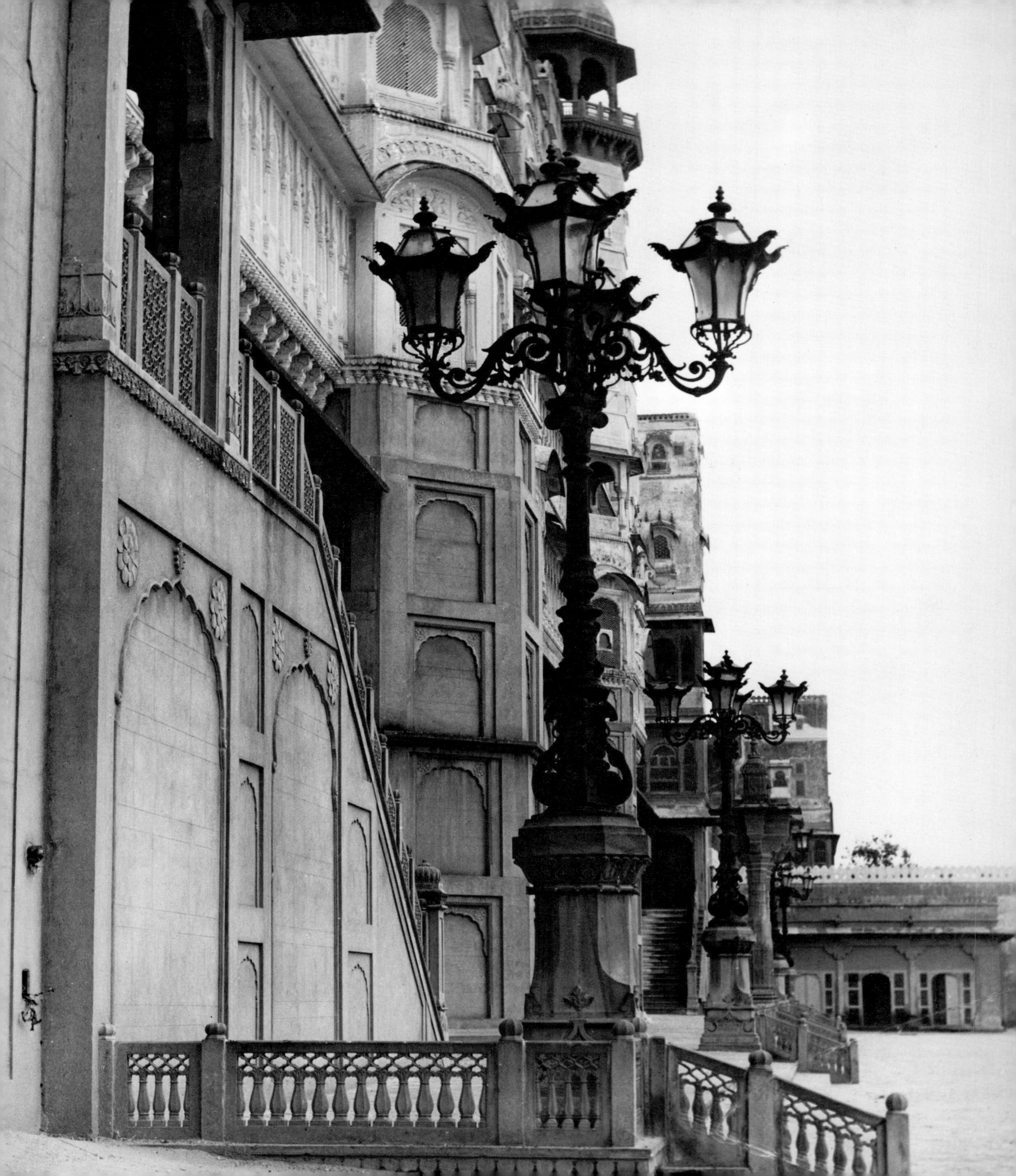

Guru there wasn't enough power to supply the palace as well as our lights, so a very large generator, used for location shooting, had to be brought all the way from Bombay. Our requirements of space grew and grew. We were shooting in only a few of the hundreds of rooms in the palace, but we needed many others besides: to store our equipment in at night; to use for our wardrobe; to use as production offices. We began to crowd the Maharaja, an avid painter of abstract canvases, whose pictures were hanging all over one of our main sets. There were more than fifty people around all the time, either actively working or on call. They had to be fed and facilities found for them in a building where modern plumbing was almost nonexistent. The stars of the film had to have some place they could call their own.

There was always the problem of maintaining the location itself: film companies are notoriously lax about other people's property. Fortunately, there were no valuable objects around to be broken or stolen, since the Bikaner Fort was almost unfurnished. (It must have been so even when it was inhabited by the Maharaja, his family, and all their retainers. The classical Indian interior never had much furniture—just a bed, a few boxes and mats and cushions, a mirror or two. It is only since the Maharajas became gentlemen in the English style that they had to have a lot of objects around.)

Besides observing the physical integrity of the Fort—being careful not to chip the stuccowork or scrape the painted walls—we had to respect its sacred character: it is, after all, the symbolic seat of the ruling family of one of the oldest and proudest Rajput states. The Indian members of the crew and cast had an instinctive sense of this, but the foreign members had to be reminded. *I* had to be reminded: one day, while we were working in the Hall of Private Audience, I was feeling exhausted and sat down for a moment on the *gadi*, or cushion, which serves as the throne of an Indian prince. It really was only for a moment; the reminder came at once in the form of the most delicate, the most subtle of suggestions that I should perhaps sit somewhere else.

Our work was always watched by a palace servant or two. They were there to see that the decorum of the place was maintained; to keep unauthorized people out; to open locked doors with a big key; and to report back to the palace custodian on whatever was happening. These old men who work for the Maharajas have

Bikaner. The Exterior of the Fort from the Front. This is the view the arriving visitor would see first. Maharaja Ganga Singh brought a lot of trophies home from his European trips. These Paris (or Vienna?) street lamps are an example; inside the palace one can see the bullet-riddled fuselages of several fighter planes shot down in the First World War.

A Royal Servant—in This Case, from Jodhpur. Many of these old men are so closely identified with their royal masters, have served them for so long, that they have gained an authority which seems quite out of proportion to the lowly-sounding office they actually hold. Sometimes they have to be firm, sometimes cunning, sometimes vigilant where their master's vices are concerned: they can be a controlling influence on rulers addicted to alcohol or opium. Their loyalty to the family they serve makes them a part of the dilemma of the princes today: how to care for these old retainers and their dependents now that the allowances are gone.

amazing aplomb. Most Indian servants seem to belong to a frieze of comic figures beneath the serious composition that is the world of their employers. In the world of Maharajas it is often the reverse: the servants are the serious composition.

We didn't sleep in the Fort. I don't think anybody wanted to. Some stayed in the guest quarters of Largarh Palace; some stayed in the Circuit House; some in the Dak Bungalow. We all ate together at lunch in a courtyard of the Fort; at night we went back to our own quarters to eat.

The Guru was a tense, unhappy film to make. People didn't get on well together. The atmosphere was poisoned by all the catty things that were said. Each new person joining the company was expected to take sides—either against "management" and the crew, or against the actors. Sometimes the actors turned against one another. Here are two entries from my journal which give a good idea of what those days were like:

February 14, 1968

Last night Nadira, the Courtesan, made her first appearance at dinner. She laughed a lot and flashed her eyes and told risqué stories. We all tried to have a good time with her, tried to make her feel

Another Servant, Again from Jodhpur. This old man is the custodian of a royal farm.

welcome, but I felt uneasy. There is always something a bit out of control about her; you never know what she will say or do next. The Memsahibs think she possesses evil powers, that she's a kind of witch, and they attributed the day's misfortunes to her arrival upon the scene: a camera jam, the jeep breaking down on its way from the palace to the set with the crew's lunch, Rita's sudden migraine. Utpal encourages the Memsahibs in all of this nonsense; it's rather unbecoming of him. Nadira has no use for the Memsahibs, makes a pained face when she's forced to talk to them—Would you pass the pickle, *please?*—dismisses their flat English figures, straight yellow hair, and sun-reddened skin. After she left the table the witch-talk went on for a long time. Now they feel they really have something to blame on her and are making the most of it.

When I went back to my room Michael and Pat (York) called me into theirs. They had something to tell me, a great announcement to make! This was that they had decided, that very evening, to get

Bikaner. A Scene from *The Guru.* Rita Tushingham, as Jenny, peers during her nightmare into the locked-up rooms of the palace.

126

married. I was the first person to be told. After I congratulated them I went off to my room again. But in a couple of hours I was waked up by a lot of running along the passage outside, by a lot of whispering, by doors opening and banging shut. I went to look and found Pat in the throes of some dread seizure. She lay on her bed, twisting and moaning. Michael, looking frightened and helpless, held her hands. She had an agonizing pain in her stomach; the doctor had been sent for, but appendicitis was ruled out as she'd already had that. All we could do was stand around and see what would happen next. The moans became screams, the twisting a demented, frenzied writhing. She wanted us to massage her feet and we all took turns doing this while Michael bent over her, whispering encouragement. Then she became hysterical, demanded that the servant be sent away: there was something malignant in his presence that frightened her. I can imagine how that might be: he is only five feet tall, including turban. That wizened face peering up at her all

Bikaner. Another Scene from *The Guru*: a Concert in the Old Palace. Utpal Dutt (seated on the floor facing the camera) plays the title role, a sitar virtuoso named Ustad Zafar Khan.

the time must have made her think of some dwarf in an evil fairy tale. Then the doctor came; he stood at the foot of the bed and watched her for a while. He was a tall, grave, distinguished-looking man. We all felt reassured. He said that before diagnosing he preferred to observe for a day. There was nothing to do now. I left this tableau—reminiscent of some Victorian hospital scene before the invention of chloroform—and went back to bed.

February 15, 1968

Today Pat is much worse. We tried to take a shot for the last scene of the film, where Tom walks Jenny through a ruinous landscape to the sound of the Ustad's sitar recital coming from inside, but Michael naturally was too upset to do anything more than mope across. He looked more gaunt and touching than usual, in his black velvet suit and purple shirt from Trend of Simpson's, Piccadilly. This evening—to liven things up, she said—Nadira decided to throw

Bikaner. A Scene from *The Guru.* Nadira, as the courtesan, in Jenny's nightmare.

a barbecue for her fellow actors and the higher echelon of crew. No one had the heart for it but she insisted and—yes—a witch's fire was built for her by the front steps of the guest house. She was crouched over it, turning gobbets of goat meat on a spit, when Michael passed on the way to the hospital with Pat in his arms. He was very shaken when he got back. The hospital had turned out to be a tin-roofed, mud-walled sort of place, full of peasants and their grieving families. You read in his eyes that he thought Pat might never come out of there alive. Nadira, excited, flushed, and high, brought a plate of cold, charred meat to him in his room. She perched gaily on the arm of his chair as he sat staring into the fire, calling him "darling" and caressing his neck as she poked the over-cooked meat at him on a fork. He was wonderfully patient with her, never lost his temper; you have to hand it to the English sometimes. We managed finally to coax her out. He says the doctor is preparing to operate for an intestinal obstruction.

We rearranged our shooting schedule and took the series of shots which, when edited, became "Jenny's Vision." Michael didn't have to appear in any of them. I suppose the reason that this sequence is so long is that we had nothing else to do while Michael looked after Pat: we were forced to concentrate on Rita's nightmare search through the rooms of the Fort. A pall of fear hung over our work during those days. We expected Pat to die—we really did; the bad news would be brought by a shaken Ismail. But the surgeon was skilled and Pat was stronger than she looked. We heard he removed eight feet of her intestine, and somebody told the grisly story that after the operation when he took it out in the sunlight in a basin to have a good look, a big carrion crow swooped down and flew away with it.

VI

Autobiography of a Princess

On the set during the shooting of
Autobiography of a Princess, March 1974.
Madhur Jaffrey, James Mason, and myself.

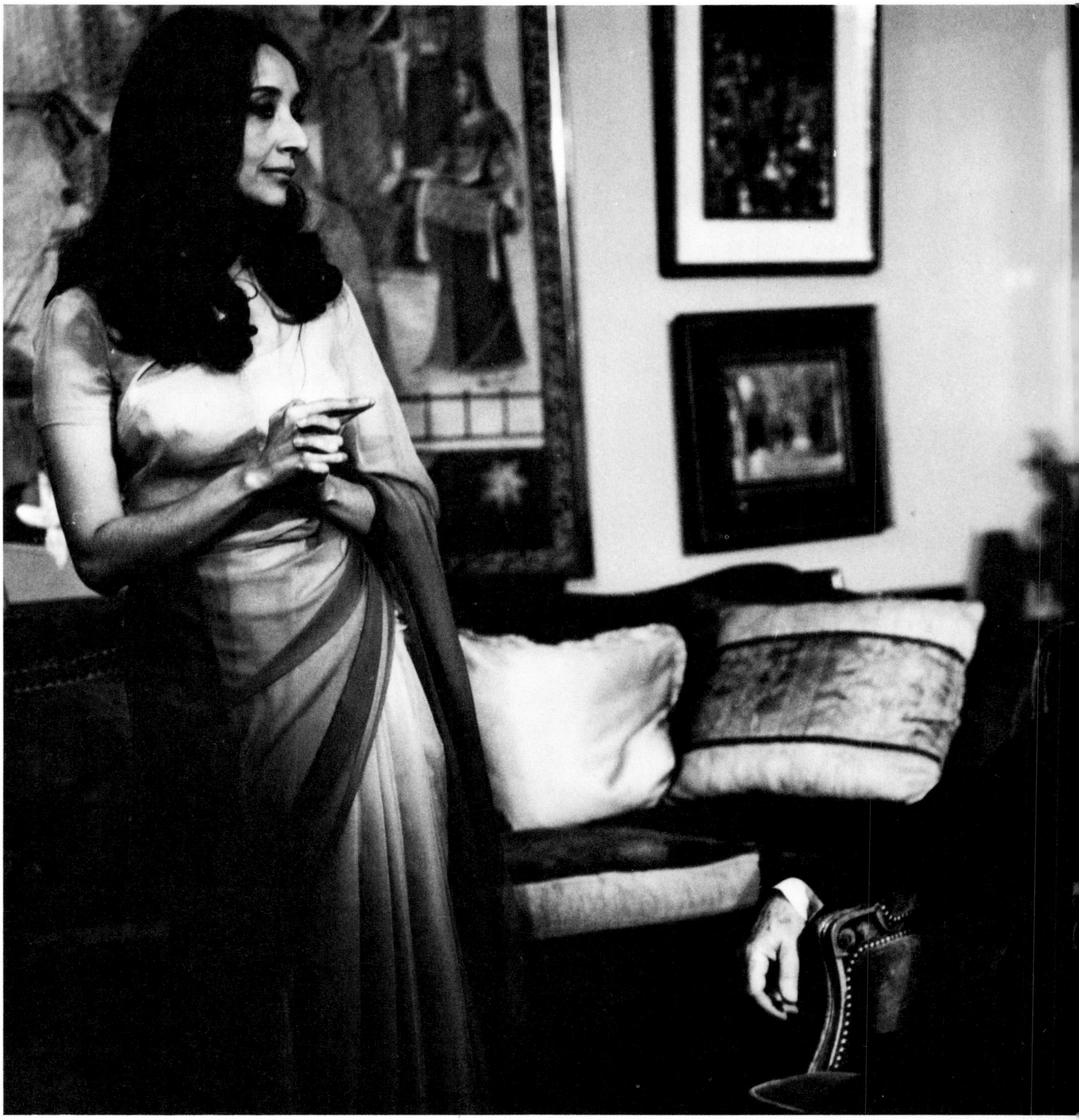

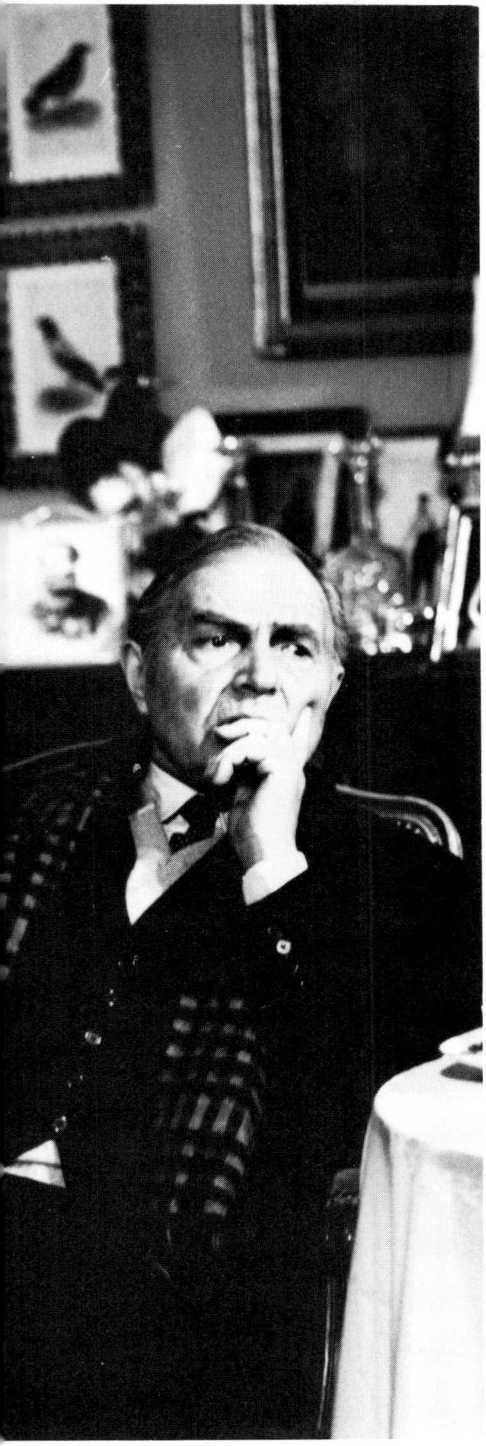

THE idea for our next Royal Indian film, *Autobiography of a Princess,* really began with our discovery of the old archive footage in various palace cellars. Besides that, we also had a lot of miscellaneous footage of our own—views of palaces, landscapes, interviews with the Maharajas. It was all something of a jumble. But the subject of Royal India has always been a jumble, with everything all mixed up together: Rolls-Royce cars and rat temples, dancing girls and Queen Victoria's marble bust and the Maharajas' Gypsy Moth airplanes.

Whenever we looked at the archive footage, we found it hard to keep it all straight. Often it was impossible to know what we were looking at, or to sort out the various ceremonies and occasions one from the other. As Cyril Sahib remarks in the film:

> Somehow it all ran together—being married, dying—it was all part of the same process . . . What is this box? I think it is the Queen Mother being carried in purdah to some ceremony. . . . [*Box in the film within the film is tipped onto pyre.*] Ah no, this appears to be a funeral.

The episodes had a way of breaking off suddenly and starting with something else. That decomposing footage was like the Dead Sea Scrolls: if you tried to see what it was, to follow the story, it turned to dust in your hands. Whatever we were able to put onto safety film is what we're left with. But that was enough to intrigue us, to keep us interested in the whole subject.

Then in 1973 I went to India to see friends. While we were there, Ismail decided to accept a long-standing invitation from the former Maharaja of Jodhpur to visit him; this provided an opportunity to do a little shooting there to add to our miscellaneous stock of royal footage. So we went—Ismail, Ruth Jhabvala, and myself, with a two-man camera crew from Bombay. It was the first week of April, and the heat in Jodhpur was intense. That seemed to be the only thing I could think about. It was grueling to go up to the Fort, to visit the bazaar, to do anything. I wanted only to lie on my bed in the palace under the fan. When I looked out my window everything was obscured by a haze of blowing dust. Usually storms excite me, but this one made me impatient. I was impatient with myself. I felt I knew it all now anyway; why had I come back here? Meanwhile, somewhere downstairs in some dim room crammed with ten-foot-tall Japanese vases and grandfather clocks that didn't run anymore, I knew the shooting must have begun. Then I began to feel guilty. It was wrong to lie up there while everybody worked. I got up and dressed—I saw my white sahib's legs reflected in the dark glass of the wardrobe door and thought, Ugh!—and went to find the others.

They were taking a close-up of the Maharaja's desk. There was a doodle on the white blotter; I felt it must have been a long time since anybody had actually worked at that desk, had put the silver pen into the silver ink pot, or blotted the crested paper with the rocking silver blotter. I sat in a chair and watched all the fussing with the lights. For some reason, I began to think of what Bai-ji, the Jodhpur princess, had told us in her interview about her life here, about going to school in Switzerland and then coming back to Jodhpur, and how everybody had tried to force her into purdah. Suddenly I thought of the actress Madhur Jaffrey: what a princess she would make! And there it was, in however vague a form—a new film.

I told Ismail what I was contemplating: a film that would be a mixture of the documentary footage we had already shot, fictional sequences with Madhur playing an Indian princess, and, of course, our archive material. From now on everything that we did in Jodhpur had to work into this new idea; I had to look around me a bit more carefully, find my raw material. It was then that I began to appreciate the Umaid Bhavan Palace for what it is: the final stupendous palace-city to be erected in India, the last in a line going back a thousand years or more—and furthermore, to see it as the setting of my new film. After this, though I suffered from the heat, I didn't think about it all the time. There was too much to do.

By the time we got back to New York, we had decided that the setting for the fictional part of our film must be London, where our fictional Indian princess would be living in a sort of self-imposed exile from present-day India. By then we had also added another character: Cyril Sahib, an aging Englishman retired from India, a friend of the Princess's, sharing her memories—but with a different view of them.

It was an enjoyable film to make, without mishaps or arguments. It took six days to shoot; the first was used as a rehearsal with the two main actors, Madhur Jaffrey and James Mason, who was playing Cyril Sahib. We had to work very fast in order to keep within the budget—and for another reason: the jewelry Madhur was wearing had been lent by Garrads, the jewelers on Regent Street (very appropriately, for Maharajas loved to shop there), and it had to be returned to the company's safe every night at six o'clock. There was a representative from Garrards and two armed guards on the set at all times; they got very nervous one day when all the lights went out. This jewelry was valued at a quarter of a million pounds. It consisted of a necklace and matching earrings of emeralds and diamonds, a large emerald ring, and a wristwatch with diamonds set around the dial, which had to be held on with Scotch tape because Madhur's wrists are so tiny.

The film is basically one long scene, with flashbacks, "visions," and digressions by way of the old footage that Cyril Sahib and the Princess are projecting in her drawing room. I had never played a whole film in one room, with only two actors. I was afraid it might become boring or be too static. But I don't think it has turned out that way.

Cyril Sahib: James Mason
The Princess: Madhur Jaffrey
Deliveryman: Keith Varnier
The Blackmailers: Diane Fletcher / Timothy Bateson / Johnny Stuart
Papa: Nazrul Rahman

Producer: Ismail Merchant
Director: James Ivory
Writer: Ruth Prawer Jhabvala
Photography: Walter Lassally
Editor: Humphrey Dixon
Music: Vic Flick
Sets: Jacquemine Charrot-Lodwidge

*A first-floor flat in a large, old house in Kensington that has been
converted into apartments. Through the tall windows there is a
view of a similar house opposite. The flat belongs to a middle-aged
Indian princess living in exile in London. It is full of heavy old
furniture and mementoes of the native state in India which was
her girlhood home. A large and imposing portrait of a Maharaja
in the uniform of a British Army regiment dominates the room.
The man in the painting—a strikingly handsome man—wears
decorations of the First World War and a turban with a diamond
aigrette in it. In the middle of the room a delivery man is setting
up a 16mm film projector and adjusting a screen. He works in a
slapdash way; at one point the top of the screen gets entangled with
the crystal chandelier. He curses under his breath.*

In her bedroom, the Princess is getting herself ready at her dressing table. An elaborate routine.

From the next room:

YOUNG MAN: I'll be going then.

PRINCESS: One moment.

She goes into the other room. The YOUNG MAN *has finished setting up the projector. The* PRINCESS *looks at it and is not pleased. She shakes her head and clicks her tongue.*

PRINCESS: But this is quite the wrong place. Quite wrong. No, this won't do. It will have to be moved.

YOUNG MAN: Bit late to tell me now, isn't it.

PRINCESS: But don't you see—it's in the way of my preparations.

She waves her hand at an elaborately set tea table. When the YOUNG MAN *is not helpful, she begins to move the projector herself. She is ineffecutal but determined. She pulls at things indiscriminately.*

YOUNG MAN: Here—look out. This is expensive equipment. Cost me my job if anything happened to that.

PRINCESS: It will have to be moved.

She goes on tugging with determination so that the YOUNG MAN *is forced to help. He grumbles as he does so.*

YOUNG MAN: I should have been told . . . I got another job waiting . . . Haven't got all day . . . Wasting my time . . . (*etc.*)

The PRINCESS *ignores this. She gives orders quite briskly as to where she wants the projector. She is obviously used to commanding, and although the* YOUNG MAN *is not used to obeying, he has no alternative. She watches him critically—warns him "Be careful" when he comes too near her tea table or threatens some precious object. The* YOUNG MAN *goes on grumbling while he is forced to work—about how she should have said—that he's got a job to go to right across London and how did she think he was going to get there on time. She ignores all this completely, intent only on getting the projector exactly where she wants it. She does not hesitate to make him change it several times till she gets it entirely to her satisfaction.*

PRINCESS (*rather grandly*): That will do.

YOUNG MAN (*with heavy sarcasm*): Oh, thanks very much.

PRINCESS: No, thank *you*. You've done very well. You may call for it in the morning. But please *not* before eleven o'clock.

YOUNG MAN: We'll have to see about that. It depends on my day.

This is his last attempt to salvage some vestige of British independence. Of course she doesn't hear it. He retires with a rather routed air. She calls after him, as a gracious afterthought:

PRINCESS: Thank you. You have been very kind.

She forgets—dismisses—him at once. She fusses about her room, her tea things, and—catching glimpses of herself in the mirror—about herself. She has a pleased air of anticipation. Obviously she is waiting for someone. When she hears the doorbell, she opens the French windows, steps onto her balcony, and sings down, "The door is open! Come right up!"

She watches from the landing of the stairs as CYRIL SAHIB *puts away his umbrella in the umbrella stand and hangs up his coat and hat. He ascends the stairs—a slow-moving, elderly Englishman. At the right moment she says in welcome, "Cyril Sahib!" She receives him at the top of the stairs, stretching out both her hands to him. He seizes one of them and kisses it, murmuring, "May I." His old-fashioned courtliness pleases her. She glows. She draws him into the room, chattering effusively.*

PRINCESS: How was the journey? Tiresome, I'm sure. That dreadful little train from Turton. Now I want you to be absolutely comfortable—no, you must sit here, this is your chair, right here by the fire—and this for your back—no, you must put your feet up—that's right—

When she has seated him to her satisfaction, she steps back to look at him as if he were an art object she has arranged.

PRINCESS: Wonderful to see you. On *our* day.

CYRIL SAHIB: My dear Princess.

138

PRINCESS: Our very own day. Another year has gone and you look just the same. (*As he ruefully passes his hand over his head.*) Exactly the same. You haven't aged a day.

CYRIL SAHIB (*sincerely and with feeling, not as polite compliment*): You are younger and more beautiful than ever.

PRINCESS: Oh, but of course! Of course! (*She pretends to speak ironically but is really very pleased.*) Now I'm going to get your tea—everything is ready—no, you're not to move—I absolutely forbid it . . .

She goes and he sinks down again into his chair. He looks round the room—at the hangings, the objects salvaged from palaces and now come to rest in this old-fashioned, high-ceilinged Kensington room. His gaze finally stays on the portrait above the mantlepiece. It is garlanded. He gets up to look at it. As CYRIL SAHIB *stands there, the* PRINCESS *returns with the tea.*

PRINCESS: I had such trouble with his birthday garland again this year. These London florists simply don't know how to make a garland. I had to show the girl myself. Come along now, I'm pouring your tea. (*Watching him with amusement, as he lingers by the portrait.*) I know you can't tear yourself away.

He smiles and returns to his chair.

CYRIL SAHIB: He certainly was a handsome man.

PRINCESS: Oh, Cyril Sahib! Handsome! Papa was the—the—(*Words fail her—finally she comes out with this schoolgirl expression.*) he was tops.

CYRIL SAHIB: Quite.

PRINCESS: In everything . . . Well, shall we drink to our birthday boy? (*Raising her teacup to the portrait.*) In *tea*. Drinking to Papa in tea! (*Giggles.*)

CYRIL SAHIB: He was always amused by my drinking habits. Or rather, my non-drinking habits. A mild man, he called me.

She laughs.

PRINCESS: How is Turton-on-Sea, Cyril Sahib? And the research?

CYRIL SAHIB: Turton is quiet—and mild. Very suitable. And the research is coming along, slowly along. I shall have a book one of these days.

PRINCESS (*with meaning*): You know the book I want you to write.

He doesn't answer. There is a slightly awkward pause, which she then bridges over with a deliberate change of subject and tone. She gets up to fiddle around with the projector.

PRINCESS: Everything is ready, you see, for our annual birthday treat. And I have the tapes for the interviews as well. Such a nice young man brought them over from the BBC. He said I could keep them as long as I liked. A charming boy. We became friends . . . No, I don't want you to move. First I shall put on our films and after that if you like—if you're not too tired—we can see the interviews. No, I don't need help—you will sit absolutely still—and drink more tea. There. And I know you like these—go on—I insist (*handing him some Indian delicacy*).

CYRIL SAHIB: Very well, Princess. Turn me into a greedy old man.

The films begin. The PRINCESS *comments on the state of the footage—its physical deterioration since they saw it last year—some vague intentions of doing something to have it restored, she doesn't know exactly what. It's so precious, she says, that it has to be saved because when that's gone, then everything is gone.*

We see a polo match: some very good footage here—polo at its best.

PRINCESS (*voice-over*): It was a good team, wasn't it? Although of course not up to Jodhpur. Or Patiala . . . It wasn't quite Papa's favourite sport. He found it a bit tame. What did he always say? "Sitting on a horse to run after a ball." When *he* sat on a horse— it wasn't to run after a ball.

Hunting scenes of various kinds—culminating in pig-sticking.

This was more his kind of game. Our hunts were famous. Everyone came from all over India, from all over the world. And he loved doing daredevil things. Once, when there was a royal visitor from England who couldn't shoot properly—he was so clumsy—he wounded a tiger and let him get away—of course that was terribly dangerous, so Papa said he would go and look for it. He wouldn't allow anyone to come with him except Purush Chand, his favourite Shikari. They couldn't find the tiger for a whole day and were just going to turn back when he surprised them. He mauled Purush Chand and would have killed him on the spot if Papa hadn't fired. He and that tiger were at a distance of less than one foot from each other. Papa called it the closest shave he ever had, and that tiger's skin was afterwards hung up in his own study. He was a beauty. . . . Purush Chand died of his wounds, which was a tragedy, but Papa was very generous with the widow. You know how he was. No wonder the poor adored him.

CYRIL SAHIB *looks a bit uneasy by the end of this story; they have been watching a leopard tear a tethered kid to pieces; the* PRINCESS *is excited, a bit out of breath.*

She tells these old stories as if she were telling them for the first time and as if it were all new to CYRIL SAHIB. *By now we have come to the pig-sticking.*

PRINCESS: Of course pig-sticking was his favourite sport of all. He called it a real man's sport. Because he said there wasn't anything between you and the pig except steady hands and steady nerves and a brave heart. . . . I think what he really loved was danger. *That* was his sport. Whether it was animals or aeroplanes.

The pig-sticking has given way to the private airplanes.

He was one of the first princes to get a pilot's license. And ours was one of the first aerodromes in India. . . . That was a great day for him, the inauguration of the hangar . . .

The old Jodhpur footage here, with speech by Sir John Steel.

We were terrified out of our wits whenever Papa went out to fly. Especially after Bajapur was killed in *his* plane. We thought after that perhaps Papa would be more careful—but not a bit of it. All he said was "When your time has come, it has come . . ." Sir John Steel came specially from Delhi for the inauguration. There was such a big party. Papa was in seventh heaven. You know how good he was at parties . . .

Footage of Europeans—especially the footage of sahibs and memsahibs having fun at some hunt.

They had such fun. Papa loved fun. And he never spared expense —quails from Isphahan—and champagne—and fireworks . . . He loved jokes too. Making people laugh. Once he made an apple-pie bed with his own hands for the Resident, Sir Philip Rough. Next morning at breakfast he said, "Well, Sir Philip, I hope you had a good night." "Excellent, Your Highness. Thanks to your very *personal* efforts." Sir Philip was a good sport— which is more than can be said for some of the Indian princes. The stuffier ones refused to come to us because of Papa's jokes. Silly they were. It was all just harmless fun. Whenever he was in London, he bought up the joke shops in Tottenham Court Road. He brought back trunkfuls of squeaking cushions, exploding cigars, things like that. There were a few accidents because of his sense of humour—but he always made it up to people afterwards . . .

Footage of royal weddings and suchlike grand occasions has started.

. . . Where are we? Is this Fatehpur—Princey and Pussy? Or is it Indu and Meher? No, it must be Princey and Pussy—because there's Uncle Rajkumar, and he was no longer there for Indu's wedding . . . From the moment the guests came in the special train . . . till they left there wasn't a moment's rest. One thing after another.

We are now in the middle of footage showing various stages of, or happenings at, Indian weddings. With explanatory and other comments here and there by the PRINCESS.

People came for a month—and stayed for three . . . with all their servants, naturally.

The wedding footage is followed by home movies of two children riding tricyles on some royal lawn. The Princess sighs:

Poor Babli . . . She is in Mexico now, with that—person she married . . . He is still in the sanitarium near Lausanne . . . He was such a wonderful rider. And dancer.

Then shots of guest suites, sitting rooms, bedrooms, bathrooms.

This is the suite done up in '38 for the Jaisalmer wedding.

Of the paintings and decorations by a European artist:

Aren't they spiffing? They're very valuable now, of course. Art Deco . . . They were all done by a German artist—or was it Austrian? He was called Paul Merkler. He could turn his hand to anything. He sewed the curtains in the ballroom and designed a new uniform for the palace guard . . . He stayed with us for fifteen years and we thought he would be there forever but I don't know what happened to him—one day he suddenly decided he must go back to Germany. Or was it Austria? After fifteen years! And he was in the middle of doing terrazzo murals for the indoor swimming pool—it was left unfinished—a whole mythological scene with Neptune and mermaids . . .

Back at London tea party:

PRINCESS: Are you tired?

CYRIL SAHIB: Not at all. (*But he does look exhausted.*)

PRINCESS: We'll have a break, shall we?

She sits close to him. She makes a fuss over him. She draws an affectionate forefinger over his sleeve.

PRINCESS (*in a wheedling voice*): Cyril Sahib . . . (*She is a person who wants something.*) What is your book about?

CYRIL SAHIB: You ask me that every year . . . And in your Christmas card as well.

PRINCESS: I always forget . . . No, no, I remember. It is about— about—the life of some Englishman—

CYRIL SAHIB: Denis Lever.

PRINCESS: He lived in Assam for donkey's years.

CYRIL SAHIB: Thirty-five. And not Assam but Orissa, Princess. He made the most comprehensive record of local history, poetry, and song ever assembled. An enormously valuable work. And at the same time he was a first-class administrator who left his district among the most prosperous and progressive in the country.

PRINCESS: Wonderful . . . What about the other book? *Our* book?

He is silent.

If you don't write it, who will? . . . Oh, what a shame that would be, if it were all to vanish into thin air! What a loss to humanity!

He is still silent.

What's left of Royal India now except what people like us remember? We owe it to posterity to put it all down. It is a sacred debt . . .

She gets up and puts another reel on the projector.

I want you to see the interviews the young man from the BBC left with me . . . I looked at them last night. I had meant to wait till today, till you came—but I couldn't resist temptation. And then afterwards I cried and cried . . . I told myself, you silly goose, what is there to cry for? That's the way it is now . . .

Excerpts from interviews. First their attitude to politics:

RAJMATA OF JAIPUR: *Her bitterness about the dispossession of the princes and how it was done.*

JODHPUR: *His description of how he and his mother got into politics—how they felt it to be their duty. His bitterness about the attitude to the princes—*"We are Public Enemy No. 1."

Then they talk more generally, giving the impression of up-rooted, lost, unwanted people:

JODHPUR: *His dilemma between England and India.*

PRINCE JAGAT: *His indecision: Where to start? What to do? Impossible to decide on a career—*"Can't say I'll be a painter, I'll be a banker . . ."

RAJMATA OF JAIPUR: *How she wants to spend her time—six weeks of skiing, six weeks by the sea.*

Back at the London tea party. After pause:

PRINCESS: And who was he anyway? Denis Lever. That you should spend all that time and work on such a person.

CYRIL SAHIB: He was—an Englishman in India.

PRINCESS: My goodness, there were enough of those. Papa only had to snap his fingers and they would come running. To shoot our tigers and drink our liquor. *How* they drank. Claret and Scotch for breakfast, port and champagne all night.

CYRIL SAHIB: Denis Lever was not entertained by Maharajas. He was too busy sinking wells and building schools. Whatever spare time he had he spent riding around the country. He sat days and nights with the villagers to listen to their songs and stories.

The PRINCESS *yawns.*

Unfortunately he did not live to complete his *magnum opus.* He died in the cholera epidemic of '17, a year before he was due to retire. The book was published posthumously.

A silence.

PRINCESS: How long were *you* in India, Cyril Sahib?

CYRIL SAHIB: A long time . . .

PRINCESS: Yes, and always with us. You were one of us. The British never liked it. Papa had terrible rows with them about you. Sir Philip wanted to appoint some English officer as Papa's tutor, and then afterwards when Papa made you his private secretary, they were all furious. It went right up to the Viceroy. Terrible pressure was put, but Papa stuck up for you. He was loyal. A true Rajput . . . Loyalty was something he prized above everything else. He was terribly disappointed when people failed him—as they often did.

An awkward silence. During which she offers him a pastry.

When Paul Merkler wanted to leave after all those years, Papa offered him everything he could think of if only he would stay. But still he wouldn't. Papa was so hurt. He said, "You see, he didn't love us as we loved him."

Another silence.

CYRIL SAHIB: One day Merkler came to my room. It was in the afternoon. It was very hot and a dust storm had been blowing for several days. Out of the palace window you couldn't see anything but dust and sun and desert. Merkler told me that he couldn't stand it any more. That he just wanted to leave and go home. He didn't have to say much to me because I knew only too well what he meant. I too had been in India for a long time. No—wait, Princess. It is true that I was living in undreamed-of luxury—in a palace, waited on hand and foot, eating rich food, with plenty of time to do everything

146

I wanted. Read. Write. Study. Everything. Only most of the time I did nothing. I lay on my soft bed and felt as if I were rotting away with heat and boredom.

A pause. The Princess changes reels.

When I first came out to be your father's tutor, I thought I would never want to go home again. I wanted only to be in India, to be part of it. I dressed up in Indian clothes—His Highness showered me with silk turbans and brocade coats and dressed me up in them himself—and then stood back to have a hearty laugh at me. I dare say I looked very ridiculous . . . I learned to eat curry with my fingers. To chew betel. Even to smoke a hookah. I sat cross-legged on the floor with the other courtiers and we played rough-and-tumble games like boys and card games for high stakes at which we all cheated like hell. Then I don't know what happened. Why it stopped being fun.

Here the footage of shabby processions and confused events starts.

Although in the beginning I was excited by all the processions and ceremonies, after a time they all seemed the same. The weddings. The birthdays. The funerals. There were always crowds. It was always very hot. Once I fainted and had to be carried back to the palace. His Highness showed such kindness and concern—he left the ceremony and all his guests to enquire after me, to sit by my bedside. After that he would no longer allow me to come out in the sun . . . Always crowds. Crowds. The city streets full of crowds . . . There was a lot of waiting. Hours of waiting in the sun. Everyone had to wait—His Highness too. He accepted it. It was part of the ceremony. There was a great deal of confusion. Moments when no one knew what was to be done next and they argued about it—"It has always been done this way." "No, that way." Each stated his case at length. Meanwhile we waited. Sometimes the elephant didn't turn up, or the mahout was missing; or the Rolls had a puncture and the man who knew how to fix it was visiting his elder brother in hospital.

Of some mysterious-looking event in the footage:

I can't remember what this was . . . One would have thought that, as the years went by, all these ceremonies would become more familiar to me. Not at all. They became more mystifying. More mysterious. I was able less and less to keep them apart, or to know what was going on. Somehow it all ran together— being married, dying—it was all part of the same process . . . What is this box? I think it is the Queen Mother being carried in purdah to some ceremony . . .

The box is tipped onto funeral pyre.

Ah no, this appears to be a funeral . . . What is going on here? I think it is a birthday weighing ceremony—afterwards the gold or silver would be distributed among the poor. This is not a palace but the cenotaph for His Highness's father . . . This too is a cenotaph . . . The ashes of a king had to be palatially housed . . . But it is disconcerting when you're not sure whether a palace is for a live king or a dead one . . . Ah, I remember this, the cenotaph of the dead queens. This is where they were brought when their lives in the purdah palaces were finished. It is the other side of the coin. It was more quiet and empty and lonely than any other place I know on earth . . . Nothing there except a few vultures . . . I thought the cenotaphs themselves resembled vultures. Or some extinct species of bird come to roost in the desert . . . I was haunted by the place. I used to think of it on the oddest occasions . . .

We are now in the middle of the Jodhpur singing-and-dancing-girl footage.

Even when the singing and dancing girls came to entertain—I would think of those dead queens out there . . . Perhaps because the songs the girls sang weren't as gay as they were supposed to be. I always found them rather sad. And the girls too, in their tawdry dresses. Some of them were no longer in their first youth.

What happens to the singing and dancing girls when they get old? When I asked His Highness, he said, "They die of pox in the bazaar." He laughed when he said it, so I suppose he was joking . . .

At the end of the singing-and-dancing-girl sequence, we are back at the London tea party.

PRINCESS: I don't think ours was a *very* backward state. Not compared with some of the others.

CYRIL SAHIB: That's true. Yes. There were worse.

PRINCESS: Much worse! Think of Thugpur. Why, they were still living in the Dark Ages. There were many terrible things that happened there. Even child sacrifice. Oh, it's horrible to think of. And so many cases of suttee. *We* hardly had any suttee at all . . .

CYRIL SAHIB: What about your great-aunt?

PRINCESS: That was different . . . I mean, it wasn't religious, but because she *loved* her husband. When he died, she just didn't want to live anymore. Everyone who was there said it was very beautiful, the way she climbed on the funeral pyre and lay down beside his corpse. Sacred and beautiful . . .

A pause.

The reason we were a progressive state was because of Papa. He had a really modern mind. He couldn't stand all those old superstitions, and if he had had a free hand, he would have swept many of them away. But of course he was hampered all the time by the traditionalists—the priests and the old aunts and all those orthodox people. He tried to fight them but what could he do singlehanded? But one thing he did insist on, and there no one could stand in his way—and that was about me. My education. Oh, and for that I'm eternally grateful to him—what he did for his motherless child!

She clasps her hands in gratitude to the portrait above the mantelpiece. In spite of this melodramatic expression, there is no doubt about her sincerity.

Can you imagine, Cyril Sahib, if it hadn't been for him I would have been like all the others: my whole life spent in a purdah palace, never allowed out except in a closed carriage and family servants riding before and behind . . . Yes, and then what would have become of me—afterwards? What would I have done? It's as if he foresaw all that would happen and how in later life I would have to stand on my own two feet. As if he knew all that. I was only four when he engaged my first English governess, Miss Simpkins, from Shropshire . . . And I still remember the fearful row the aunts made when I was to leave for Switzerland. But he insisted. He wouldn't budge. And when I was fifteen and they wanted to bring me home to get me married, he sent me to my English boarding school instead. He wouldn't even let me come home for the hols for fear they would get at me. Of course I was homesick quite a lot all those years abroad, but now I see how wise he was. Because that was the way to make me a truly independent woman so that today I can take my place in the modern world along with everyone else . . .

She trails off. Her eyes look sadly out the window, at the Kensington houses opposite, the uncompromising London street. Those eyes were perhaps meant to look out at different scenes—how else to account for their melancholy?

(*Snapping out of her mood with determined gaiety.*) And now I'm going to make us some more tea.

She goes out. Left alone, CYRIL SAHIB *begins to leaf through some of the many photograph albums scattered about. He lingers over the portraits of the Princess's father. They are mostly of him in the prime of life—a magnificent young Prince. But out of the back of one of the albums, forgotten, unstuck—another picture flutters out and onto the floor.* CYRIL SAHIB *stoops painfully to pick it up. This too is of the Princess's father, though we do not recognise him because he is now a gross, dissolute, middle-aged man.* CYRIL SAHIB *turns the picture over. There is a newspaper clipping stuck to the back of it. The headline reads:* Indian Maharaja in London Hotel Scandal.

The PRINCESS'S *voice from the kitchen:*

PRINCESS: I won't be a jiffy! It's just brewing . . . I do hate these tea bags, don't you? They are a horrible invention . . .

When she enters, he quickly replaces the picture in the back of the album and concentrates on studying the earlier photographs. She looks over his shoulder.

That was at the time of the Princes' Assembly. The newspapers always made such a fuss of him—India's Fairy Prince, they called him. Beside him the other princes did cut a sorry figure, poor things.

She pours his tea and hands it to him.

That was why they were all jealous of him. When his trouble came on, there wasn't one of them that stood up for him. But he didn't mind about them—he knew they were not his friends and never had been. He only minded when he felt betrayed by those he thought *were* his friends . . .

A pause. CYRIL SAHIB's *hands are trembling somewhat with emotion.*

I shall never forget the way he said about Paul Merkler: "He didn't love us as we loved him" . . . I know you were fond of him—

Another pause.

(*With a change of tone, rather accusing now.*) But if you had loved him as he did you, wouldn't you have stood up for him— at that time? You who had known him longer than anyone, you could have told them.

CYRIL SAHIB (*with great self-control*): What, Princess? What should I have said?

PRINCESS: That he was completely innocent! . . . As if someone like him was ever capable of anything base. He was a king through and through and there wasn't one of them fit to judge him, let alone do what they did . . . (*Her voice breaks.*)

CYRIL SAHIB: Princess. Princess.

PRINCESS (*with brave defiance*): Don't think I care. *He* never did.

152

Because he knew it didn't mean a thing. There wasn't a power on earth that could depose him. Whatever they may have written on paper, in reality—and in the hearts of his people—he was *still* the Maharaja. No little tribunal or commission could take that away from him.

CYRIL SAHIB *is still turning the pages of the album—in self-defence, to hide the expression on his face. Suddenly she puts her hand on the page he has come to.*

PRINCESS: Don't look at that.

CYRIL SAHIB: Your wedding pictures.

PRINCESS: I hate them. It's the one thing I can't forgive him for . . . I don't mean that. Of course he was thinking—as always—only of my good, and how was he to know that Bunny wasn't going to turn out the most wonderful husband in the world . . . He wasn't a bad sort, really. He was just weak and spoiled, like all that family. Papa took opium too, but he knew how to control himself if necessary. But Bunny would go mad—literally insane—if he couldn't get it. (*Looking briefly at Bunny's picture, in bridegroom attire.*) He wasn't bad-looking. (*Flicking over the page.*) But of course nothing—nothing—compared to *him*.

She lovingly looks at the splendid pictures of her splendid father, but then the other photo drops again. CYRIL SAHIB *picks it up and lays it aside. There is a silence.*

PRINCESS: It was all a frame-up, everyone knows that. He was completely innocent. They were just two common blackmailers. Common criminals. To take away his throne because of two creatures like that . . . He should have shot that woman long ago . . . Why don't you speak! When it's time to speak, then you are silent. Now—and at that time too. Don't think he didn't feel it. He never complained—he was far too proud for that—but he felt it. I know. It was just another stab in the back.

CYRIL SAHIB: No. You mustn't say that to me.

PRINCESS: It's true. You can't deny it.

CYRIL SAHIB: I do deny it, Princess.

PRINCESS: You can't. If you had cared for him, you would have spoken up for him.

CYRIL SAHIB: And if I had, who would have listened? What was I? An Englishman who had stayed too long. His Highness's parasite.

PRINCESS: No one called you that.

CYRIL SAHIB: Not aloud, no . . .

A silence.

PRINCESS: We all loved and respected you. You were part of the family.

He walks around the room in agitation. Finally he stands opposite the Princess who has seated herself on a sofa.

CYRIL SAHIB: I came out for one year. I really did mean to go home. My college was offering me a fellowship, I was to write a thesis on—some very learned subject. By the end of the year, I said next year. And then next year . . . By that time I could no longer live without him. I couldn't bear to have him out of my sight for as much as an hour. He knew it of course and loved to tease me. He would go off for days on end without telling me. When he came back, he'd say, "Where *were* you, Cyril Sahib? I've been looking for you everywhere." When I reproached him, he laughed. Next day he would be off again and stay away for another week. By the time he came back I was frantic. I made scenes like a woman. He enjoyed it for a time, but then he got bored and avoided me. He made jokes about me with the fawners round him . . .

PRINCESS: He fought for you! He stuck up for you against the Viceroy and all of them!

CYRIL SAHIB: Whenever there was a party of English visitors, I would be sent for. When I tried to withdraw—I didn't like them any better than they did me, as he well knew—but when I tried to go, he wouldn't let me. And afterwards he would ask me—with that innocent air he had when he knew something would hurt a person—"Why do they hate you?" I never answered and he would go on needling me: "Is it because you don't play any games? Can't shoot straight? Can't even sit on a horse properly?" Once he told me, "Mrs. Purblock says you are a degenerate." Then he asked, "What is a degenerate?" . . . But he always knew when he had gone too far. Then he would turn round completely and be—the soul of kindness. Showing the most delicate personal attentions, as only he knew how. He could really make one feel —loved. And it was genuine . . . When the telegram came to say my mother had died, he wouldn't leave my side for days on end. He slept in my room, I on the bed and he at the foot of it. He sent for an Anglican priest all the way to Ambala because he said he wanted me to have the comfort of my religion. And he sat through the service weeping like a child . . . But very often I was afraid of him.

Cyril Sahib sits down next to the Princess.

CYRIL SAHIB (*voice-over*): There were many things I was afraid of. For no reason at all. Except that I began to feel how alien everything was to me. Strange and alien. All those strange ceremonies, and priests, and idols . . . An alien land . . .

A series of quick flashbacks begin: An idol being offered something in a golden cup to drink; the idol, wearing a gauzy dress, being carried in procession; then the Rat Temple.

CYRIL SAHIB: This is the temple sacred to the rat. I found it difficult to go near the place. Even to think of it . . . I began to be very careful about myself. I became fussy about what food I ate and drinking only boiled water. I swallowed quantities of quinine. All the time I felt I had to protect myself. I don't know against what exactly . . .

The squirming, squealing rats fade gradually.

The sports events and the religious ones became mixed up in my mind. Sometimes in my dreams . . . This was a festival to honour the goddess Kali . . . There were always two goats and a young bull.

The animal sacrifice at Jodhpur. The swords come down, the heads are struck off with one blow, the cannons fire from the ramparts, and the little boys touch their foreheads with fingers dipped in blood.

Back at the tea party:

PRINCESS: Many foreigners don't understand our Indian philosophy. There is creation and destruction. Both are aspects of life.

CYRIL SAHIB: I never could understand that. Or accept it . . . No more than I could accept what was happening to him . . .

He draws out the photograph of the ageing Maharaja which he had laid aside. She snatches it from him and tears it up and throws it on the fire.

PRINCESS: Of course people grow older. Everyone does. (*With an ironic laugh.*) That would be very nice if we all stayed young and beautiful forever.

CYRIL SAHIB: He changed so much. His whole face changed.

PRINCESS: It was that woman. If I were not a modern person I would say she had used spells. And some did say that. If not, how could she get such power over him? How was it possible?

CYRIL SAHIB: He was always—forgive me, Princess—susceptible.

PRINCESS: At least all the others had something! Even Sultana—at least she was a film star, she had looks and talent to attract him! But that common Englishwoman. A person from the lowest class. She was despicable . . . You know, she is still alive. She has the impudence to write me begging letters. Of course I tear them up at once and then my fingers feel soiled . . . Ugh . . .

Flashback to a suite in a luxurious London hotel, like the Savoy, circa 1945. A blowsy Englishwoman is urging the Maharaja to come to bed. She is no longer in her first youth; her hair is bleached; she is wearing a satin nightgown. The Maharaja, in his dissolute aspect, is drawn down onto the bed by the Englishwoman. They lie full-length for a moment. Suddenly the door bursts open and a man jumps into the room. He is a photographer. He starts taking pictures with a flash camera. Another man comes into the room, short, wearing a raincoat and carrying an umbrella. The Maharaja leaps out of bed, starts around it towards a bureau opposite. The short man starts belaboring him with the umbrella. The Maharaja manages to get his pistol out of the bureau drawer. He aims it and fires. After the shot, there is a silence. (This whole scene—silent and melodramatic—is as dated as a silent film; as dated as the hotel suite, itself.)

CYRIL SAHIB: What about the man?

PRINCESS: He disappeared long ago. I never believed that was her husband. It was all a plot to blackmail Papa. I wish he had shot them both! The one time in his life that he missed!

CYRIL SAHIB: Thank God he did. Thank God.

PRINCESS: What worse thing could have been done to him than was done? . . . I begged him that time: don't go to London, Papa. We'll go together in June, for Ascot. It was as if I had some premonition. But no, he would not listen. He followed that creature and then everything happened . . . He fell into their trap.

Back at the tea party:

CYRIL SAHIB: They called it "The Shot That Shattered a Throne." They do love a headline . . . (*Looking towards the window, where evening is drawing in.*) I'm afraid it's getting time . . .

PRINCESS: Not yet! There is still such a lot to talk about . . . Oh, this is pure selfishness on my part. Of course you have to get back to Turton.

CYRIL SAHIB: I would prefer to avoid the rush hour . . .

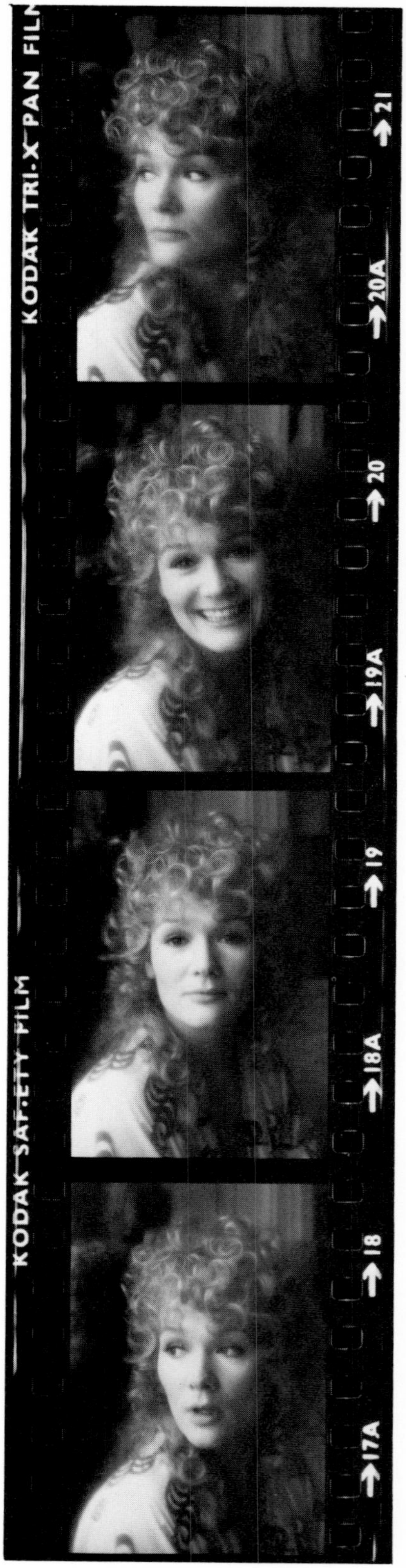
KODAK TRI-X PAN FILM
21
20A
20
19A
19
KODAK SAFETY FILM
18A
18
17A

PRINCESS: I don't suppose anyone ever offers you a seat. It wouldn't occur to them . . . You have to learn to push, that's the only way. I do it. (*She begins to gather up the remains of sandwiches and other refreshments that are abundantly left. She ties them up in a napkin.*) I insist. You are not to say no. (*As* CYRIL SAHIB *tries to protest.*) It will do for your supper.

CYRIL SAHIB: It *would* save that bit of cooking tonight . . .

PRINCESS (*in pity and annoyance*): Really, it's terrible that there is no one to look after you.

CYRIL SAHIB: Oh, I manage very well. Mrs. Parrot comes in once a week for the cleaning—or used to, just recently she has been laid up . . .

PRINCESS: These people are always laid up . . . Well, that's the way it is. We just have to learn to manage. (*She gathers up more food for him: a whole cake.*)

CYRIL SAHIB: Princess! Please!

PRINCESS: It will do for tomorrow's lunch as well . . . I wish you lived in town. At least I could look in every now and then . . . It must get lonely for you down there.

CYRIL SAHIB: Not a bit. I keep busy. With my research. My bit of writing. My walks by the sea . . . Sometimes I imagine it's not the sea at all but the desert of Rajasthan . . . Which is of course as endless as the sea . . . Well, you will laugh at me but at my age it's sometimes difficult to distinguish between past and present. Between the desert and the sea. (*He laughs.*)

PRINCESS (*who has been sorting out the reels of film and now comes across a forgotten one*): Oh, but I've left out the most important thing! I've been saving it for you. It won't take long and you'll love it . . . You know when I was home last I went to see Bari Moti Bai.

CYRIL SAHIB: She must be over eighty now.

PRINCESS: She is better than ever. You'll see . . . Of course like all
the old court musicians she is living in very straitened circum-
stances now . . . At first I felt so sad to find her living in that
place. I think it was part of the palace stables, or perhaps even
the sweepers' quarters . . . It's no more than a hole in the wall,
and she doesn't have anything there except a mat to sleep on
and one old cooking pot. She is all alone and suffers terribly
with gall stones. But gay! Like a bird. She seems happy about
everything. As if all the good things that happened in the past
are still there and even better ones to come . . .

160

Footage of eighty-year-old woman singer of Jaisalmer. She sings love songs in her old voice, with coquettish looks. She is gay and like a bird. After a time, and with the singer still singing, we see the PRINCESS *escorting* CYRIL SAHIB *down the stairs. She helps him on with his hat and coat and hands him his umbrella and the parcel of food she has tied up for him. She is very careful and protective about him. They go down together to the street and say goodbye. She watches him walk down the darkening London street. The* PRINCESS *shivers and draws her thin silk sari around her and goes in, closing the door.*

Autobiography of a Princess is a special presentation of WNET/13, New York, over the Public Broadcasting Service. The film was sponsored by Volkswagen of America, Inc. The American distributor is Cinema 5, 595 Madison Avenue, New York 10021.

VII

Sets for a Film to Come

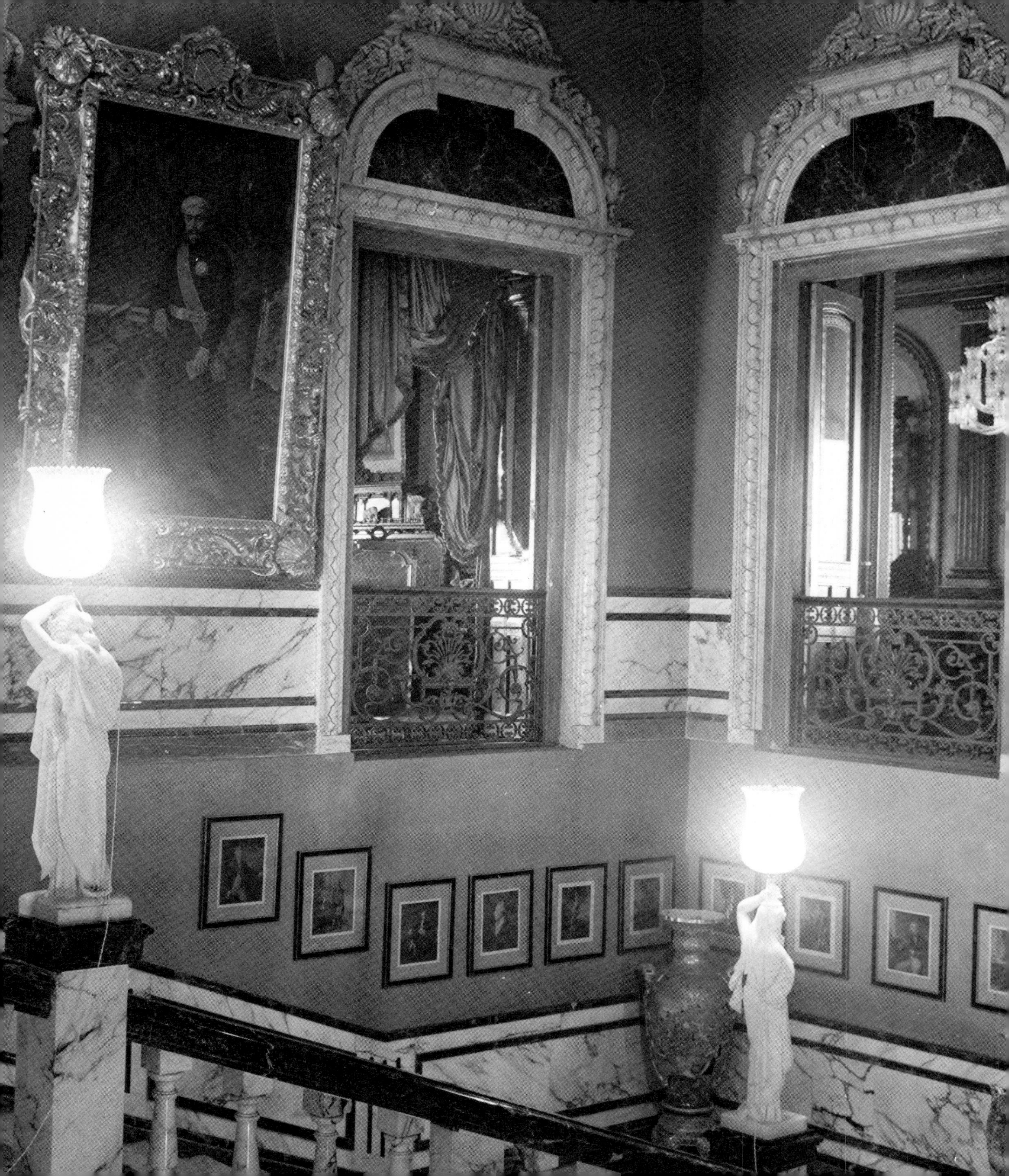

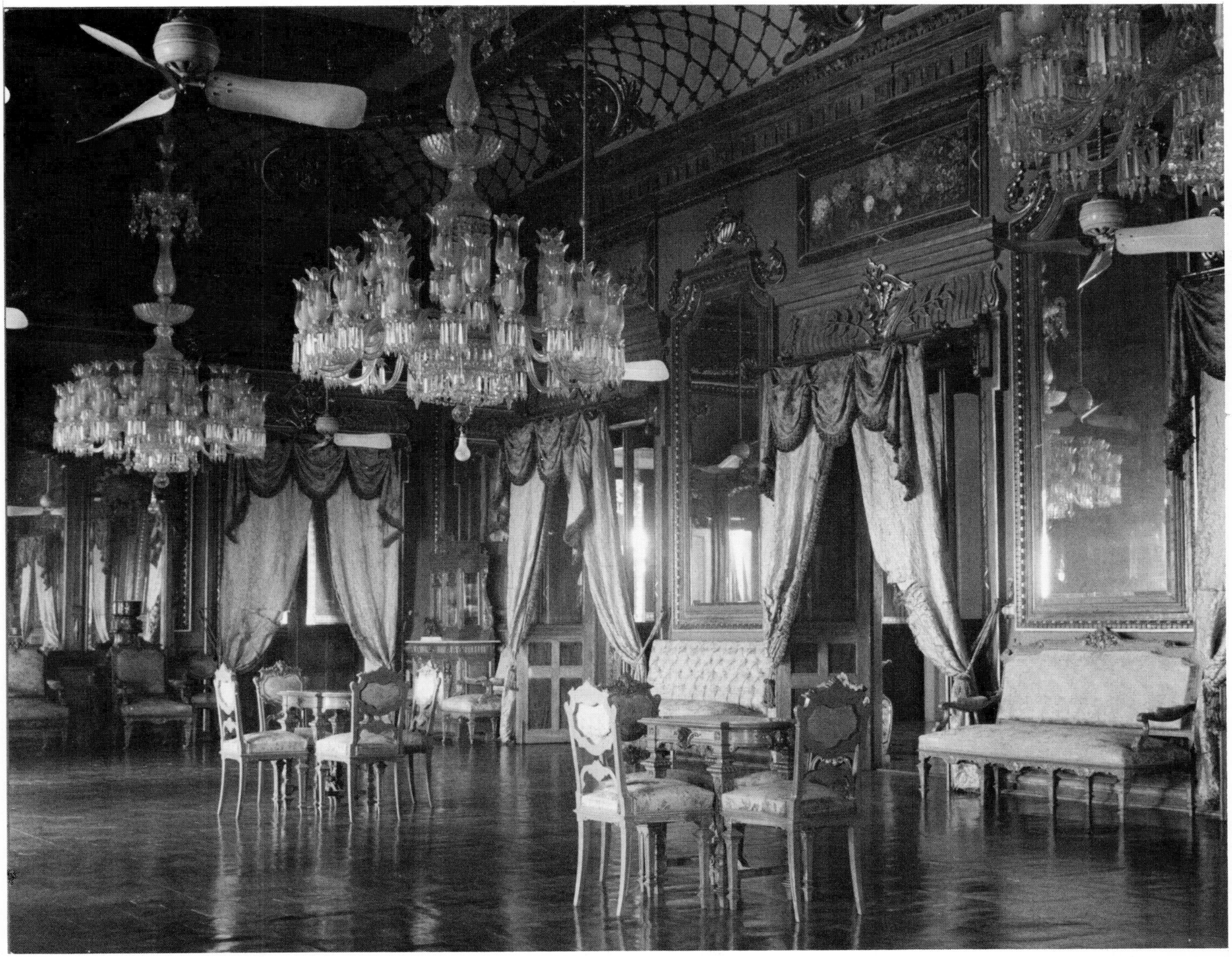

Hyderabad. Faluknamah Palace.

◄ Hyderabad. Faluknamah Palace.
The Grand Staircase, with
Portraits of the British Viceroys.

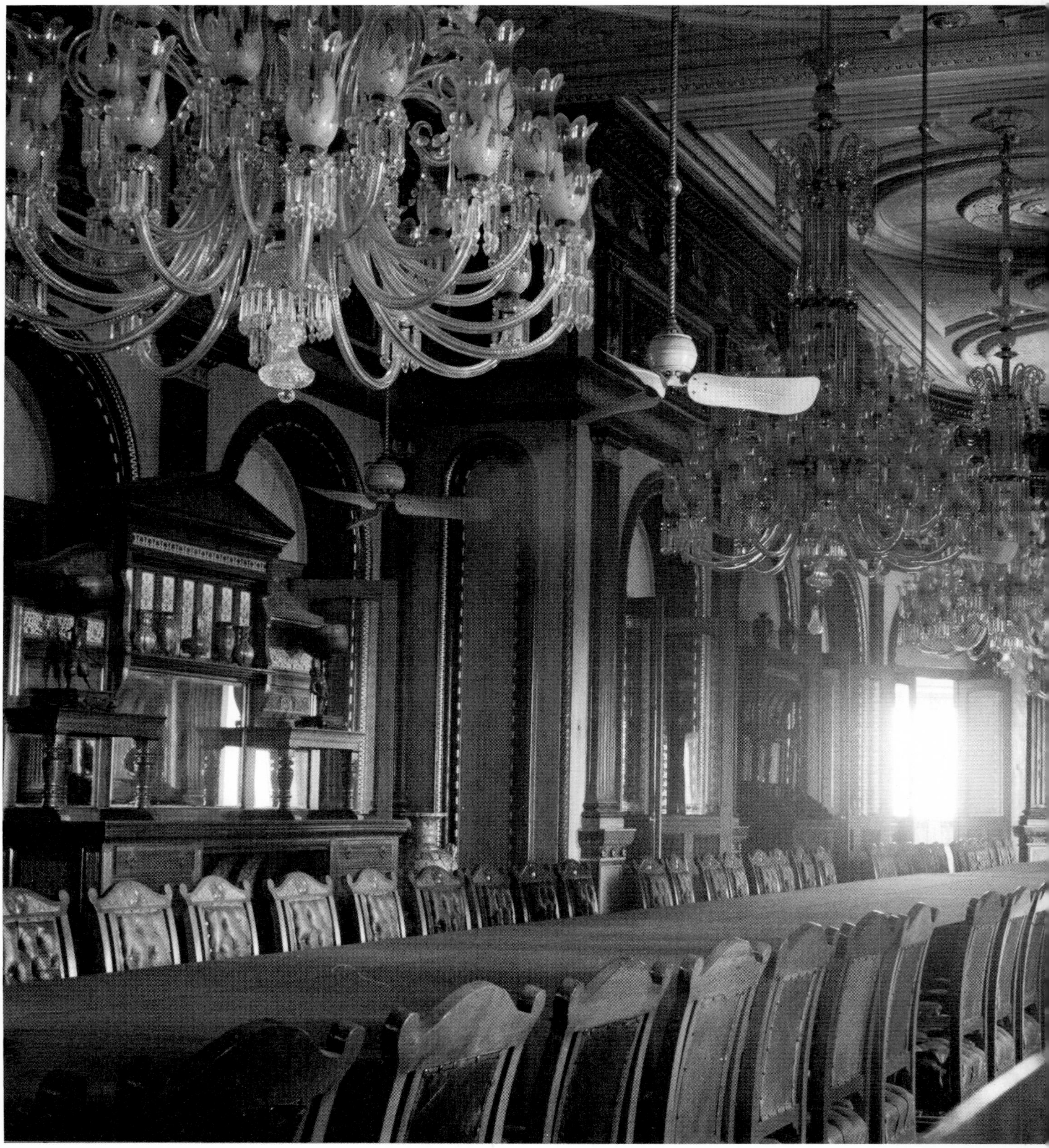

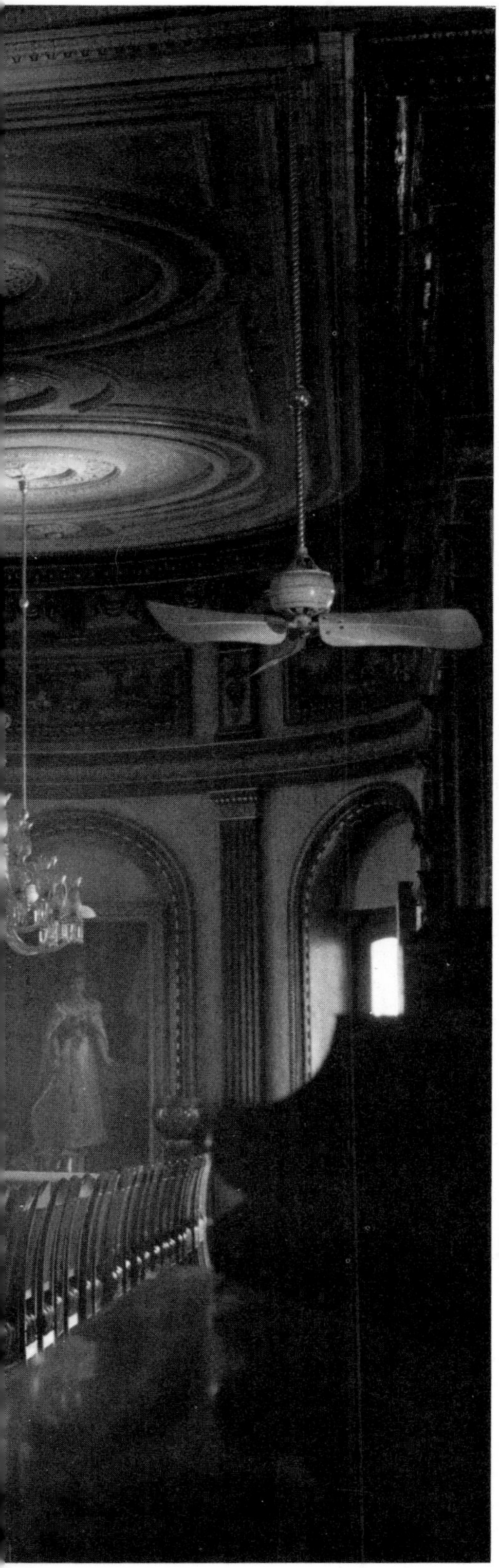

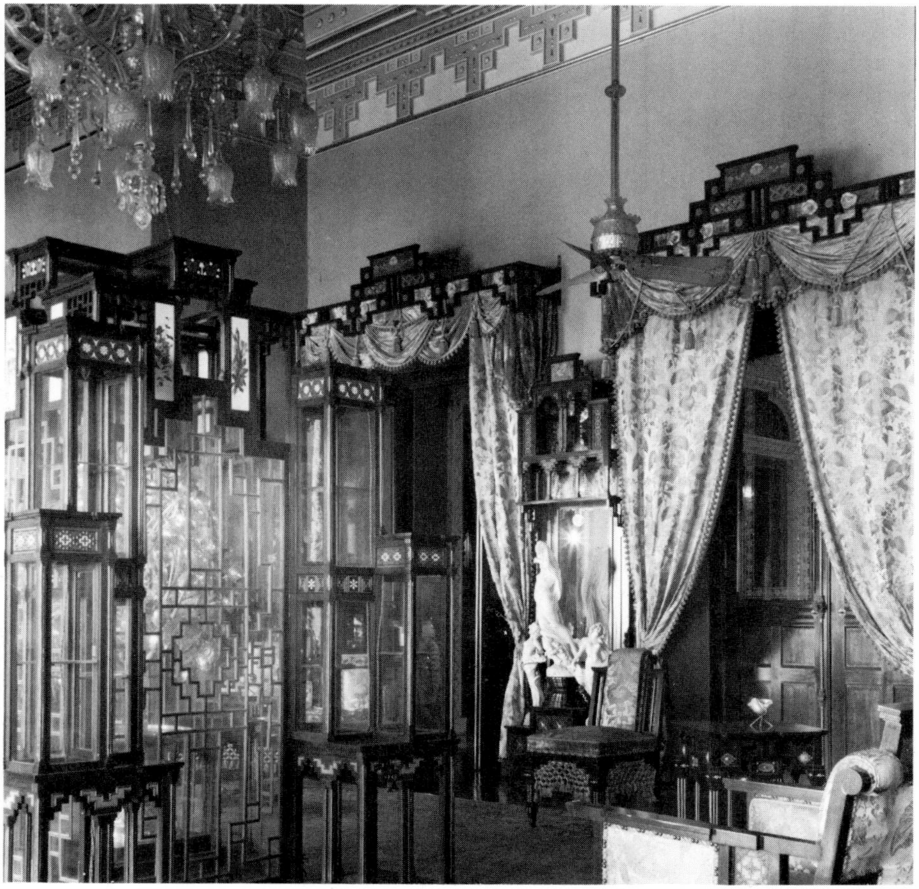

Hyderabad. Faluknamah Palace.

Hyderabad. The State Dining
Room in Faulknamah Palace.

Hyderabad. Detail of a Guest
Bedroom in Faluknamah Palace.

Hyderabad. Faluknamah Palace.

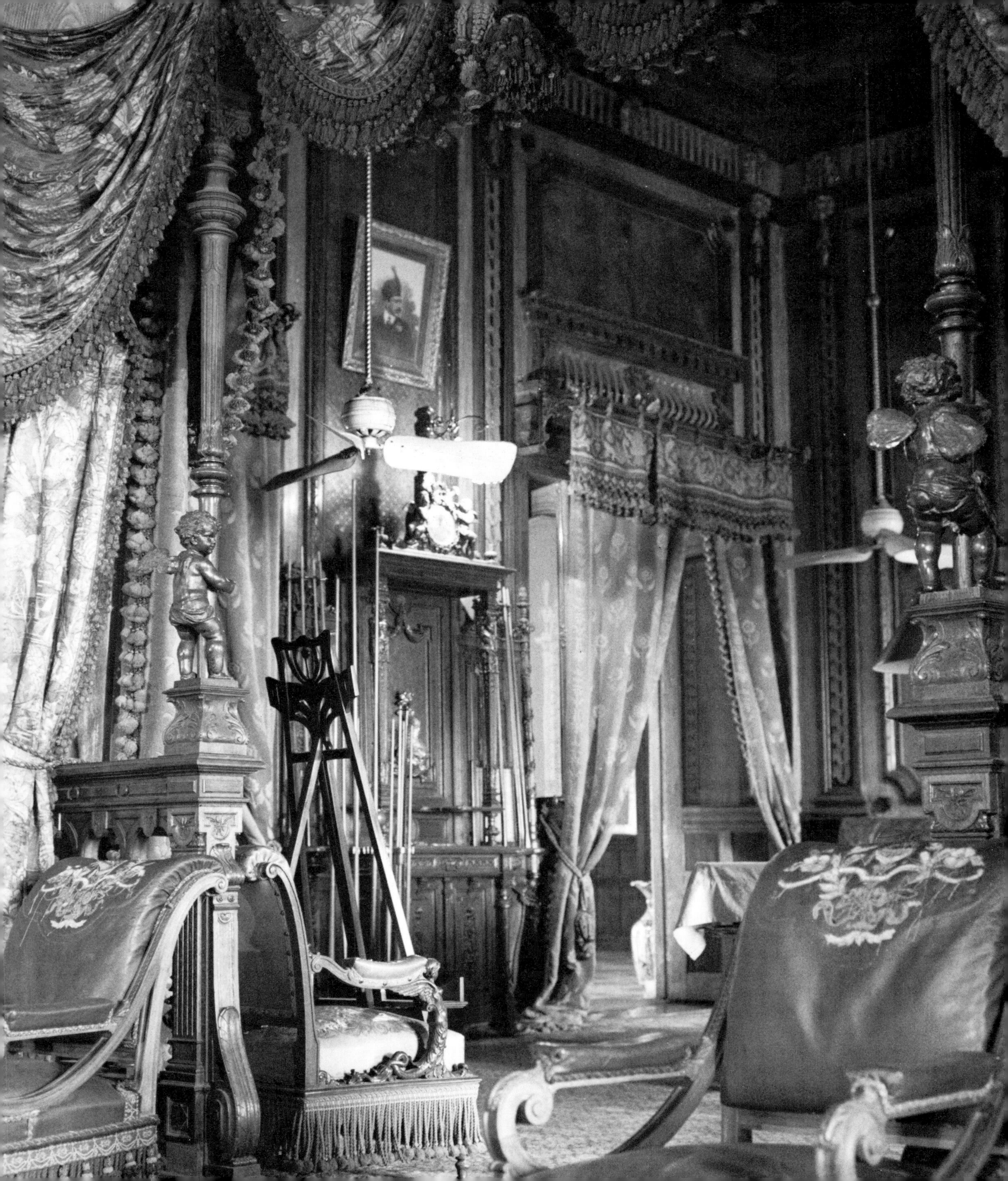

Hyderabad. Guest bathroom in Faluknamah Palace.

Glossary

Ashram. A retreat, usually under the supervision of a swami, where the inmates live simply in order to develop spiritually.

Bara Sahib. An important Englishman.

Chattri. Literally, an umbrella. Used as an architectural term, however, the word applies not only to the little domed pavilions dotting the Indian countryside which mark the spot where some important person was cremated or a saint lived, but also to the graceful structures—shelters from sun or rain—poking up all over Indian palaces. In its mortuary aspect, a *chattri* was often a palatial affair, rather than a simple, open-air pavilion.

Chela. The disciple of an Indian maestro, artistic or musical; also the devotee of an Indian sage.

Dak Bungalow. *Dak* means the post, or mail. A dak bungalow is a government-maintained rest house for the accommodation of travelers, providing for humble essentials of shelter, bed and table, a bathroom, and a servant furnishing food at a very moderate cost. These were built in Victorian times on main roads every ten or fifteen miles so that a traveler could make his journey by marches without carrying a tent. They still come in very handy today.

Darshan. A higher form of the *Durbar,* with mystical overtones, and not restricted to kings. Holy men in India give *darshan,* and so do other men esteemed for their integrity or wisdom. The definition is complicated: *darshan* means letting the assembled persons experience the benefit of the presence of an exalted being. To give *darshan* is a kind of communion too, a two-way thing, with emanations of power both temporal and spiritual flowing one way, and respect (or sometimes even love) flowing the other.

Durbar. To sit in audience. In the large Indian courts there were two kinds of durbar: a large-scale one, which usually took place in the *Diwan-i-Am,* a many-pillared hall, in which all the nobles and chieftains would assemble before the ruler; and a smaller, more intimate affair, which took place in the *Diwan-i-Khas,* often the most sumptuously decorated apartment in the palace. The first was a show of state, the second was for more private business. In India, as at seventeenth-century Versailles with its similar system of *petites* and *grandes entrées,* the basic function of the durbar was to reinforce the awesome thought in the minds of the king's subjects that he was *there.* ["The tenth of January, I went to Court at foure in the evening to the Durbar, which is the place where the Mogoll sits out daily, to entertaine strangers, to receive Petitions and Presents, to give Commande, to see and to be seene . . ." (Sir Thomas Roe, Ambassador of James I, describing the Emperor Jehangir's durbar in 1616.)]

Fakir. A holy man.

Har. Literally, a necklace. Also a garland, usually of fresh flowers, especially marigolds, but sometimes of sandalwood shavings, of tinsel and ribbon, or of one-rupee notes, as at Punjabi weddings.

Itr. Attar; a perfumed essence.

Maharaj Kumar. A crown prince.

Memsahib. An Englishwoman, or any European lady.

Mohur. A gold coin of the realm. Also a seal.

Nawab. The Muslim equivalent of a Maharaja. His consort is called a Begum.

Pan. A brilliant green leaf very cunningly folded over a mixture of spices, lime, tobacco, and betel nut, which is then put in the mouth and chewed. A *pan* tastes best after a meal and is a passion with most Indians. Knowing how to make a *pan* is one of the most esteemed of the housewifely arts.

Puja. A Hindu religious ritual performed in the temple or at home.

Purdah. The forced seclusion of women. The word literally means a curtain. Purdah is supposed to have been introduced by the Muslim invaders; before that, Indian women are said to have been very free.

Raja. A king, or ruler. A Maharaja was a more important ruler, either because of the size and strength of his state (and sometimes his dynasty's pedigree), or because the British, for reasons of policy, designated him as such.

Rajmata. The Queen Mother.

Rajput. A proud member of one of the proud clans from the desert states of Rajasthan.

Rani. A queen; the foremost wife of an Indian ruler, when Hindu. If her consort was a Maharaja, she would then be a Maharani.

Rao. A noble.

Sarangi. A stringed instrument played with a bow and used throughout North India to accompany dancers and singers. The *sarangi* is very old; angels play its European equivalent in medieval paintings.

Sati. Also *suttee*. The self-immolation of a widow on her husband's funeral pyre. Some women threw themselves into the flames because they were mad with grief, and a widow's life in orthodox Hindu society was frightful anyway; others were persuaded for reasons of family honor: a *sati* became a goddess. The British outlawed the practice in the early nineteenth century.

Swami. A holy man.

Tabla. The little pair of drums, beaten and slapped with the fingertips and the heel of the hand, which provides the rhythmic accompaniment to North Indian music.

Zenana. The women's quarters, and the part of the palace where the ruler lived with his family and women.

Photo Credits

The *Focal Encyclopedia of Photography* provides the following information about Samuel Bourne (1834–1912): ". . . English photographer of Indian views. Took up photography in the mid-1850's and c. 1860 became a partner in the firm founded by Shepherd in Simla, 1843 (later also in Calcutta). Bourne became famous for his photographs of the Himalayas taken on expeditions lasting several months and requiring up to 60 porters to carry the wet collodion equipment and other baggage. In 1868 he photographed at an altitude of 18,600 feet—a record held until 1880 . . ."

The *Encyclopedia* is silent on Bourne's partner, Shepherd. It would be fascinating to see his Simla views, taken in the 1840s. Perhaps some of them have survived and will turn up one day.

John Swope: Pages vi, viii, 33, 55, 61, 64, 65, 66–67, 69, 70, 73, 76–77, 79, 82, 83, 84, 85, 86–87, 88, 90–91, 92–93, 94, 95, 96, 97, 98, 100, 102–103, 105, 111, 112, 116, 117, 118–119, 120–121, 124, 125, 163, 164, 166, 167, 168, 169, 170, 171, 172, and 177.

Bourne & Shepherd: Pages 1, 2, 4, 5, 6, 8, 10, 11, 12, 13, 14–15, 16–17, 18–19, 22–23, 24, 25, 26, 28, and 31.

F. Bremner: Page 39.

James Ivory: Pages 56, 80, 106, 108, 109, 110, and 122.

Mary Ellen Mark: Pages 58, 59, and 63.

Lawrence Copley Thaw: Page 62.

Subratra Mitra: Pages 113, 126, 127, and 128.

Nigel Cooke: Pages 131, 132–133, 136, 139, 147, 149, 154, 156, and 158.

Pincho Kapoor: Page 160.

Photographs in the book appear through the courtesy of the following individuals and institutions: The India Office Library; Sven Gahlin; Kasmin; The Photographic Collection, Humanities Research Center, The University of Texas, Austin; Mohan Singh; Lloyd and Susanne Rudolph; Lee Thaw; and Merchant Ivory Productions.

Grateful acknowledgment is made for permission to reprint the following:

Excerpts from *Courts and Camps of India* by Yvonne Fitzroy. Published by Methuen & Co. Ltd. Reprinted by permission of Associated Book Publishers Ltd.

Excerpts from *The Viceroy's Wife* by Iris Butler. Published by Hodder & Stoughton, Ltd. Reprinted by permission of the publisher.

Maharaja Ganga Singh of Bikaner Being Weighed Against Treasure.